# First World War
## and Army of Occupation
# War Diary
## France, Belgium and Germany

35 DIVISION
104 Infantry Brigade
Lancashire Fusiliers
17th Battalion
28 January 1916 - 31 March 1919

WO95/2484/1

The Naval & Military Press Ltd
www.nmarchive.com
**Published in association with The National Archives**

Published by

The Naval & Military Press Ltd

Unit 10 Ridgewood Industrial Park,
Uckfield, East Sussex,
TN22 5QE England
Tel: +44 (0) 1825 749494

www.naval-military-press.com
www.nmarchive.com

*This diary has been reprinted in facsimile from the original. Any imperfections are inevitably reproduced and the quality may fall short of modern type and cartographic standards.*

# Contents

| Document type | Place/Title | Date From | Date To |
|---|---|---|---|
| Heading | WO95/2484/1 | | |
| Heading | 35th Division 104th Infy Bde 17th Bn Lancs Fus. Jan 1916-Mar 1919 | | |
| Heading | War Diary of 17th (Service) Battn. Lanc. Fus. S.E.L. From Jan 28th 1916 To Feb 27th 1918. Vol I. | | |
| War Diary | Park House Camp. | 28/01/1916 | 28/01/1916 |
| War Diary | Salisbury. | 28/01/1916 | 28/01/1916 |
| War Diary | Le. Havre. | 29/01/1916 | 30/01/1916 |
| War Diary | St. Omer. | 31/01/1916 | 31/01/1916 |
| War Diary | Wizernes | 31/01/1916 | 09/02/1916 |
| War Diary | Wardrecques. | 09/02/1916 | 18/02/1916 |
| War Diary | Thiennies. | 19/02/1916 | 19/02/1916 |
| War Diary | Robecq. | 20/02/1916 | 20/02/1916 |
| War Diary | Gorre. | 21/02/1916 | 27/02/1916 |
| Heading | War Diary. of 17th (Service) Battn. Lanc. Fus. S.E.L. From March 1st. 1916 To March 31st. Volume II. | | |
| War Diary | Leslobes. | 01/03/1916 | 01/03/1916 |
| War Diary | Robecq-Calonne. | 02/03/1916 | 07/03/1916 |
| War Diary | Richebourg | 08/03/1916 | 08/03/1916 |
| War Diary | St. Vaast. | 08/03/1917 | 08/03/1917 |
| War Diary | Plum Street to Boar's Head. | 09/03/1916 | 14/03/1916 |
| War Diary | No Mans Land | 12/03/1916 | 13/03/1916 |
| War Diary | Left Subsector | 14/03/1916 | 16/03/1916 |
| War Diary | Richebourg St. Vaast. | 17/03/1916 | 23/03/1916 |
| War Diary | Front Line Trenches. | 24/03/1916 | 24/03/1916 |
| War Diary | S.10.2 S.10.3 | 24/03/1916 | 24/03/1916 |
| War Diary | Richebourg St. Vaast. | 25/03/1916 | 25/03/1916 |
| War Diary | Paradis. | 26/03/1916 | 26/03/1916 |
| War Diary | Pacaut Area. | 28/03/1916 | 28/03/1916 |
| War Diary | Leslobes. | 01/03/1916 | 01/03/1916 |
| War Diary | Calonne Area. | 07/03/1916 | 07/03/1916 |
| War Diary | Plum St to Quinque Rue. | 08/03/1916 | 08/03/1916 |
| War Diary | Richebourg St Vaast | 08/03/1916 | 24/03/1916 |
| War Diary | Pacaut Area. | 27/03/1916 | 27/03/1916 |
| Heading | War Diary of 17th (Service) Battn. Lanc. Fus. S.E.L. 1916 From April, 1st. To April 30th. Volume III. | | |
| War Diary | Sailly Sur La Lys. | 01/04/1916 | 01/04/1916 |
| War Diary | Sailly | 02/04/1916 | 04/04/1916 |
| War Diary | Right Subsector Trenches. N.8.3 to N.9.4. | 05/04/1916 | 07/04/1916 |
| War Diary | Petillon Section of Brigade Trench Map Area "L". | 04/04/1916 | 16/04/1916 |
| War Diary | Right Subsection N.8.3 to N.9.4. | 07/04/1916 | 08/04/1916 |
| War Diary | Right Reserve Billets H.31, G36, G.32. | 09/04/1916 | 10/04/1916 |
| War Diary | Right Reserve Billets. | 11/04/1916 | 11/04/1916 |
| War Diary | Right Subsection Trenches. N.8.3 to N.9.4. | 12/04/1916 | 16/04/1916 |
| War Diary | Reserve Billets H31, G36, G32. | 17/04/1916 | 18/04/1916 |
| War Diary | Sailly. | 19/04/1916 | 19/04/1916 |
| War Diary | Estaires | 20/04/1916 | 20/04/1916 |
| War Diary | Vielle Chapelle. | 22/04/1916 | 28/04/1916 |
| War Diary | Left Subsection Trenches Neuve Chapelle Area. | 28/04/1916 | 30/04/1916 |
| War Diary | Right Subsection Trenches. | 30/04/1916 | 30/04/1916 |

| | | | |
|---|---|---|---|
| War Diary | N.8.3 to N.8.4. | 04/04/1916 | 04/04/1916 |
| War Diary | Front Line-H.31, G.36, G.32. | 08/04/1916 | 08/04/1916 |
| War Diary | Sailly. | 12/04/1916 | 12/04/1916 |
| War Diary | Petillon Section. | 12/04/1916 | 12/04/1916 |
| War Diary | Right Sub Section Trenches. | 16/04/1916 | 16/04/1916 |
| War Diary | Reserve Billets. G.36, G.22, H.31. | 16/04/1916 | 16/04/1916 |
| War Diary | Right Reserve Billets. | 19/04/1916 | 19/04/1916 |
| War Diary | Estaires. | 20/04/1916 | 20/04/1916 |
| Heading | War Diary of 17th (Service) Battn. Lanc. Fus. S.E.L. 1916. From May 1st/16 To May 31st/16. Volume IV. | | |
| War Diary | Left Subsection Trenches. Neuve Chapelle. | 01/05/1916 | 02/05/1916 |
| War Diary | Croix Barbee | 03/05/1916 | 05/05/1916 |
| War Diary | Left Subsection Trenches Neuve Chapelle | 06/05/1916 | 10/05/1916 |
| War Diary | Croix Barbee. | 10/05/1916 | 14/05/1916 |
| War Diary | Vieille Chapelle | 14/05/1916 | 22/05/1916 |
| War Diary | Vieille Chapelle to Richebourg (Fme Du Bois) Section. | 22/05/1916 | 22/05/1916 |
| War Diary | Left Subsection Trenches. Ferme Du Bois Section | 22/05/1916 | 26/05/1916 |
| War Diary | Richebourg St. Vaast. | 27/05/1916 | 30/05/1916 |
| War Diary | Left Subsection Trenches-Ferme Du Bois Sector | 30/05/1916 | 31/05/1916 |
| Diagram etc | No Mans Land of the Ferme Du Bois Section. May 28th 1916. | | |
| Heading | War Diary of 17th Service (1st S.C) Bn., Lancashire Fusiliers 1916 Volume V June 1st-June 30th | | |
| War Diary | Left Sub Section Trenche Fme Du Bois Section | 01/06/1916 | 05/06/1916 |
| War Diary | Richebourg St. Vaast. | 06/06/1916 | 11/06/1916 |
| War Diary | Left Subsection Trenches-Fme Du Bois Section | 11/06/1916 | 16/06/1916 |
| War Diary | Les Caudrons. | 17/06/1916 | 19/06/1916 |
| War Diary | Bethune | 20/06/1916 | 30/06/1916 |
| Heading | 104th Bde. 35th Div. War Diary 17th Battalion Lancashire Fusiliers 1st to 31st July 1916. | | |
| Heading | War Diary of 17th Service (1st S.E.L.) Battalion, Lancashire Fusiliers From July 1st 1916 To July 31st 1916. (Volume 6) | | |
| War Diary | Bethune | 01/07/1916 | 02/07/1916 |
| War Diary | Bouquemaison | 03/07/1916 | 06/07/1916 |
| War Diary | Bus-Les-Artois | 09/07/1916 | 09/07/1916 |
| War Diary | Lealvillers | 10/07/1916 | 10/07/1916 |
| War Diary | Aveluy Wood | 13/07/1916 | 13/07/1916 |
| War Diary | Happy Valley | 14/07/1916 | 18/07/1916 |
| War Diary | Maricourt | 19/07/1916 | 19/07/1916 |
| War Diary | Talus Boise | 20/07/1916 | 20/07/1916 |
| War Diary | Bernafay Wood | 21/07/1916 | 21/07/1916 |
| War Diary | Front Line. | 22/07/1916 | 23/07/1916 |
| War Diary | Talus Boise. | 24/07/1916 | 25/07/1916 |
| War Diary | Dublin Trench | 26/07/1916 | 26/07/1916 |
| War Diary | Front Line. | 29/07/1916 | 30/07/1916 |
| War Diary | Minden Post. | 31/07/1916 | 31/07/1916 |
| Heading | 35th Division. 104th Infantry Brigade. 1/17th Battalion Lancashire Fusiliers August 1916 3 Sketch maps attached. | | |
| Heading | War Diary of 17th Service (1st S.E.L.) Battalion, Lancashire Fusiliers. From:- 1st August, 1916, to:- 31st August, 1916 (Volume 7.) 35th Divn 104th Bde | | |
| War Diary | Happy Valley. | 01/08/1916 | 02/08/1916 |
| War Diary | Vaux-Sur-Somme | 03/08/1916 | 05/08/1916 |
| War Diary | Montagne-Le-Fayel. | 06/08/1916 | 10/08/1916 |

| | | | |
|---|---|---|---|
| War Diary | Vaux-Sur-Somme | 11/08/1916 | 15/08/1916 |
| War Diary | Happy Valley | 15/08/1916 | 18/08/1916 |
| War Diary | Talus Boise | 19/08/1916 | 19/08/1916 |
| War Diary | Dublin Trench. | 20/08/1916 | 22/08/1916 |
| War Diary | Trenches. | 23/08/1916 | 25/08/1916 |
| War Diary | Casement Trench. | 26/08/1916 | 26/08/1916 |
| War Diary | Citadel. | 27/08/1916 | 30/08/1916 |
| War Diary | Candas. | 31/08/1916 | 31/08/1916 |
| Map | Extract from Trench Map 62c N.W.1. Disposition on Aug 23rd 1916. Appendix 1. | | |
| Map | Sketch From Trench Map 62c N.W.1 Disposition on Aug. 24th 1916, Before Forward Movement. Appendix 2. | | |
| Map | Sketch From Trench Map 62c N.W.1 Disposition on Aug 24th 1916, After Forward Movement. Appendix 3. | | |
| War Diary | Ivergny. | 01/09/1916 | 01/09/1916 |
| War Diary | Grand Rullecourt | 02/09/1916 | 02/09/1916 |
| War Diary | Fosseaux | 03/09/1916 | 03/09/1916 |
| War Diary | Dainville. | 04/09/1916 | 08/09/1916 |
| War Diary | Arras | 09/09/1916 | 09/09/1916 |
| War Diary | Trenches | 09/09/1916 | 15/09/1916 |
| War Diary | Arras. | 15/09/1916 | 15/09/1916 |
| War Diary | Dainville. | 16/09/1916 | 21/09/1916 |
| War Diary | Trenches. | 21/09/1916 | 28/09/1916 |
| War Diary | Arras | 29/09/1916 | 30/09/1916 |
| Operation(al) Order(s) | 17th (S) Battalion, lancashire Fusiliers. Honours & Rewards. Brigade Order No.180 dated 28.9.16. Appendix 2. | 28/09/1916 | 28/09/1916 |
| Miscellaneous | 17 Lancashire Fusiliers | 28/09/1916 | 28/09/1916 |
| Map | Appendix 1. | | |
| Heading | War Diary of 17th Service (1st S.E.L.) Battalion Lancashire Fusiliers. From:- 1st October, 1916. To:- 31st October, 1916. (Volume 9) | | |
| War Diary | Arras. | 01/10/1916 | 05/10/1916 |
| War Diary | Trenches | 05/10/1916 | 11/10/1916 |
| War Diary | Arras | 12/10/1916 | 17/10/1916 |
| War Diary | | 12/10/1916 | 14/10/1916 |
| War Diary | | 15/10/1916 | 16/10/1916 |
| War Diary | Arras | 17/10/1916 | 17/10/1916 |
| War Diary | Trenches. | 17/10/1916 | 23/10/1916 |
| War Diary | Trenches | 17/10/1916 | 23/10/1916 |
| War Diary | Arras | 24/10/1916 | 29/10/1916 |
| War Diary | Trenches. | 29/10/1916 | 31/10/1916 |
| Miscellaneous | Battalion 17 Lancashire Fusiliers | 06/10/1916 | 06/10/1916 |
| War Diary | Battalion 17th Lancs Fus | 08/10/1916 | 08/10/1916 |
| Map | 1 Sector-Showing Detail 1 (1) | | |
| Heading | War Diary of 17th Service (1st S.E.L.) Battalion Lancashire Fusiliers From:- 1st November, 1916. To:- 30th, November, 1916. (Volume 10.) | | |
| War Diary | Trenches. | 01/11/1916 | 04/11/1916 |
| War Diary | Arras. | 04/11/1916 | 10/11/1916 |
| War Diary | Trenches. | 10/11/1916 | 16/11/1916 |
| War Diary | Arras. | 16/11/1916 | 22/11/1916 |
| War Diary | Trenches | 22/11/1916 | 26/11/1916 |
| War Diary | Arras. | 26/11/1916 | 30/11/1916 |

| | | | |
|---|---|---|---|
| Heading | War Diary of 17th Service (1st S.E.L.) Battalion, Lancashire Fusiliers. From:- 1st Decr,1916. To:- 31st Decr,1916. (Volume 11.) | | |
| War Diary | Arras. | 01/12/1916 | 02/12/1916 |
| War Diary | Trenches. | 03/12/1916 | 04/12/1916 |
| War Diary | Dainville. | 04/12/1916 | 28/12/1916 |
| War Diary | Dainville. | 12/12/1916 | 19/12/1916 |
| War Diary | Agnez. | 21/12/1916 | 21/12/1916 |
| War Diary | Dainville. | 27/12/1916 | 27/12/1916 |
| War Diary | Dainville. | 04/12/1916 | 28/12/1916 |
| War Diary | Manin. | 28/12/1916 | 31/12/1916 |
| Heading | War Diary of 17th (S) Battalion, Lancashire Fusiliers. From 1st January 1917 to 31st January 1917. Volume 12. | | |
| War Diary | Manin | 01/01/1917 | 05/01/1917 |
| War Diary | | 01/01/1917 | 16/01/1917 |
| War Diary | | 08/01/1917 | 31/01/1917 |
| War Diary | | 12/01/1917 | 31/01/1917 |
| War Diary | | 18/01/1917 | 31/01/1917 |
| Heading | War Diary of 17th (S.) Battalion, Lancashire Fusiliers. From 1st February 1917 To 31st February 1917. (Volume 13.) | | |
| War Diary | Arras. | 01/02/1917 | 02/02/1917 |
| War Diary | Wanquetin | 03/02/1917 | 03/02/1917 |
| War Diary | Liencourt. | 04/02/1917 | 06/02/1917 |
| War Diary | Ransart | 07/02/1917 | 07/02/1917 |
| War Diary | Beauval | 08/02/1917 | 08/02/1917 |
| War Diary | Naours. | 09/02/1917 | 17/02/1917 |
| War Diary | Wiencourt | 18/02/1917 | 18/02/1917 |
| War Diary | Rosieres. | 19/02/1917 | 26/02/1917 |
| War Diary | Camp Decauville | 27/02/1917 | 28/02/1917 |
| Heading | War Diary of 17th Service (1st S.E.L.) Battalion, Lancashire Fusiliers. From:- 1st March, 1917-To 31st. March, 1917 (Volume 14) | | |
| War Diary | Camp Decauville | 01/03/1917 | 05/03/1917 |
| War Diary | Trenches | 06/03/1917 | 09/03/1917 |
| War Diary | Support Trenches. | 10/03/1917 | 13/03/1917 |
| War Diary | Trenches. | 14/03/1917 | 18/03/1917 |
| War Diary | Fouquescourt. | 19/03/1917 | 28/03/1917 |
| War Diary | Etalon. | 29/03/1917 | 29/03/1917 |
| War Diary | Bacquencourt | 30/03/1917 | 31/03/1917 |
| Operation(al) Order(s) | 17th (S.) Battalion, Lancashire Fusiliers Operation Order No S9. by Lt. Col. A.M. Mills. D.S.O. Commanding. Appendix 1. | 05/03/1917 | 05/03/1917 |
| Heading | War Diary of 17th (S) (1st. S.E.L.) Battalion, Lancashire Fusiliers. From:- 1st April, 1917. To:- 30th April, 1917. (Volume 15) | | |
| War Diary | Bacquencourt | 01/04/1917 | 01/04/1917 |
| War Diary | Toulle. | 02/04/1917 | 02/04/1917 |
| War Diary | Germaine. | 03/04/1917 | 06/04/1917 |
| War Diary | Ugny & Lanchy. | 07/04/1917 | 10/04/1917 |
| War Diary | Marteville. | 11/04/1917 | 11/04/1917 |
| War Diary | Line. (Fresnoy-Le Petit) | 12/04/1917 | 14/04/1917 |
| War Diary | Line (Gricourt) | 14/04/1917 | 14/04/1917 |
| War Diary | Fresnoy-Le-Petit. | 15/04/1917 | 15/04/1917 |
| War Diary | Trefcon. | 16/04/1917 | 23/04/1917 |

| | | | |
|---|---|---|---|
| War Diary | Line. (Maissemy) | 24/04/1917 | 24/04/1917 |
| War Diary | Line. | 25/04/1917 | 27/04/1917 |
| War Diary | Villecholles. | 28/04/1917 | 30/04/1917 |
| Miscellaneous | 17th Service (1st S.E.L.) Battalion, Lancashire Fusiliers. Appendix "B" to War Diary (Volume 15) for April, 1917. | | |
| Map | Situation At. 3.30 PM. | | |
| Map | Sketch Map. Shewing Positions at 7.45 PM 4/4/17 to 12.45 AM 15/4/17. | | |
| Heading | War Diary of 17th Service (1st S.E.L.) Battalion, Lancashire Fusiliers. From:- 1st May 1917.-To:- 31st May, 1917. (Volume 16). | | |
| War Diary | Villecholles | 01/05/1917 | 01/05/1917 |
| War Diary | Line. | 03/05/1917 | 06/05/1917 |
| War Diary | Villecholles. | 07/05/1917 | 08/05/1917 |
| War Diary | Maissemy. | 10/05/1917 | 14/05/1917 |
| War Diary | Poeuilly. | 15/05/1917 | 21/05/1917 |
| War Diary | Peronne. | 22/05/1917 | 23/05/1917 |
| War Diary | Nr. Heudicourt. | 24/05/1917 | 25/05/1917 |
| War Diary | Line. | 26/05/1917 | 31/05/1917 |
| Miscellaneous | 17th Service (1st S.E.L.) Battalion, Lancashire Fusiliers. Appendix "A" to War Diary (Vol:16) Operations on Night of 5/6th May 1917. | 05/05/1917 | 05/05/1917 |
| Map | Sketch Maps Shewing Positions at 9.40 P.M. & 12 Mdnt Nights 5/6 May 1917. | | |
| Heading | War Diary of 17th Service (1st S.E.L.) Battalion, Lancashire Fusiliers. From:- 1st June 1917 To:- 30th June 1917. (Volume 17) | | |
| War Diary | Trenches. | 01/06/1917 | 02/06/1917 |
| War Diary | Nr. Heudicourt. | 03/06/1917 | 10/06/1917 |
| War Diary | Nr. Aizecourt-Le-Bas. | 11/06/1917 | 18/06/1917 |
| War Diary | Trenches. | 19/06/1917 | 26/06/1917 |
| War Diary | In Support. | 27/06/1917 | 30/06/1917 |
| Heading | War Diary of 17th Service (1st S.E.L.) Battalion, Lancashire Fusiliers From 1st July 1917 To:- 31st July 1917. (Volume 18) | | |
| War Diary | Villers-Guislain. | 01/07/1917 | 01/07/1917 |
| War Diary | Aizecourt-Le-Bas. | 02/07/1917 | 14/07/1917 |
| War Diary | Epehy. | 14/07/1917 | 23/07/1917 |
| War Diary | Trenches. | 24/07/1917 | 31/07/1917 |
| Heading | War Diary of 17th Service (1st S.E.L.) Battalion, Lancashire Fusiliers. From:- 1st August, 1917. To:- 31st. August 1917. (Volume 19.) | | |
| War Diary | Support Line | 01/08/1917 | 05/08/1917 |
| War Diary | Supports. | 06/08/1917 | 07/08/1917 |
| War Diary | Gurlu Wood. | 08/08/1917 | 19/08/1917 |
| War Diary | Trenches. | 20/08/1917 | 31/08/1917 |
| Operation(al) Order(s) | 17th Service (1st S.E.L.) Battalion, Lancashire Fusiliers. Operation Order No.S/49. Appendix. | 16/08/1917 | 16/08/1917 |
| Miscellaneous | 17th Service (1st S.E.L.) Battalion, Lancashire Fusiliers. Amendments to Operation Order No.S/49. | 18/08/1917 | 18/08/1917 |
| Miscellaneous | 17th Service (1st S.E.L.) Battalion, Lancashire Fusiliers. Amendments to Operation Order No.S/49. | 20/08/1917 | 20/08/1917 |
| Map | Map Ref. Sheet 66D S.W. | | |

| | | | |
|---|---|---|---|
| Miscellaneous | 17th Service (1st S.E.L.) Battalion, Lancashire Fusiliers. Daily Intelligence Summary from 6 a.m. 20/8/17 to 6 a.m. 21/8/17. | 20/08/1917 | 20/08/1917 |
| Heading | War Diary of 17th Service (1st S.E.L.) Battalion, Lancashire Fusiliers. From:- 1st September 1917.-To:- 30th September, 1917. (Volume 20) | | |
| War Diary | Trenches. | 01/09/1917 | 06/09/1917 |
| War Diary | Templeux-La-Fosse. | 08/09/1917 | 11/09/1917 |
| War Diary | Trenches. | 12/09/1917 | 19/09/1917 |
| War Diary | St. Emilie. | 20/09/1917 | 24/09/1917 |
| War Diary | Gillemont Sectr | 24/09/1917 | 24/09/1917 |
| War Diary | St. Emilie. | 25/09/1917 | 26/09/1917 |
| War Diary | Templeux-La-Fosse. | 27/09/1917 | 29/09/1917 |
| War Diary | Peronne. | 30/09/1917 | 30/09/1917 |
| Heading | War Diary of 17th Service (1st. S.E.L.) Battalion, Lancashire Fusiliers. From:- 1st October, 1917. To:- 31st October, 1917. (Volume 21.) | | |
| War Diary | Peronne. | 01/10/1917 | 02/10/1917 |
| War Diary | Aubigny. | 03/10/1917 | 03/10/1917 |
| War Diary | Lattre St. Quentin. | 04/10/1917 | 13/10/1917 |
| War Diary | Eringhem. | 14/10/1917 | 15/10/1917 |
| War Diary | Proven. | 16/10/1917 | 16/10/1917 |
| War Diary | Front Line. | 17/10/1917 | 18/10/1917 |
| War Diary | Camp. | 19/10/1917 | 20/10/1917 |
| War Diary | Front Line. | 21/10/1917 | 23/10/1917 |
| War Diary | Baboon Camp. | 24/10/1917 | 24/10/1917 |
| War Diary | Dykes Camp. | 25/10/1917 | 30/10/1917 |
| War Diary | New Boesinghe Camp. | 31/10/1917 | 31/10/1917 |
| Miscellaneous | 17th Service (1st S.E.L.) Battalion, Lancashire Fusiliers. Report on Operations 15th to 18th October, 1917. Appendix "A". | 15/10/1917 | 15/10/1917 |
| Miscellaneous | 17th Service (1st S.E.L.) Battalion, Lancashire Fusiliers. Report on Operations of October 22nd 1917. Appendix "B". | 22/10/1917 | 22/10/1917 |
| Diagram etc | Sketch Maps of Operations Houthulst Wood Oct 22/23rd. 17. | | |
| Heading | War Diary of 17th Service (1st. S.E.L.) Battalion, Lancashire Fusiliers. From:- 1st November, 1917. To:- 30th. November, 1917. (Volume 22) | | |
| War Diary | Camp. | 01/11/1917 | 04/11/1917 |
| War Diary | Purbrook. | 05/11/1917 | 06/11/1917 |
| War Diary | Herzeele. | 07/11/1917 | 17/11/1917 |
| War Diary | Siege Camp. | 18/11/1917 | 20/11/1917 |
| War Diary | Canal Bank. | 22/11/1917 | 22/11/1917 |
| War Diary | Front Line. | 24/11/1917 | 24/11/1917 |
| War Diary | Camp. | 25/11/1917 | 01/12/1917 |
| War Diary | Front Line | 02/12/1917 | 03/12/1917 |
| War Diary | Canal Bank | 04/12/1917 | 05/12/1917 |
| War Diary | Camp. | 06/12/1917 | 07/12/1917 |
| War Diary | Canal. | 08/12/1917 | 08/12/1917 |
| War Diary | Watou | 15/12/1917 | 15/12/1917 |
| War Diary | Houtkerque Area. | 16/12/1917 | 31/12/1917 |
| War Diary | Houtkerque. | 01/01/1918 | 07/01/1918 |
| War Diary | Canal Bank. | 08/01/1918 | 08/01/1918 |
| War Diary | Trenches. | 10/01/1918 | 10/01/1918 |
| War Diary | Supports. | 12/01/1918 | 12/01/1918 |

| | | | |
|---|---|---|---|
| War Diary | Trenches. | 14/01/1918 | 14/01/1918 |
| War Diary | Supports. | 16/01/1918 | 16/01/1918 |
| War Diary | Turco Camp. | 17/01/1918 | 24/01/1918 |
| War Diary | Trenches. | 26/01/1918 | 26/01/1918 |
| War Diary | Supports. | 28/01/1918 | 28/01/1918 |
| War Diary | Trenches. | 30/01/1918 | 30/01/1918 |
| War Diary | Supports. | 31/01/1918 | 31/01/1918 |
| Heading | War Diary of 17th Service (1st. S.E.L.) Battalion, Lancashire Fusiliers From:- 1st February 1918 To:- 28th February 1918. (Volume 25.) | | |
| War Diary | Turco Camp | 01/02/1918 | 08/02/1918 |
| War Diary | Irish Farm | 05/02/1918 | 05/02/1918 |
| War Diary | Turco Camp | 06/02/1918 | 06/02/1918 |
| War Diary | Trenches | 09/02/1918 | 09/02/1918 |
| War Diary | Support | 14/02/1918 | 14/02/1918 |
| War Diary | Cambridge Camp | 16/02/1918 | 21/02/1918 |
| War Diary | Larry Camp | 22/02/1918 | 28/02/1918 |
| Heading | 104th Inf. Bde. 35th Div. War Diary 17th Battn. The Lancashire Fusiliers. March 1918 | | |
| War Diary | Larry Camp. | 01/03/1918 | 23/03/1918 |
| War Diary | Maricourt | 24/03/1918 | 25/03/1918 |
| War Diary | Bray | 26/03/1918 | 26/03/1918 |
| War Diary | Buire Sur L Ancre. | 27/03/1918 | 30/03/1918 |
| War Diary | La Housslye | 31/03/1918 | 31/03/1918 |
| Miscellaneous | Marching Out State W. Company. | 22/03/1918 | 22/03/1918 |
| Miscellaneous | Marching Out State | 22/03/1918 | 22/03/1918 |
| Miscellaneous | C.O. Jahan | 28/03/1918 | 28/03/1918 |
| Miscellaneous | W Corps | 28/03/1918 | 28/03/1918 |
| Miscellaneous | W Coy 17th Lancs Fus. Casualty Reference from Noon 29.3.18 to Noon 30.3.18 | 29/03/1918 | 29/03/1918 |
| Heading | War Diary of 17th Service (1st S.E.L.) Bn., Lancashire Fusiliers From:- 1st April 1918-To:- 30th April, 1918. Volume 27. | | |
| War Diary | La Houssoye. | 01/04/1918 | 08/04/1918 |
| War Diary | Trenches | 08/04/1918 | 08/04/1918 |
| War Diary | Bonnay. | 09/04/1918 | 09/04/1918 |
| War Diary | Hedauville. | 10/04/1918 | 11/04/1918 |
| War Diary | Trenches | 12/04/1918 | 17/04/1918 |
| War Diary | Hedauville. | 18/04/1918 | 20/04/1918 |
| War Diary | Trenches. | 21/04/1918 | 26/04/1918 |
| War Diary | Bivouacs | 27/04/1918 | 29/04/1918 |
| Heading | War Diary of 17th Service (1st S.E.L.) Bn Lancashire Fusiliers From-1st May 1918. To-30th May 1918 Volume 28. | | |
| War Diary | Trenches | 01/05/1918 | 02/05/1918 |
| War Diary | Reserve | 03/05/1918 | 03/05/1918 |
| War Diary | Toutencourt | 04/05/1918 | 20/05/1918 |
| War Diary | Trenches | 21/05/1918 | 25/05/1918 |
| War Diary | Reserves | 26/05/1918 | 29/05/1918 |
| War Diary | Trenches | 30/05/1918 | 31/05/1918 |
| Heading | War Diary of 17th Service (1st S.E.L.) Battalion, Lancashire Fusiliers. From 1st June 1918 to 30th June 1918. Volume 29. | | |
| War Diary | Aveluy Wood | 01/05/1918 | 01/05/1918 |
| War Diary | Hedauville. | 02/06/1918 | 05/06/1918 |
| War Diary | Trenches. | 05/06/1918 | 18/06/1918 |

| | | | |
|---|---|---|---|
| War Diary | Warloy | 18/06/1918 | 18/06/1918 |
| War Diary | Beauquesne | 19/06/1918 | 30/06/1918 |
| Miscellaneous | Casualties For Month. | | |
| Miscellaneous | 17th Service (1st S.E.L.) Battalion, Lancashire Fusiliers. Appendix to War Diary for June, 1918. Extract from Battalion Orders dated 28th June, 1918. | 28/06/1918 | 28/06/1918 |
| Heading | War Diary of the 17th Service (1st S.E.L.) Batt. Lancashire Fusiliers From 1st July 1918-To 31st July 1918 Volume No.30. | | |
| War Diary | St Omer. | 01/07/1918 | 01/07/1918 |
| War Diary | Bois De Beauvoorde | 02/07/1918 | 08/07/1918 |
| War Diary | Boeschepe | 09/07/1918 | 31/07/1918 |
| Heading | War Diary of 17th Service (1st S.E.L.) Battalion, Lancashire Fusiliers 1-8-18 to 31-8-18. Volume 31. | | |
| War Diary | Locre | 01/08/1918 | 31/08/1918 |
| Miscellaneous | Casualties for month. | | |
| Heading | War Diary of the 17th Service (1st S.E.L.) Battalion, The Lancashire Fusiliers From:- 1.9.18 to:- 30.9.18. Volume No.32. | | |
| War Diary | Cassel | 01/09/1918 | 02/09/1918 |
| War Diary | Herzeele | 03/09/1918 | 05/09/1918 |
| War Diary | Erie Camp. | 06/09/1918 | 07/09/1918 |
| War Diary | Front Line | 08/09/1918 | 12/09/1918 |
| War Diary | Bde. Res. | 13/09/1918 | 30/09/1918 |
| Miscellaneous | Casualties for month:- | | |
| Operation(al) Order(s) | Operation Order R23. | 27/09/1918 | 27/09/1918 |
| Map | Parts of Shts. 28 N.W., 28 N.E., 28 S.W. & 28 S.E. | | |
| Miscellaneous | | | |
| Map | Parts of Shts. 28 N.W., 28 N.E., 28 S.W. & 28 S.E. | | |
| Miscellaneous | | | |
| Map | Message Map Scale 1/40,000 Part-Sheet 28. | | |
| Miscellaneous | Operation Order S.14. Egy Appendix 2. | 18/08/1917 | 18/08/1917 |
| Heading | War Diary of the 17th Service (1st S.E.L) Battalion, The Lancashire Fusiliers From 1.10.18 to 31.10.18 Volume No 33. | | |
| War Diary | W of Wervicq-America Cabt. | 01/10/1918 | 02/10/1918 |
| War Diary | Zillebeke Lake. | 03/10/1918 | 06/10/1918 |
| War Diary | Front Line | 07/10/1918 | 08/10/1918 |
| War Diary | J 20. | 09/10/1918 | 11/10/1918 |
| War Diary | Front Line. | 12/10/1918 | 14/10/1918 |
| War Diary | Elba Corner. L.27.f.2.8. | 15/10/1918 | 18/10/1918 |
| War Diary | Marcke. | 19/10/1918 | 19/10/1918 |
| War Diary | Marionnette-Berg | 20/10/1918 | 20/10/1918 |
| War Diary | N.35.a. | 21/10/1918 | 21/10/1918 |
| War Diary | Courtrai. | 21/10/1918 | 25/10/1918 |
| War Diary | Avelghem. | 26/10/1918 | 27/10/1918 |
| War Diary | Krote | 28/10/1918 | 30/10/1918 |
| War Diary | Avelghem. | 31/10/1918 | 31/10/1918 |
| Miscellaneous | Casualties for month:- | | |
| Miscellaneous | Honours Gained by the Battalion during the Period 1st-31st October, 1918. | 01/10/1918 | 01/10/1918 |
| Miscellaneous | ZOVI. Preliminary Instructions for Attack. | 10/10/1918 | 10/10/1918 |
| Miscellaneous | Adjt | | |
| Operation(al) Order(s) | 17th (S) Lancashire Fusiliers Operation Order R27. | 30/10/1918 | 30/10/1918 |
| Map | | | |
| Map | No. 9308. | | |

| | | | |
|---|---|---|---|
| Map | | | |
| Map | No. 9308. | | |
| Map | No. 9252. | | |
| Map | | | |
| Map | No.9252. | | |
| Map | | | |
| Heading | The 17th Services (1st S.E.L.) Battalion The Lancashire Fusiliers From 1-11-18 To 30-11-18. Volume No.34. | | |
| War Diary | Tenhove | 01/11/1918 | 01/11/1918 |
| War Diary | O.2.b. | 02/11/1918 | 02/11/1918 |
| War Diary | Hooge. | 03/11/1918 | 07/11/1918 |
| War Diary | Esscher. | 08/11/1918 | 09/11/1918 |
| War Diary | Berchem. | 10/11/1918 | 10/11/1918 |
| War Diary | Audenhove. | 11/10/1918 | 11/10/1918 |
| War Diary | Vicinity of Grammont. | 12/10/1918 | 13/10/1918 |
| War Diary | Schoorisse | 14/10/1918 | 18/10/1918 |
| War Diary | Berchem. | 19/10/1918 | 19/10/1918 |
| War Diary | Harlebeke | 20/10/1918 | 29/10/1918 |
| War Diary | Menin | 30/11/1918 | 30/11/1918 |
| Miscellaneous | Honours Gained by the Battalion during the period 1st-30th November, 1918. | 01/11/1918 | 01/11/1918 |
| Miscellaneous | Casualties for month:- | | |
| Heading | The 17th Service (1st S.E.L.) Battalion The Lancashire Fusiliers From 1-12-1918 to 31-12-1918. Volume No.35. | | |
| War Diary | Vlamertinghe | 01/12/1918 | 01/12/1918 |
| War Diary | St. Sylvestre Cappel | 02/12/1918 | 02/12/1918 |
| War Diary | Merckeghem | 03/12/1918 | 31/12/1918 |
| Miscellaneous | Casualties for month | 02/01/1918 | 02/01/1918 |
| Miscellaneous | Honours Gained by the Battalion during the period 1st-31st December, 1918. | 01/12/1918 | 01/12/1918 |
| Heading | The 17th Service (1st S.E.L.) Battalion The Lancashire Fusiliers. From 1-1-1919 to 31-1-1919. Volume 36. | | |
| War Diary | Merckeghem | 01/01/1919 | 29/01/1919 |
| War Diary | Calais | 30/01/1919 | 31/01/1919 |
| Miscellaneous | Honours joined by the Battalion during the period 1st-31st January, 1919. | 01/01/1919 | 01/01/1919 |
| Miscellaneous | Casualties for month | 03/02/1919 | 03/02/1919 |
| War Diary | Calais | 01/02/1919 | 02/02/1919 |
| War Diary | Coijlogne | 02/02/1919 | 10/02/1919 |
| War Diary | Calais | 10/02/1919 | 27/02/1919 |
| War Diary | Beaumarais | 28/02/1919 | 28/02/1919 |
| Miscellaneous | Honours joined by the Battalion during the period 1st-28th February 1919 | 01/02/1919 | 01/02/1919 |
| Miscellaneous | Casualties for the month | 03/03/1919 | 03/03/1919 |
| Heading | The 17th Service (1st S.E.L.) Battalion. The Lancashire Fusiliers. From 1-3-19 to 31-3-19. Volume 38 | | |
| War Diary | Beaumarais | 01/03/1919 | 04/03/1919 |
| War Diary | Merceghem | 05/03/1919 | 31/03/1919 |
| Miscellaneous | Honours joined by the Battalion during the period 1st-31st March 1919. | 01/03/1919 | 01/03/1919 |
| Miscellaneous | Casualties for the month. | 31/03/1919 | 31/03/1919 |

WO 95/2484/1

35TH DIVISION
104TH INFY BDE

17TH BN LANCS FUS.

~~FEB~~ 1916-MAR 1919
JAN

# CONFIDETIAL.

## WAR DIARY

of

17th (Service) Battn. Lanc. Fus. S. E. L.

From JAN 28TH 1916 To FEB 27TH 1916

Instructions regarding War Diaries and Intelligence Summaries are contained in F. S. Regs., Part II. and the Staff Manual respectively. Title Pages will be prepared in manuscript.

# WAR DIARY
or
~~INTELLIGENCE SUMMARY~~
*(Erase heading not required.)*

Army Form C. 2118

| Place | Date 1916 | Hour | Summary of Events and Information | Remarks and references to Appendices |
|---|---|---|---|---|
| PARKHOUSE CAMP. SALISBURY | JAN. 28TH | | LIEUTS. JOBLING & ROBINSON were left with the Details at PARKHOUSE CAMP. | |
| LE. HAVRE. | JAN. 29TH | 9-30am<br>5.0pm | The Battn. disembarked at LE HAVRE and proceeded to No.5 DOCK REST CAMP. – After settling down, fires lighted &c to prepare a hot meal, orders were received to proceed to No1 REST CAMP, distance 7 miles. In a very short time the Battn. was on parade in marching order, everyman carrying his blankets and waterproof sheet and proceeded through the town, arriving at its destination about 5p.m. Here orders were awaiting to entrain the following morning. | |
| LE. HAVRE | JAN 30TH | 12p.m<br>2.30pm | "W" Coy under Major BROWN-HOVELT entrained at No. 4. LE HAVRE; the remainder of the Battn under the C.O. at No.3. LE HAVRE and left at 12 noon and 2.30 p.m respectively. | |
| ST. OMER<br>WIZERNES | JAN 31ST<br>" | 10a.m<br>" | "W" Coy detrained at ST. OMER and the Battn at WIZERNES at about 10a.m. where we were billetted until the 9th February | |
| WIZERNES | FEB 8TH | | CAPTS CROOK, RENNISON CHRISTIE, COWAN together with 2 N.C.Os per company were attached to the Headquarters of the GUARDS' DIVISION for instruction in Trench warfare. | |
| WIZERNES<br>WARDRECQUES | FEB. 9TH.<br>FEB 9TH | 10-45 a.m. | The Battalion marched to WARDRECQUES and took over Billets from the 17th Bn. ROYAL SCOTS & was inspected en route by the C.in.C. SIR D. HAIG. LIEUT. R.C. DOIDGE 17th LAN. FUS. promoted to temporary rank of CAPTAIN (without pay and allowances) with effect from the 8th February 1916, whilst holding appointment of Brigade Grenade Officer 104th Infantry Brigade. | ARMY COUNCIL No 50 of 1916<br>APPENDIX. I. |
| WARDRECQUES | FEB. 11th. | 11a.m. | The Battalion was inspected by Field Marshal Lord KITCHENER, who expressed his approval of the smart appearance of the men. | |

1875 Wt. W593/826 1,000,000 4/15 J.B.C. & A. A.D.S.S./Forms/C. 2118.

Instructions regarding War Diaries and Intelligence Summaries are contained in F. S. Regs., Part II. and the Staff Manual respectively. Title Pages will be prepared in manuscript.

# WAR DIARY
*or*
~~INTELLIGENCE SUMMARY~~
*(Erase heading not required.)*

Army Form C. 2118

| Place | Date 1916 | Hour | Summary of Events and Information | Remarks and references to Appendices |
|---|---|---|---|---|
| ARDRECQUES | FEB 14TH | | CAPTAINS CROOK, RENNISON, CHRISTIE, COWAN, with the 2 NCOS per company returned from the GUARDS' DIVISION.<br>The G.O.C XI Army Corps lectured to all Officers of the 104th Brigade at AIRE. | |
| WARDRECQUES | FEB. 18TH. | 10.30 a.m. | The Battalion marched from WARDECQUES to THIENNES where it was billetted for the night. | APPENDIX I. |
| THIENNIES. | FEB. 19TH | 9.30 a.m. | Marched to ROBECQ - CALONNE area where it was billetted for the night. | APPENDIX I |
| ROBECQ. | FEB. 20TH. | 7.0 a.m. | Marched to GORRE, where it was attached to the 113th Infantry Brigade, 38th WELSH DIVISION, for instruction in Trench warfare.<br>The Battalion was attached as under:-<br>"W" Coy attached to 16th Royal WELSH FUSILIERS.<br>"X" Coy " " 13th " " "<br>"Y" Coy " " 14th " " "<br>"Z" Coy " " 15th " " " | APPENDIX I |
| GORRE. | FEB 21st. | | The following casualties occurred on this date :- 5 men wounded. | |
| GORRE. | FEB. 22nd | 8.45am | 2/LIEUT. LAYMAN was fatally wounded - he died about 12 noon at the 33rd CASUALTY CLEARING STATION | |
| GORRE | FEB 23rd. | | One private of Y Coy was killed on this date<br>Copy of letter received from the G.O.C. 113th Infantry Brigade, dated 22.2.16<br>"Please convey to your Battalion, my appreciation of the spirit they showed in the recent encounter they had with the enemy. The readiness of the listening patrol in allowing the enemy to approach them and then dealing with them is also an excellent sign."<br>(Sd). L. PRICE DAVIES. BGDR. GEN. | 113th Inf Bde No. B.M. 621. 22/2/16. |

1875 Wt. W593/826 1,000,000 4/15 J.B.C. & A. A.D.S.S./Forms/C. 2118.

Army Form C. 2118

# WAR DIARY
*or*
~~INTELLIGENCE SUMMARY~~
*(Erase heading not required.)*

Instructions regarding War Diaries and Intelligence Summaries are contained in F. S. Regs., Part II. and the Staff Manual respectively. Title Pages will be prepared in manuscript.

| Place | Date | Hour | Summary of Events and Information | Remarks and references to Appendices |
|---|---|---|---|---|
| GORRE | FEB 24th | 2 P.M. | 2/LT. LAYMAN. D.A.C. was buried at COLLEGE ST. VAAST, BETHUNE. | WH |
| GORRE | FEB. 26TH. | – | The following casualties occurred this day:- 3 men wounded | WH |
| GORRE | FEB 27TH | – | The Battalion came out of the trenches after completing its instruction, and marched from GORRE to LESLOBES to take over the billets vacated by the 15th CHESHIRE REGT., thus being temporarily attached to the 105TH Infantry Brigade. It remained in these billets as a reserve until MARCH 1ST. | 1/40.000 SHEET BETHUNE. APPENDIX I. WH |

W Hesson Capt for Lt Colonel Commdg 17th (Service) Battn. Lanc. Fus. B. F. L.

1875 Wt. W593/826 1,000,000 4/15 J.B.C. & A. A.D.S.S./Forms/C. 2118.

35

17 Lan Fus

Vol 2

CONFIDENTIAL.

# WAR DIARY.

OF

17th (Service) Battn. Lanc. Fus. S. E. L.

1916.

FROM MARCH 1ST. TO MARCH 31ST.

VOLUME II.

2. V.
9 sheets

Instructions regarding War Diaries and Intelligence Summaries are contained in F. S. Regs., Part II. and the Staff Manual respectively. Title Pages will be prepared in manuscript.

# WAR DIARY
*or*
# INTELLIGENCE SUMMARY
*(Erase heading not required.)*

Army Form C. 2118

| Place | 1916. Date | Hour | Summary of Events and Information VOLUME II MARCH 1916. | Remarks and references to Appendices |
|---|---|---|---|---|
| LESLOBES | MARCH 1st. | 8.0 a.m. | The Battalion marched from LESLOBES to ROBECQ-CALONNE area to rejoin the 104th Infantry Brigade. KH | 1/40.000 SHEET BETHUNE APPENDIX II. |
| ROBECQ - CALONNE. | MARCH 2nd. | 3.30pm | CAPT DOIDGE, 104th Brigade Bombing Officer, was accidentally killed whilst carrying out Bomb Instruction | KH |
| ROBECQ - CALONNE | MARCH 3rd. | 10 a.m. | The Battalion was inspected by Brigadier General G.M. MACKENZIE<br>Transferrence of 1 N.C.O to DIVISIONAL CAMP COMMANDANT.<br>" 11 men to 75th SANITARY SECTION, ST VENANT.<br>Received preliminary instructions re relief of 58th Brigade. | |
| | | 4pm. | Funeral of Capt DOIDGE at CALONNE CHURCH. | KH |
| ROBECQ - CALONNE. | MARCH 5TH | 4pm. | Received Brigade Operation Order No. 6. re relieving the 58th Brigade in the sector QUINQUE RUE – PLUM STREET. | KH |
| ROBECQ. - CALONNE. | MARCH 6TH. | 9.30am. | The C.O., 2nd in Command, and Coy. Commanders reported to Headquarters 9th CHESHIRE REGT (LEFT RESERVE BATTALION) to obtain all available | |
| | | 4pm. | information – returned to ROBECQ-CALONNE Area at 4p.m. | KH |
| ROBECQ - CALONNE | MARCH 7th. | 10am | The Battalion left ROBECQ area en route for RICHEBOURG ST. VAAST – arrived at 10 am and relieved the 9th CHESHIRES. – thus taking LEFT RESERVE BATTALION. | KH |
| RICHEBOURG ST VAAST | MARCH 8th. | 6.10pm | Took over the left subsector of the Sector QUINQUE RUE – PLUM STREET from the 20th LANCASHIRE FUSILIERS – relief completed without interruption or casualty by 7.47 pm. | KH |
| | | 7.47pm | | |

1875 Wt. W593/826 1,000,000 4/15 J.B.C. & A. A.D.S.S./Forms/C. 2118.

Instructions regarding War Diaries and Intelligence Summaries are contained in F. S. Regs., Part II. and the Staff Manual respectively. Title Pages will be prepared in manuscript.

Volume V.

# WAR DIARY
*or*
# ~~INTELLIGENCE SUMMARY~~
*(Erase heading not required.)*

Army Form C. 2118

| Place | 1916. Date | Hour | Summary of Events and Information | Remarks and references to Appendices |
|---|---|---|---|---|
| LUM STREET TO BOAR'S HEAD. | MARCH 9th. 5am to MARCH 10th 5am | 5am<br>3.45pm | Situation unchanged - some shelling - wind N.N.E.<br>Situation unchanged - enemy very quiet - snipers rather active - wind N. | LH |
| LUM STREET TO BOAR'S HEAD. | MARCH 10th, to MARCH 11th | 5am<br>5am | Situation normal - Snipers persistant - enemy's artillery bombarded our support trenches in the morning at RIGHT GUARDS and COPSE STREET - retaliation by own artillery - Several enemy working parties dispersed - The searchlight in enemy's lines causes a great deal of inconvenience to our working parties. Much work was done, eg repairing parapets, strengthening wires and draining trenches.<br>One casualty occurred during the day - one man being wounded | LH |
| LUM STREET TO BOARS HEAD. | MARCH 11TH to MARCH 12th | 5am<br>5am | Slight shelling by enemy on GUARDS KEEP & GUARDS TRENCH - snipers very active especially at night.<br>Front line trenches cleared at 2.45pm between S.10.2 & S.10.3 to enable our Howitzer Battery to fire on enemy front line. Much damage apparently done.<br>During the day the wind veered from NE to S.<br>Work as described 10.3.16 carried on with considerable progress.<br>Casualty - one man wounded. | LH |
| LUM STREET TO BOARS HEAD. | MARCH 12th to MARCH 13th | 5am<br>5am | Enemy particularly active - enemy working party opposite S.10.3 caught by machine gun and rapid rifle fire. Patrols report NO MAN'S LAND in front of S.16.3 in very bad state.<br>Enemy's Trench mortars shelled junction of front line trench and COPSE ST.<br>One man was fatally wounded and another wounded during the day.<br>The Searchlight was again visible & fired on by D Battery - result unknown as yet. | LH |
| LUM STREET TO BOARS HEAD | MARCH 13th to MARCH 14th | 5am<br>5a.m. | Patrols sent out to locate snipers' position. LIEUT. NUTTALL wounded and one man killed by sniper - NO MANS LAND patrolled (See sketch over). Rifle Grenades fired by enemy opposite S.10.3 - retaliation by D Battery - enemy artillery bombarded trenches S.10.3<br>Snipers still active<br>Casualties 2 men killed 1 Officer and 1 man wounded. | LH |

1875 Wt. W593/826 1,000,000 4/15 J.B.C. & A. A.D.S.S./Forms/C. 2118.

Instructions regarding War Diaries and Intelligence Summaries are contained in F. S. Regs., Part II. and the Staff Manual respectively. Title Pages will be prepared in manuscript.

Volume V.

Army Form C. 2118

# WAR DIARY
*or*
# ~~INTELLIGENCE SUMMARY~~
*(Erase heading not required.)*

| Place | Date | Hour | Summary of Events and Information | Remarks and references to Appendices |
|---|---|---|---|---|
| NO MANS' LAND | MARCH 12th to MARCH 13th | | SKETCH OF NO MANS LAND 14.3.16 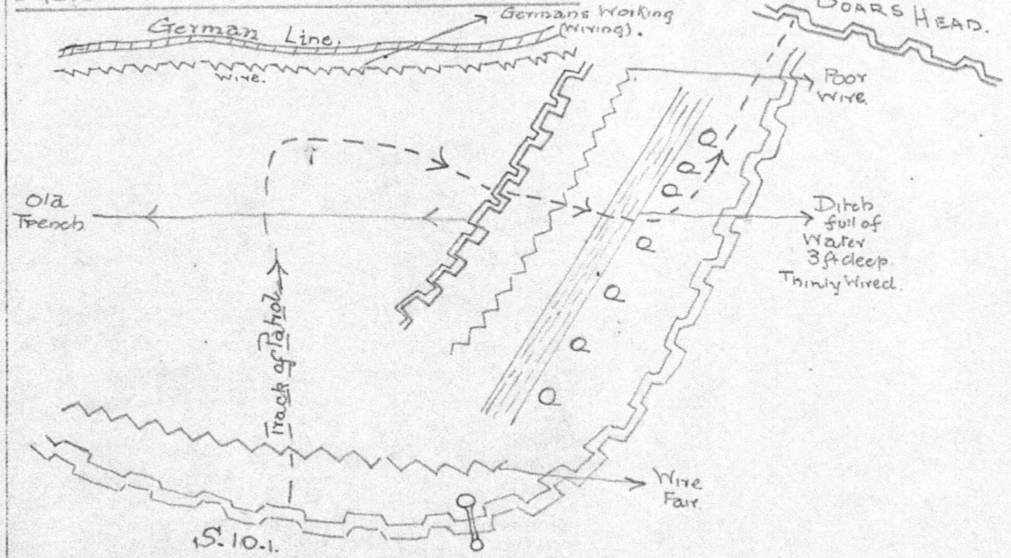  STATE of Ground<br>Very Muddy.<br>Impossible to cross ditch without making much noise. | [illegible] |
| LEFT SUBSECTOR | MARCH 14th to MARCH 15th | 5 am<br>5 a.m. | Very quiet day - heavy firing on our left about 6am and on right in late afternoon and evening. - enemy working parties dispersed - sniper located at BOARS HEAD wearing sandbag with eye slits over his head. Our artillery fired at enemy's wire opposite S.10.3 - causing much damage. Aeroplanes active, one of ours was brought down in our lines in the afternoon, an enemy aeroplane on being fired at by our machine guns, changed direction and got out of range.<br>Casualties - 1 man killed and 1 man wounded. | [illegible] |
| LEFT SUBSECTOR. | MARCH 15TH to MARCH 16TH. | 5 a.m<br>5 a.m. | Up to 9am. situation normal - then enemy shelled BUTE ST. breastworks followed by rifle grenade attack in morning and afternoon. The latter was silenced by our having obtained a bigger stock between the attacks. Two scares of gas originated from the Brigade on our left. Mining experts report mining to be impossible at present in this sector.<br>Casualties:- 2/Lt FARRAR fatally wounded<br>CAPT. CHRISTIE severely wounded<br>3 men wounded. | [illegible] |

1875 Wt. W593/826 1,000,000 4/15 J.B.C. & A. A.D.S.S./Forms/C. 2118.

Instructions regarding War Diaries and Intelligence Summaries are contained in F. S. Regs., Part II. and the Staff Manual respectively. Title Pages will be prepared in manuscript.

Volume II

# WAR DIARY
*or*
# ~~INTELLIGENCE SUMMARY~~
*(Erase heading not required.)*

Army Form C. 2118

| Place | Date 1916. | Hour | Summary of Events and Information | Remarks and references to Appendices |
|---|---|---|---|---|
| LEFT SUBSECTOR | MARCH 16th | 5am to 9am | Our parapet breached at certain points by own Artillery firing at enemy's wire. Enemy reply was feeble. The Battalion was relieved by the 20th Batt. LANCS. FUS and the relief was completed without interruption or casualty by 9 pm. Took over Left Reserve Billets at RICHEBOURG ST VAAST. Casualties during the day were 4 men wounded. | LSH |
| RICHEBOURG ST. VAAST. | MARCH 17th | 12.45am | 2/Lt. FARRAR died of wounds (received 16.3.16) at 32nd Casualty Clearing Station, ST. VENANT and was interred there in the afternoon. | LSH |
| RICHEBOURG ST VAAST. | MARCH 18th | | 2/Lt. C. THIELE joined the Battalion for duty and posted to "X" Coy. | LSH |
| RICHEBOURG ST. VAAST | MARCH 18th to MARCH 23rd. | | The Battalion during this period supplied working parties for the repairing of various front line, support and communication trenches. | LSH |
| FRONT LINE TRENCHES. | MARCH 24th | 9.0pm. | A raid was made by a party of 3 officers and 50 other ranks on the enemy's salient opposite S.10.2 and S.10.3. A covering party of 2 officers and 100 other ranks supported the raiding party in the front line. The Battalions on the Left and Right, namely, 7th Kings Own Lancaster Regt., and the 18th Lancashire Fusiliers together with the Supporting Artillery Brigade were all instructed how to act in case of counter attacks by the enemy. The preliminary arrangements, eg the previous observation of the salient under consideration by the Officer i/c of raiding Party, the training of the men selected for the raiding party and the various means of exit, of bridging the ditch and of return were all carried out in accordance with Operation orders received on the 29th inst. The raid was postponed from 9 pm until 9.35 pm. as the enemy's searchlight was not put out of action, although rifle fire and artillery fire was directed at it. | LSH |
| | | 9.35pm | At 9.35 pm the raiding party crept forward, reached and | |

1875 Wt. W593/826 1,000,000 4/15 J.B.C. & A. A.D.S.S./Forms/C. 2118.

Instructions regarding War Diaries and Intelligence Summaries are contained in F. S. Regs., Part II. and the Staff Manual respectively. Title Pages will be prepared in manuscript.

# WAR DIARY
*or*
~~INTELLIGENCE SUMMARY~~
*(Erase heading not required.)*

Army Form C. 2118

| Place | Date | Hour | Summary of Events and Information | Remarks and references to Appendices |
|---|---|---|---|---|
| S.10.2<br>S.10.3 | MARCH 24TH | 9.35 p.m. | passed the enemy's wire, when an exchange of hand grenades took place ~~thus~~ + the enemy opened rapid fire causing our men to retire. The following casualties occurred:- 1 man fatally wounded and died before reaching the Dressing Station.<br>2/LT. WILLIAMS wounded.<br>10 other ranks wounded<br>4 other ranks slightly wounded and still doing duty. | |

SKETCH SHOWING BRITISH & ENEMY SALIENTS DURING ABOVE RAID.

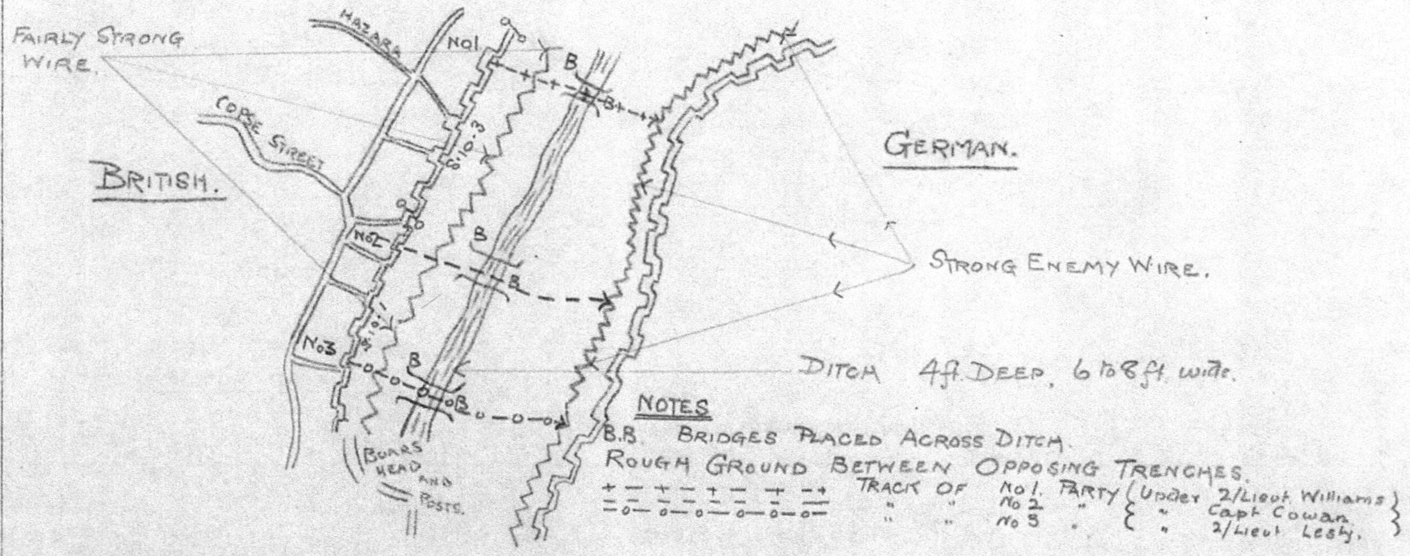

Instructions regarding War Diaries and Intelligence Summaries are contained in F. S. Regs., Part II. and the Staff Manual respectively. Title Pages will be prepared in manuscript.

Army Form C. 2118

# WAR DIARY
*or*
~~INTELLIGENCE SUMMARY~~
*(Erase heading not required.)*

Volume II

| Place | Date | Hour | Summary of Events and Information | Remarks and references to Appendices |
|---|---|---|---|---|
| [R]ICHEBOURG ST. VAAST. | MARCH 25th. | 9.30 am to 12.30 am. | The Battalion marched from the Reserve Billets at RICHEBOURG ST. VAAST, where it was relieved by the 9th Cheshire Regiment, to the PACAUT area. | APPENDIX II<br>LSH |
| PARADIS. | MARCH 26TH | 12 noon. | The G.O.C. 35th Division lectured to the C.Os., Adjutants and Coy. Commanders of the 104th Brigade at the School, PARADIS. | LSH |
| PACAUT AREA. | MARCH 28th. | 9.45 am | The Battalion marched from the Billets at PACAUT to SAILLY where it came in the Brigade Reserve.<br>Transference of 1 N.C.O. and 7 men to 181st Tunnelling Company R.E. at LAVENTIE. | MAP SHEET 36, EDITION 6.<br>LSH |

[signature] Lieut. Colonel.
Commdg. 17th (Service) Battn. Lanc. Fus. S. E. L.

1875 Wt. W593/826 1,000,000 4/15 J.B.C. & A. A.D.S.S./Forms/C. 2118.

Instructions regarding War Diaries and Intelligence Summaries are contained in F. S. Regs., Part II. and the Staff Manual respectively. Title Pages will be prepared in manuscript.

# WAR DIARY
*or*
~~INTELLIGENCE SUMMARY~~
*(Erase heading not required.)*

Army Form C. 2118

APPENDIX II — ROUTE · MOVEMENTS - OPERATION ORDERS. VOLUME II.

| Place | Date | Hour | Summary of Events and Information | Remarks and references to Appendices |
|---|---|---|---|---|
| ESLOBES | MARCH 1st | 8am | MOVE FROM LESLOBES TO ROBECQ-CALONNE AREA.<br>CROSS ROADS R.31a - Cross Roads R.25c - Cross Roads Q30b - Cross roads Q28d Cross Roads Q28b - via H in BOHEME - Cross Roads Q9b - Cross Roads Q9c - CALONNE.<br>STARTING POINT:- 100 yards South of LE in LE-LOBES.<br>ORDER:- Advanced Guard - 1 platoon X Coy<br>X Coy less 1 platoon.<br>Y "<br>Z "<br>W " less 2 platoons.<br>Rear Guard. 2 platoons W Coy | SHEET 6 BETHUNE. 1/40.000 |
| ALONNE AREA. | MARCH 7th | 10.a.m. | Move from CALONNE area to RICHEBOURG ST. VAAST.<br>ROUTE Road junction at Q.14 c4.5 - LE CORNET MALO - ZELOBES - VEILLE CHAPELLE - draw-bridge at R.3a - RICHEBOURG ST VAAST. | MAP SHEET BETHUNE. |
| PLUM ST TO QUINQUE RUE, | MAR 8th | | Battalion took over left section of the Brigade Sector. This section extends from PLUM ST to BOARS HEAD and posts. The front of this section is divided into 3 subsections (1) Z Coy took over right subsection ie BOARS HEAD - 5 posts and post extending from CINDER TRACK SOUTHWARD. - 2 platoons in front line; 2 platoons in support in PALL MALL TRENCH<br>(2). W Coy took over centre subsection from CINDER TRACK to COPSE STREET both inclusive, 3 platoons in front line and 1 in support in LEFT GUARDS<br>(3) X Coy took over left subsection extending from COPSE STREET and PLUM STREET with 3 platoons in front line and 1 platoon in support between HAZARD and PLUM STREET.<br>Y Coy was in support and be divided as follows:—<br>COPSE KEEP - - - - - - - 1 N.C.O & 15 men.<br>RIGHT GUARDS. - - - - - 1 NCO & 15 men<br>FACTORY POST. - - - - - 1 NCO & 3 men.<br>CATS - - - - - - - 1 NCO & 15 men.<br>STRAND. - - - - - - 2 officers 25 other ranks.<br>BUTE - - - - - - 3 officers and remainder of Company.<br>The Companies passed Windy Corner in following order with 200 yards distance between parties, no party to be more than one platoon. | BETHUNE MAP |

Army Form C. 2118

Instructions regarding War Diaries and Intelligence Summaries are contained in F. S. Regs., Part II. and the Staff Manual respectively. Title Pages will be prepared in manuscript.

# WAR DIARY
*or*
~~INTELLIGENCE SUMMARY~~
*(Erase heading not required.)*

| Place | Date | Hour | Summary of Events and Information — APPENDIX II — VOLUME II. | Remarks and references to Appendices |
|---|---|---|---|---|
| RICHEBOURG ST VAAST | MARCH 8" | 6.10<br>6.20<br>6.30<br>6.40. | W Coy, met by 4 guides passed WINDY CORNER at 6.10 pm.<br>X " " " 4 " " " " 6.20 pm<br>Y " " " 6 " " " " 6.30 pm<br>Z " " " 4 " " " " 6.40 pm.<br>BATTN. HEADQUARTERS AT. S9. a Y5.<br>REGTL. AID POST " S9. d. 2.8. | BRIGADE TRENCH MAP AREA H. |
| RICHEBOURG ST VAAST | MARCH 24th. | am 9.30<br>10.30<br>11.30<br>12.30pm | ROUTE FROM RICHEBOURG ST. VAAST TO PACAUT AREA.<br>W Coy, X Coy, Z Coy, Y Coy } Companies moved EAST of LAWE CANAL by platoons at 200 yds distance.<br>ROUTE. QUEEN MARY'S ROAD – R. 35. d 5.4 – X. 5. A.5 8 – DRAW BRIDGE, R.34.a.6.8 – VEILLE CHAPELLE – ZELOBES. – thence to Billets by shortest route. | MAP BETHUNE COMBINED SHEET |
| PACAUT AREA. | MARCH 27th. | 9.45 a.m. | ROUTE FROM PACAUT AREA TO SAILLY-SUR-LA-LYS.<br>Head of "W" Coy at road junction 100 yds WEST of P in PARADIS, followed by Y & Z Coys.<br>"X" Coy marched by shortest route and was at same place at that hour.<br>ADVANCED GUARD. 2 platoons "W" Company<br>REAR GUARD. 1 platoon X Company.<br>ROUTE. LESTREM – PONT RIQUEUL – Cross Roads at R.5a – thence NORTH EAST to road junction at G. 32. a. 2.1 – road junction at G. 26. C. 3.8. | BETHUNE COMBINED SHEET<br>2{SHEET 36 {EDITION 6 |
| | | | [signature] Lieut Colonel,<br>Commdg. 17th (Service) Battn. Lanc. Fus. S. E. L. | |

1875 Wt. W593/826 1,000,000 4/15 J.B.C. & A. A.D.S.S./Forms/C.2118.

CONFIDENTIAL.

XXXV

17 Lan Fus
Vol 3

# WAR DIARY

OF

17th (Service) Battn. Lanc. Fus. S. E. L.

1916.

From April, 1st.

To April 30th.

## VOLUME III

S. V.
13 sheets

Instructions regarding War Diaries and Intelligence Summaries are contained in F. S. Regs., Part II. and the Staff Manual respectively. Title Pages will be prepared in manuscript.

# WAR DIARY
*or*
~~INTELLIGENCE SUMMARY~~
*(Erase heading not required.)*

Army Form C. 2118

VOLUME III. APRIL 1916.

| Place | 1916 Date | Hour | Summary of Events and Information | Remarks and references to Appendices |
|---|---|---|---|---|
| SAILLY SUR LA LYS. | APRIL 1ST | 10.15 a.m. | The G.O.C. 35th DIVISION, MAJOR-GENERAL R. J. PINNEY, inspected the Battalion in the field in rear of the farm at G.23.c.5.5. The G.O.C. expressed his satisfaction at the clean smart and soldier like appearance of the men. Received preliminary Brigade Operations re taking over the PETILLON sector from the 18th H.L.I. | MAP 36 EDITION 6. KH |
| SAILLY | APRIL 2nd | 10 a.m. | The C.O., 2nd in Command and Coy. Commanders inspected the portion of the line to be taken over on Tuesday April 4th | |
| | | 12.15pm | Received Brigade Operation Order No. 10 re relieving 18th H.L.I. | KH |
| SAILLY. | APRIL 3rd. | 9.0 a.m | Transferrence of two N.C.Os as Instructors to Brigade Bomb School. | KH |
| SAILLY | APRIL 4th. | 7.15pm | The Battalion relieved the 18th H.L.I in the Right Subsector (N.8.3. to N.9.4) of the PETILLON SECTOR (N.8.3 -to- N.10.5). | MAP 36 TRENCH MAP AREA "L" APP. III. KH |
| | | 9.22pm | Relief completed by 9.22 p.m - enemy very quiet. | |
| RIGHT SUBSECTOR TRENCHES. N.8.3 to N.9.4 | APRIL 5th - to - APRIL 6TH | 5a.m - to - 5a.m. | Quiet day - tried to make things lively by firing rifle grenades from N.9.3 and N.9.4 - no retaliation from either locality. Our snipers claimed 2 Germans at N.9.c.9.1 - large fire observed behind enemy's line opposite left of N.9.4 at about 8p.m. Rapid fire practised on enemy's trenches at about 3.10 a.m. Patrol from Subsection H, Right Subsector located large working party opposite junction N.9.4 and N.10.1 - dispersed by our machine Gun fire. Casualties this day were two men wounded. | TRENCH MAP AREA "L". KH |
| N.8.3 to N.9.4 | APRIL 6th - to - APRIL 7TH. | 5a.m - to - 5.a.m. | Enemy's snipers active - during the afternoon our T.M. bombarded enemy's support trenches - enemy replied with rifle grenades which have a longer range than ours - Patrols report our wire good in some parts of the line but very bad in others. Casualties. One man fatally wounded. | KH |

1875 Wt. W593/826 1,000,000 4/15 J.B.C. & A. A.D.S.S./Forms/C. 2118.

Instructions regarding War Diaries and Intelligence Summaries are contained in F. S. Regs., Part II. and the Staff Manual respectively. Title Pages will be prepared in manuscript.

# WAR DIARY
*or*
# ~~INTELLIGENCE SUMMARY~~
*(Erase heading not required.)*

Army Form C. 2118

| Place | Date | Hour | French Subsector Occupied Summary of Events and Information by the Battalion {1. April 4th to April 8th / 2. April 12th to April 16th | Remarks and references to Appendices |
|---|---|---|---|---|
| Petillon Section of Brigade Trench Map Area "L". | 1. April 4th to April 8th<br>2. April 12th to April 16th | 7.45pm<br>9.0pm<br>7.50pm<br>9.0pm | 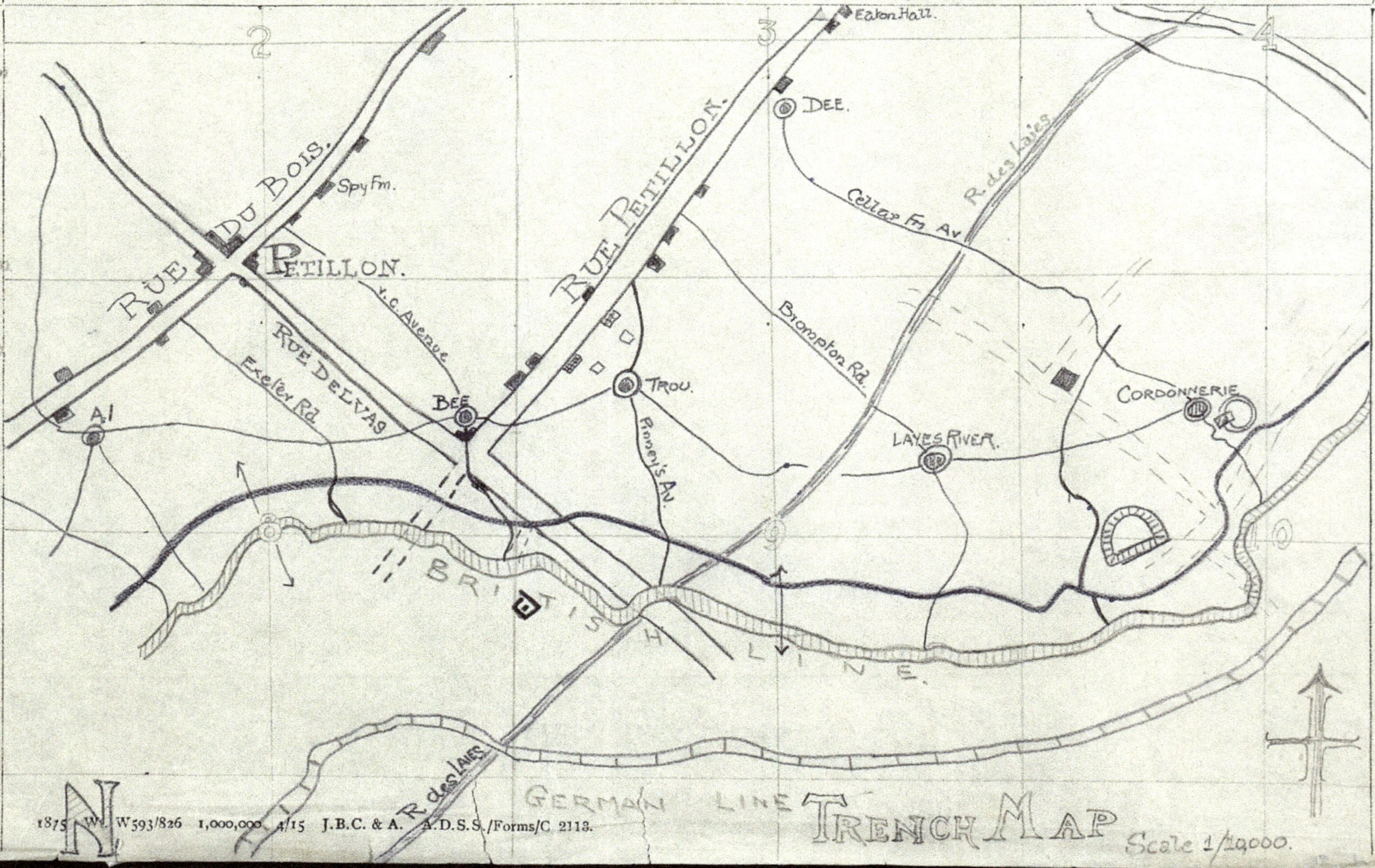 | Brigade Trench Map Area "L" |

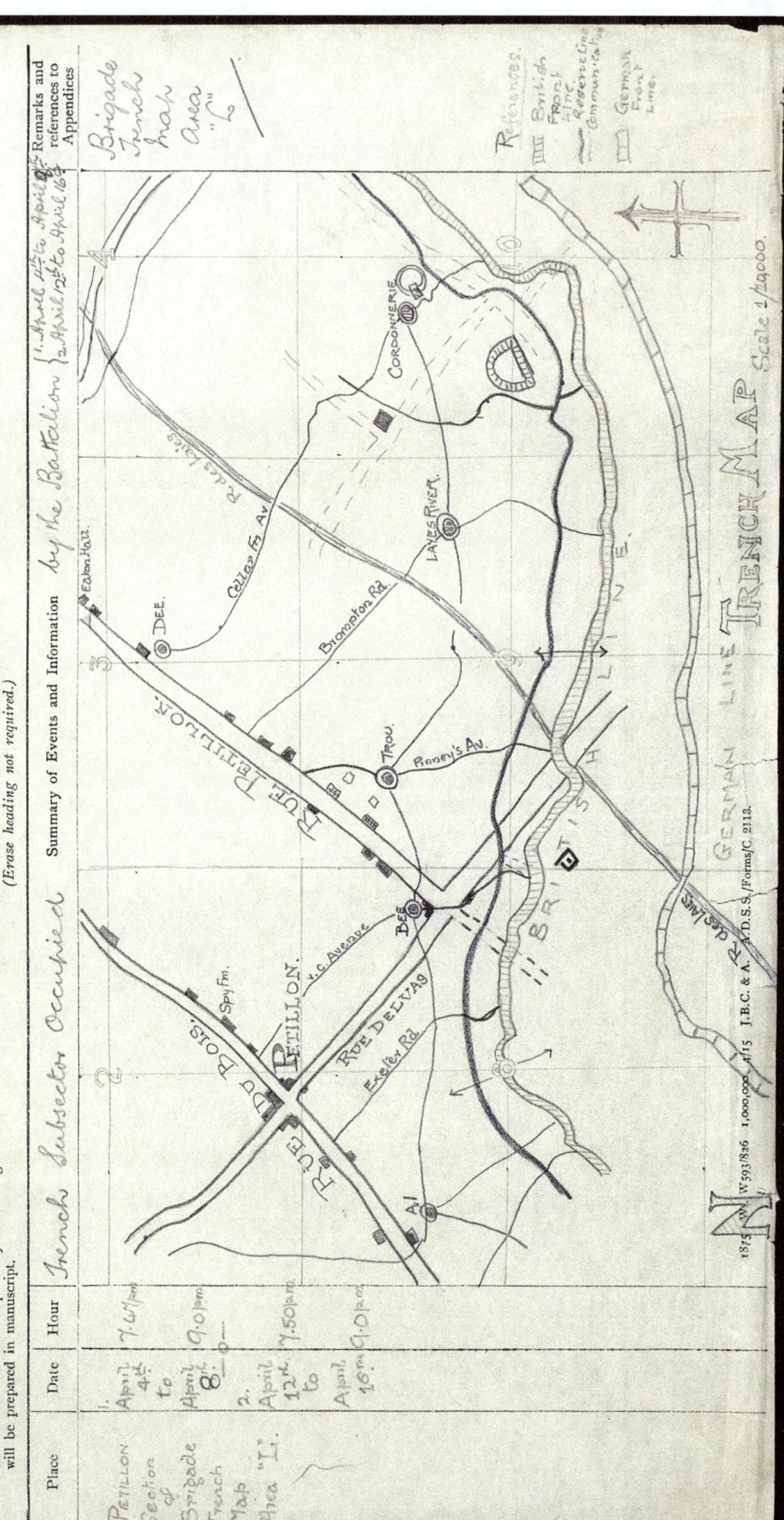

1875 Wt. W593/826 1,000,000 4/15 J.B.C. & A. A.D.S.S./Forms/C. 2118.

Instructions regarding War Diaries and Intelligence Summaries are contained in F. S. Regs., Part II. and the Staff Manual respectively. Title Pages will be prepared in manuscript.

# WAR DIARY
*or*
~~INTELLIGENCE SUMMARY~~
*(Erase heading not required.)*

Army Form C. 2118

| Place | Date | Hour | Summary of Events and Information | Remarks and references to Appendices |
|---|---|---|---|---|
| RIGHT SUBSECTION N.8.3 to N.9.4 | APRIL 7th — to — APRIL 8th | 5a.m — to — 5.a.m | Patrols having reported enemy working party at gap opposite N.9.4, three machine guns were directed to fire into this party. The party was dispersed and some of the enemy must have been wounded as groans were distinctly heard.<br>At "Stand To" on the morning of the 7th Germans threw hand grenades from their trench opposite N.9.1 and N.9.2. They must have been either nervous or have bombed their own patrol as no men of this Battalion were near that part of their parapet.<br>Our parapet was shelled with H.2 and a few larger shells between 12.30 pm. and 1.30 p.m. Of these, two hit our parapet and one hit Y.C. AVENUE. Several direct hits were made on the Second Line trenches which were not occupied. The communication with the Artillery was cut in two places. Otherwise no damage, which could not be repaired in a very short time, was done. | TRENCH MAP AREA "L". BH |
| N.8.3 to N.9.4 | APRIL 8th — to — | 5am — to — | Enemy's line shelled with rifle grenades and T.M. – the only retaliation of the enemy consisted of two rifle grenades. Artillery on both sides more active during the afternoon.<br>Two Warrant Officers (unfit to serve in Trenches) transferred to 35th Inf. Base Depôt.<br>The Battalion was relieved by the 20th Bn. Lancashire Fusiliers.<br>Relief completed by 9.55 pm. without interruption. | BH |
| RIGHT RESERVE BILLETS 4.31, G36, G.32. | APRIL 9th to APRIL 10th | | During this period, the Battalion supplied working parties by day and by night.<br>On the 10th, one of the night working parties was fired on and sustained the casualties of 1 man killed and 1 man wounded. | BH |
| RIGHT RESERVE BILLETS. | APRIL 11th | 3pm. | Great artillery activity by both sides. No damage to the billets was done.<br>2/LIEUT. DERWENT reported and joined for duty. He was posted to "X" Company. | BH |

1875 Wt. W593/826 1,000,000 4/15 J.B.C. & A. A.D.S.S./Forms/C. 2118.

Instructions regarding War Diaries and Intelligence Summaries are contained in F. S. Regs., Part II. and the Staff Manual respectively. Title Pages will be prepared in manuscript.

# WAR DIARY
*or*
# INTELLIGENCE SUMMARY
*(Erase heading not required.)*

Army Form C. 2118

VOLUME III — APRIL 1916.

RIGHT SUBSECTION TRENCHES

| Place | Date | Hour | Summary of Events and Information | Remarks and references to Appendices |
|---|---|---|---|---|
| N.8.3 to N.9.4. | APRIL 12th | 7.30 pm. | The Battalion relieved the 20th Battalion Lancashire Fusiliers in the Right Sub section trenches. During the relief one man was fatally wounded. Our motor machine guns firing from some point between V.C. AVENUE and BOND STREET, appear to have provoked retaliation, especially during the relief. The Relief was completed by 9.13 p.m. During the relief, 7 officers and 16 other ranks of the 1st Australian Infantry Battalion were attached to the Battalion together with ten cadets from the Cadet School, ST OMER. | TRENCH MAP AREA "L". KH |
| N.8.3 to N.9.4. | APRIL 12TH —to— APRIL 13th | 7.30 pm —to— 5am. | The enemy's artillery was fairly active – over 50 shells fired at gun emplacements and cottage N.W. of Battalion Headquarters. The platoon of the 18th Battn. Lancashire Fusiliers quartered in this cottage vacated it and occupied the assembly trenches close to it. Two shells hit the Cottage but no other damage was done. The enemy also shelled TWO TREE FARM; the platoon quartered there was transferred to BEE POST. Patrols reported working parties opposite N.9.3 before dawn on the 13th. Machine gun fire was opened ~~causing~~ casualities as cries were heard. During the afternoon, six rounds were fired from a T.M in N.9.3 – most of them dropped short but considerable damaged was done to the enemy's wire, one knife rest being blown into the air. Two Platoons of 1st Bn. Australians were attached to Y Coy. The cadets returned to SAILLY. Casualties – one man wounded. | TRENCH MAP AREA "L". KH |
| N.8.3 to N.9.4. | APRIL 13th —to— APRIL 14th | 5am. —to— 5.a.m | Enemy weakly bombarded out Support Line and the RUE DE BOIS South of V.C. CORNER. Our machine Guns dispersed an enemy working party on parapet N.9.d.9.2. Enemy appears to have relieved during the night – situation very quiet. Two Platoons of 1st Bn. Australians attached to Y & Z Companies respectively. | TRENCH MAP AREA "L". KH |
| N.8.3 to N.9.4 | APRIL 14th to APRIL 15th | 5am to 5.a.m | Very quiet day – enemy fired a few shells into TROU village and RUE DE BOIS. – enemy's machine guns and snipers much less active. On left of sector, we fired rifle grenades into enemy's front trench to which he did not reply. Patrols went out as usual. Two platoons of 1st Bn. Australian Infantry were attached to "W" & "X" Companies respectively. | TRENCH MAP AREA "L". KH |

1875 Wt. W593/826 1,000,000 4/15 J.B.C. & A. A.D.S.S./Forms/C. 2118.

Army Form C. 2118

Instructions regarding War Diaries and Intelligence Summaries are contained in F. S. Regs., Part II. and the Staff Manual respectively. Title Pages will be prepared in manuscript.

# WAR DIARY
*or*
~~INTELLIGENCE SUMMARY~~
*(Erase heading not required.)*

VOLUME III — APRIL 1916. —

RIGHT SUBSECTOR TRENCHES.

| Place | Date | Hour | Summary of Events and Information | Remarks and references to Appendices |
|---|---|---|---|---|
| N.8.3 to N.9.H. | APRIL 15th to APRIL 16th | 5a.m to 5.a.m | Very quiet day – the O.C. Right Centre Company reported at 8.45 p.m on the 15th, that Red, white and green lights were seen some miles away to our right front. Situation quiet and normal. | BRIGADE TRENCH MAP AREA "L". |
| | | | LIEUT. COLONEL, W.J. McWHINNIE relinquished command of the Battalion and proceeded to England. The following was his farewell message before leaving:– "It is with the deepest regret and not from choice that I relinquish Command of the Battalion with which I have been associated since its formation. As I have been unable to find an occasion for saying "Good Bye" to you all on parade, and for thanking all Ranks for their loyal co-operation during the time we have served together, I take this opportunity of wishing you God speed and the best of Good Luck. The motto for every soldier is" Play the Game". Live up to the tradition of the Lancashire Fusiliers and the 17th Battalion will make History". | |
| | | | MAJOR. A.M. MILLS assumed Command of the Battalion from April 15th. | |
| | | | 2/LIEUT. LEAVER H. and 2/LIEUT. OPENSHAW. S.N. having joined for duty on the 15th April were posted to "W" and "X" Companies respectively. | |
| | | 10.a.m | Received Operation Order No 13. on the 15th. | KH |
| N.8.3 to N.9.H. | APRIL 16th | 6.0am to 9.30pm | Quiet day – the Left Company fired about fifty Rifle Grenades into the enemy's trenches without drawing any retaliation. Enemy shelled vicinity of RIFLE VILLA and V.C AVENUE about noon, without doing any damage. He fired about 20 shells chiefly H.E and started again at 4.30 pm with salvoes of three, about V.C. AVENUE with the same result. Inter-Battalion relief, completed at 9.35 p.m without incident. The Battalion took over the Right Reserve Billets from the 2nd Battn. Lancashire Fusiliers. | TRENCH MAP AREA "L". KH |

1875 Wt. W593/826 1,000,000 4/15 J.B.C. & A. A.D.S.S./Forms/C. 2118.

Army Form C. 2118

Instructions regarding War Diaries and Intelligence Summaries are contained in F. S. Regs., Part II. and the Staff Manual respectively. Title Pages will be prepared in manuscript.

# WAR DIARY

*or*

~~INTELLIGENCE SUMMARY~~

*(Erase heading not required.)*

| Place | Date | Hour | — VOLUME III. — Summary of Events and Information — APRIL 1918. — | Remarks and references to Appendices |
|---|---|---|---|---|
| RESERVE BILLETS H31, G36, G32. | APRIL 17th & 18th | | During these two days, the Battalion supplied working parties by day and by night in the front line and the various support and communication trenches. | KH |
| SAILLY. | APRIL 19th | 6am. | The Battalion was relieved by the 9th Battalion Australian Infantry and marched to ESTAIRES where it remained for the night. | APP. III KH |
| ESTAIRES | APRIL 20th | 10am. | The Battalion moved to VIEILLE CHAPELLE where it was placed in Divisional Reserve. | APP. III. KH |
| VIEILLE CHAPELLE. | APRIL 22nd. | 10.30 a.m. | The G.O.C. 104th Brigade inspected the Battalion which was formed up in mass in the Field at R.34. c.8.5., and remarked on the smart appearance and the manner in which the men handled their arms.<br>LIEUT. F. L. WAINWRIGT rejoined from Hospital. | MAP 36.a. KH |
| VIEILLE CHAPELLE. | APRIL 23rd | 9.0am. | The C.O inspected the NEUVE CHAPELLE section which the Battalion would take over on the 28th inst.<br>LIEUT. W. E. M. CURNOCK joined the Battalion for duty - posted to "X" Coy. | KH |
| VIEILLE CHAPELLE | APRIL 26th | 9.0am. | Company Commanders proceeded to inspect the NEUVE CHAPELLE Section | |
| VIEILLE CHAPELLE. | APRIL 27TH | 5.30pm. | The enemy fired three shells (HE) into VIEILLE CHAPELLE fatally wounding one British soldier and two middle aged French women; and severely wounding one French soldier on leave and a Frenchman. | KH |

Army Form C. 2118

Instructions regarding War Diaries and Intelligence Summaries are contained in F. S. Regs., Part II. and the Staff Manual respectively. Title Pages will be prepared in manuscript.

# WAR DIARY

*or*

# ~~INTELLIGENCE SUMMARY~~

*(Erase heading not required.)*

| Place | Date | Hour | VOLUME III — Summary of Events and Information — APRIL 1916. | Remarks and references to Appendices |
|---|---|---|---|---|
| VIEILLE CHAPELLE | APRIL 28th | 7.20 pm | The Battalion marched to relieve the 19th Battalion, Durham Light Infantry in the NEUVE CHAPELLE left sub-section trenches.<br>Companies moved in the following order:- "Y", "W", "Z", "X", Head Quarters.<br>Starting Point. Cross Roads R.28 d. Central<br>Route. Via QUEEN MARY'S ROAD, RICHEBOURG ST. VAAST, Road junction M.32. d.7.3 to Road junction M.27. d.7.3 (EUSTON CORNER)<br>From Starting Point, all movements will be by Platoons and from EUSTON CORNER by Sections.<br>Time. 1st Platoon from Starting Point at 7.20 pm and succeeding platoons at intervals of 2 minutes. | Bethune Combined 1/40,000<br>KH |
| LEFT SUBSECTION TRENCHES NEUVE CHAPELLE AREA | APRIL 28th to APRIL 29th | 10.40 p.m. 8 a.m. | Operations:- Relief completed at 10.40 p.m. – very quiet night – enemy opened rapid fire with machine gun and rifle just before stand-to, owing to our sending over rifle grenades.<br>Intelligence:- Wire examined and found to be only in a fair condition.<br>Our Artillery shelled enemy's lines and the fringe of BOIS DU BIEZ – The enemy retaliated on BALUCHI communication trench at the CHATEAU – slight damage on the latter with two direct hits – THE ORCHARD and our supports | BRIGADE TRENCH MAP AREA "I".<br>KH |
| | APRIL 29th to APRIL 30th | 8am 8a.m. | Operations:- Quiet Day – Enemy sent a few shells near "B" Line. CHATEAU & CHURCH POSTS and BALUCHI Trench between 9 and 11 a.m. They scored 2 hits on the latter but no material damage. – Left Company with Rifle Grenades & 2 Stokes Gun registered about M.35d.9.3. Patrols were hampered by large numbers of Very Lights sent up by the enemy who were nervous.<br>Intelligence:- Our wire between right and centre company is thin – pigeon from over our line alighted in rear of enemy's line.<br>Work. Putting down new duck boards – snipers' loopholes. parapet strengthened wiring in front of Right and Centre Companies. | TRENCH MAP AREA "I".<br>KH |

1875 Wt. W593/826 1,000,000 4/15 J.B.C. & A. A.D.S.S./Forms/C. 2118.

Instructions regarding War Diaries and Intelligence Summaries are contained in F. S. Regs., Part II. and the Staff Manual respectively. Title Pages will be prepared in manuscript.

Army Form C. 2118

# WAR DIARY
*or*
~~INTELLIGENCE SUMMARY~~
*(Erase heading not required.)*

VOLUME III. APRIL 1916.

| Place | Date | Hour | Summary of Events and Information | Remarks and references to Appendices |
|---|---|---|---|---|
| RIGHT SUBSECTION TRENCHES. | APRIL 30th | 8a.m to 5p.m | Throughout the day there ~~was~~ was an intermittent bombardment of the BOIS DU BIEZ area. The Germans retaliated by firing on the RIGHT SECTOR and our support line. During the morning Germans were observed pumping from their front line trench at S. 5. b. 5. 2 – wire at this point very high – nozzle apparently rests on his wire. Casualties this day were :- one man wounded and one man slightly wounded but still at Duty. | BRIGADE TRENCH MAP AREA "I" BH |

30/4/16

A. H. Mills Major,
Commdg, 17th (Service) Battn. Lanc. Fus. S. E. L.

1875 Wt. W593/826 1,000,000 4/15 J.B.C. & A. A.D.S.S./Forms/C. 2118.

Instructions regarding War Diaries and Intelligence Summaries are contained in F. S. Regs., Part II. and the Staff Manual respectively. Title Pages will be prepared in manuscript.

# WAR DIARY
*or*
# ~~INTELLIGENCE SUMMARY~~
*(Erase heading not required.)*

Army Form C. 2118

| Place | Date | Hour | Summary of Events and Information — APPENDIX III. — APRIL 1918. | Remarks and references to Appendices |
|---|---|---|---|---|
| N. 8.3 to N. 8.4. | APRIL 4TH | | The distribution of the Battalion whilst in the Right Subsector was as follows:- | MAP 36 ED. 6 |
| | | | "X" Coy. - - - - - Right Subsection. - - - - N. 8.3 and N. 8.4 (3 platoons) 1 Platoon at TWO TREE FARM. | BRIGADE TRENCH MAP AREA "L". |
| | | | "W" Coy. - - - - - Right Centre Subsection: - N. 8.5 and N. 9.1 (3 platoons). BEE & TROU POSTS (1 platoon). | |
| | | | "Z" Coy. - - - - - Left Centre Subsection - - N. 9.2 and N. 9.3 (3 platoons). Billets at N. 2. d. 2.6 (1 platoon). | |
| | | | "Y" Coy. - - - - - Left Subsection. - - - - N. 9.4 Billets at N. 2. d. 2. 6 (1 platoon). | |
| | | 7.15pm. | Guides from 18th H.L.I. met platoons at WEATHERCOCK CORNER N. 1. a 6. 9½ at 7.15pm. Companies marched in the following order:- | |
| | | | "Y" Coy to arrive at WEATHERCOCK CORNER at 7.15 p.m. | |
| | | | "W" " " " " " " 7.23 p.m. | |
| | | | "Z" " " " " " " 7.31 p.m. | |
| | | | "X" " " " " " " 7.39 p.m. | |
| | | | After passing the above point, platoons advanced at 2 minutes interval and were told off to their respective portion of the line before marching off. | |
| | | | The Posts in the Back area were relieved in daylight - the other posts were relieved during the ordinary process of relief. | WH |
| FRONT LINE | APRIL 8th. | | The distribution of Battalion whilst in Reserve was as under:- | |
| — | | | "X" Compy. - - - - WEATHERCOCK HOUSE, H. 31. c. 9. 2½ in close support to the Battalion in the Right Subsection Trenches and must be ready to turn out at a moment's notice. | |
| H. 31, G. 36, G 32. | | | "W" Compy. - - - - WINDY POST, G. 36. d. 8. 6. and found Two platoons for CHARRED POST. | |
| | | | "Y" Compy, Billets at G. 36. d. 5. 6. | |
| | | | "Z" Compy, Billets between ROUGE DE BOUT and GRANNY POST. G 22. d. 7. 6. | WH |

1875 Wt. W593/826 1,000,000 4/15 J.B.C. & A. A.D.S.S./Forms/C. 2118.

Army Form C. 2118

Instructions regarding War Diaries and Intelligence Summaries are contained in F. S. Regs., Part II. and the Staff Manual respectively. Title Pages will be prepared in manuscript.

# WAR DIARY
*or*
~~INTELLIGENCE SUMMARY~~
*(Erase heading not required.)*

| Place | Date | Hour | Summary of Events and Information — APPENDIX III. — APRIL 1916. | Remarks and references to Appendices |
|---|---|---|---|---|
| SAILLY. PETILLON SECTION. | APRIL 12TH | 7.30pm | The Battalion relieved the 20th Lancashire Fusiliers as under:-<br>RIGHT SUBSECTION TRENCHES. ------------ "X" Compy. 3 platoons front line & 1 platoon TWOTREE FARM.<br>RIGHT CENTRE SUB-SECTION " ------------ "W" " 3 " " " " 1 " BEE & TROU POSTS.<br>LEFT " " " " ------------ "Z" " 3 " " " " 1 " Billets at N.2.d. 2.6.<br>LEFT SUBSECTION ------ " ------------ "Y" " 3 " " " " 1 " " " " " " "<br>The Companies passed WEATHER COCK CORNER in the following order with intervals of 2 minutes between platoons.<br>"Y" Coy -------- 7.30 p.m.<br>"X" Coy. -------- 7.38 p.m.<br>"Z" Coy. -------- 7.46 p.m.<br>"W" Coy. -------- 8.54 p.m.<br>Machine Gunners, Bombers, Snipers and Signallers were relieved during the morning. | MAP 36 Eo 6., BRIGADE TRENCH MAP AREA "I". LSH |
| RIGHT SUB SECTION TRENCHES | APRIL 16TH | | Relieved by 20th Lancashire Fusiliers :-<br>Machine Guns relieved about 8.30 a.m.<br>Signallers " " 10.0 a.m.<br>Snipers " " 10.30 a.m.<br>Bombers " " 11.0 a.m.<br>Relief of Companies commenced about 7.45 p.m. | LSH |
| RESERVE BILLETS. G.36. G.22 H.31 | APRIL 16TH | | Distribution of Battalion whilst in Reserve :-<br>"Z" Coy, WEATHERCOCK HOUSE, H31.c.9.2½ in close support to the Battalion in the Right Sub-section Trenches, ready to turn out at a moment's notice.<br>"Y" Coy., WINDY POST, G.36.d.8.6 – two platoons for CHARRED POST.<br>"W" Coy., Billets at G.36.d.3.6.<br>"X" Coy, Billets between ROUGE DE BOUT and GRANNY POST, G.22.d.7.6.<br>BACK POSTS. (1) LAVENTIE N (G.34.b.8.3) taken over by 1 N.C.O & 3 men of Y Coy.<br>(2). NOUVEAU MONDE (G27.c.6.2) " " " " " " " Z "<br>These were relieved eventually by the 1st Battalion Australian Infantry by 12 noon and the garrisons rejoined their Companies. | LSH |

1875 Wt. W593/826 1,000,000 4/15 J.B.C. & A. A.D.S.S./Forms/C. 2118.

Instructions regarding War Diaries and Intelligence Summaries are contained in F. S. Regs., Part II. and the Staff Manual respectively. Title Pages will be prepared in manuscript.

# WAR DIARY
*or*
~~INTELLIGENCE SUMMARY~~
*(Erase heading not required.)*

Army Form C. 2118

| Place | 1916 Date | Hour | Summary of Events and Information — APPENDIX III. — APRIL 1916. | Remarks and references to Appendices |
|---|---|---|---|---|
| RIGHT RESERVE BILLETS. | APRIL 19th | 6.am | MOVE TO ESTAIRES.<br>The Battalion moved in the following order:-<br>BAND, "Z" Company, "W" Coy., "X" Coy., "Y" Coy., less 1 Platoon, Machine Gun Section, Transport, Rear Guard, 1 Platoon "Y" Coy.<br>ROUTE. Via SAILLY - Cross Roads G.16. a.3.1 - to Billets. | MAP 36 ED.6.<br>MAP 36A |
| ESTAIRES | APRIL 20th | 10am. | MOVE TO VIEILLE CHAPELLE<br>The Battalion rendezvoused with the head of the Column at the Cross Roads L.28. d central in the following order:-<br>Advanced Guard --- 2 sections "Y" Coy under an Officer<br>"Y" Coy, less 2 sections.<br>"X" Company.<br>"W" Company.<br>"Z" Company less 2 Sections.<br>Machine Gun Section<br>Transport.<br>Rear Guard --- 2 Sections "Z" Coy. under an Officer.<br>ROUTE. Cross Roads L.28. d. Central - Road junction R.4. a<br>PONT RIQUEUL - Cross Roads R.15.a - ZELOBES - VIEILLE CHAPELLE. | MAP 36A. |
| | | | A. Mills Major,<br>Commdg, 17th (Service) Battn. Lanc. Fus. B. E. F. | |

1875 Wt. W593/826 1,000,000 4/15 J.B.C. & A. A.D.S.S./Forms/C. 2118.

A.G.
3rd Echelon.
35

17th (SERVICE) BATTN. LANC. FUS. S. E. L.
22
7 - JUN 1916

Vol. 4

CONFIDENTIAL

# WAR DIARY

OF

17th (Service) Battn. Lanc. Fus. S. E. L.

1916.

From May 1st/16 To May 31st/16.

VOLUME IV.

4. V.
12 sheets

Instructions regarding War Diaries and Intelligence Summaries are contained in F. S. Regs., Part II. and the Staff Manual respectively. Title Pages will be prepared in manuscript.

# WAR DIARY
*or*
~~INTELLIGENCE SUMMARY~~
*(Erase heading not required.)*

Army Form C. 2118

| Place | Date | Hour | VOLUME IV. Summary of Events and Information MAY 1916. | Remarks and references to Appendices |
|---|---|---|---|---|
| LEFT SUBSECTION TRENCHES NEUVE CHAPELLE | MAY 1st | 8AM. 30.4.16 to 8AM. 1.5.16. | 2/LT. LESTY having proceed to England is struck off the strength from 20/4/16.<br>Operations:- Quiet day - one Company fired 10 rounds rapid at Stand to with Gas Helmets on (in practise) - bombarded enemy at same time with rifle grenades - retaliation slight. - patrols sent out as usual - no enemy patrols met. | |
| | 8.AM 1.5.16 to 8 AM 2.5.16. | | Operations:- Quiet day - enemy T.M bombs were retaliated to, with rifle grenades. - Our Stokes gun on enemy's parapet and at a board he put up, announcing fall of KUT-EL-AMARA. Enemy inclined to be impertinent - Flank companies practised rapid fire with Gas Helmets on. - this provoked a slight retaliation.<br>Intelligence:- Enemy did little firing during night - he fired very lights from middle of No MAN'S LAND.<br>Work Done:- Strengthening wire; dug-outs, parapets and parados; firing fire step - extending railway terminus at MOGG'S HOLE.<br>Casualties:- Two men slightly wounded. | |
| | | 8.15pm | The Battalion was relieved by the 18th Battn. Lancashire Fusiliers and moved into Reserve Billets at CROIX BARBÉE. Lewis Guns, Snipers and Signallers were relieved during the morning.<br>"W" Coy garrisoned EUSTON POST and LORETTO POST.<br>Relief Completed by 10 pm. without incident. | |
| CROIX BARBÉE | MAY 3rd to MAY 5th | | During this period the Battalion supplied working parties by day and by night for the repair and strengthening the various front line, support and Communication Trenches. | |

1875 Wt. W593/826 1,000,000 4/15 J.B.C. & A. A.D.S.S./Forms/C. 2118.

Instructions regarding War Diaries and Intelligence Summaries are contained in F. S. Regs., Part II. and the Staff Manual respectively. Title Pages will be prepared in manuscript.

# WAR DIARY
*or*
~~INTELLIGENCE SUMMARY~~
*(Erase heading not required.)*

Army Form C. 2118

| Place | Date | Hour | Summary of Events and Information | Remarks and references to Appendices |
|---|---|---|---|---|
| | | | VOLUME IV MAY 1916. | |
| LEFT SUBSECTION TRENCHES NEUVE CHAPELLE | MAY 6th | 8.15 p.m. | The Battalion relieved the 18th Battn. Lancashire Fusiliers in the Left Subsection Trenches NEUVE CHAPELLE. The order of Relief and times of passing EUSTON CORNER was as follows:-<br>RIGHT COMPANY ---- "Y" Coy ------- 8.17 p.m.<br>CENTAL COMPANY. ---- "W" " ------- 8.25 p.m.<br>LEFT COMPANY. ---- "Z" " ------- 8.33 p.m.<br>SUPPORT COMPANY. ---- "X" " ------- 8.41 p.m.<br>BATTN. HDQRS. ------------ 8.49 p.m<br>"X" Coy found the garrison of CURZON POST which was relieved at 8.15 p.m.<br>Companies moved by sections at intervals of 2 minutes between platoons.<br>Lewis Guns, Snipers, Signallers and Bombers were relieved during the morning and relief completed by 12 noon.<br>The Inter. Battalion relief was completed by 9.15 pm without incident. | |
| -do- | 9 pm May 6th to 8 am May 7th | | Operations. Quiet night - enemy's machine gun active about 2 a.m - patrols as usual.<br>Intelligence. Fresh timber work opposite S.5.3 - Sounds of mining heard opposite Bay 162, S.5.6.<br>Work. Practically nil.<br>2/Lt. S.R. CARTER joined for duty and posted to "W" Coy. | Brigade Trench map area I. |
| -do- | 8 am MAY 7th to 8 am. MAY 8th. | | Operations :- Registering by Stokes Gun about 11.30 am brought on quick retaliation by enemy firing bouquet of enfilade shrapnel and causing 4 casualties. Quiet night - 3 enemy working parties dispersed by our Lewis Guns - One enemy M.G. evidently put out of action by our rifle grenades. Patrols as usual.<br>Intelligence. Our M.Gs dispersed working parties in enemy C.T., and wiring parties, No sounds of mining<br>Work Done. Wiring repaired; parados and Shell proof dug outs constructed<br>Casualties CAPT E.T. COWAN, wounded. Other Ranks:- 1 Killed and 2 wounded. | |

1875 Wt. W593/826 1,000,000 4/15 J.B.C. & A. A.D.S.S./Forms/C. 2118.

Instructions regarding War Diaries and Intelligence Summaries are contained in F. S. Regs., Part II. and the Staff Manual respectively. Title Pages will be prepared in manuscript.

# WAR DIARY
or
~~INTELLIGENCE~~ SUMMARY
*(Erase heading not required.)*

Army Form C. 2118

| Place | Date | Hour | Summary of Events and Information — VOLUME IV — MAY 1916. | Remarks and references to Appendices |
|---|---|---|---|---|
| LEFT SUBSECTION TRENCHES NEUVE CHAPELLE. | 8 AM MAY 8th to 8 AM MAY 9TH | | Operations. Rifle Grenade duel opposite Left Coy, at 9 am yesterday - Stokes Gun Bombardment was not effective. All Coys. stood to at 10.15 pm. - enemy's retaliation lasted from 10.45 pm to 11.15 pm. - chiefly on 70 yds line - direct hit at Church Post - Lively night on both sides; - both enemy and our M.G. traversed each other's parapets. Enemy Snipers more active.<br>Intelligence. - Enemy imagines our Stokes Gun is located in CHATEAU ORCHARD and that we occupy the 70x line<br>Confirmed that enemy's S.O.S. signal is a Red Rocket.<br>Work Done:- Building shell proof dug-outs parados. - wire entanglements - Foliage Screen put up between CHATEAU POST and FRONT LINE to screen C.T. Casualties 1 man wounded. | |
| | 8 AM. MAY 9TH to 8 AM MAY 10TH | | Operations:- Extremely quiet day and night on both sides - Enemy's guns put 3.77 m HE into ORCHARD and CHATEAU POSTS at 9 am. This was quite unprovoked<br>Intelligence. Patrols as usual - enemy's parados reported damaged by bombardment of the 8th inst.<br>Work Done. much work done at MOGGS HOLE - wiring of "B" Line - wire entanglements in Front Line. | |
| | 8 am MAY 10th to 9 pm MAY 10th | | Operations Quiet day and night - enemy shelled "B" Line with H.E. Several shells dropping in close proximity to Bn Hqrs.<br>Intelligence very little to report - suspected O.P in the BOIS DU BIEZ.<br>WORK DONE. Yesterday's work continued.<br>The Battalion was relieved by the 18th Lancashire Fusiliers and proceeded to Reserve Billets at CROIX BARBÉE.<br>Lewis guns, Snipers, Signallers and Bombers were relieved during the preceding night. Inter Battalion relief completed by 9.40 p.m. | |

1875 Wt. W593/826 1,000,000 4/15 J.B.C. & A. A.D.S.S./Forms/C. 2118.

Instructions regarding War Diaries and Intelligence Summaries are contained in F. S. Regs., Part II. and the Staff Manual respectively. Title Pages will be prepared in manuscript.

# WAR DIARY
*or*
# INTELLIGENCE SUMMARY
*(Erase heading not required.)*

Army Form C. 2118

| Place | Date | Hour | Summary of Events and Information | Remarks and references to Appendices |
|---|---|---|---|---|
| CROIX BARBÉE. | MAY 10th | | Major A.E. BROWN-HOVELT having proceed to England is struck off the strength from 8/5/16.<br>Casualties during relief were two men wounded. | |
| -do- | MAY 11th<br>MAY 12th | | The Battalion supplied working parties by day and by night during this period. | |
| -do- | MAY 13th. | | 2/Lt. BYTHAM W. H. having proceeded to England is struck off the strength from the 12/5/16.<br>Working parties as usual.<br>2/Lt. A.M. (WILLIAMS proceeded this day to ENGLAND. Sick) | |
| CROIX BARBÉE | MAY 14th | 5p.m. | The Battalion was relieved by the 15th Cheshire Regiment and marched to VIEILLE CHAPELLE by the Route M.20.c.1.1.<br>The Brigade then came into Divisional Reserve. | |
| VIEILLE CHAPELLE. | MAY 14th to MAY 15th | | The following programme was carried out whilst in Divisional Reserve:-<br>7.15 am to 7.45 am. Physical Drill<br>9.30 am to 12.30 am. Rifle Exercises, Rapid Loading, Close Order Drill, Ceremonial Guard Duties etc., Wiring, Dummy Bomb Throwing, Inspection of Gas Helmets.<br>Afternoon : Games and Concerts. | |
| VIEILLE CHAPELLE. | MAY 17TH | 11.15 am. | The Battalion was inspected by the G.O.C. XI Army Corps, Lt General Sir. R.C.B HAKING, K.C.B., in the Field at R.34.a.3.9. The G.O.C expressed his satisfaction at the clean turnout and smartness of the Battalion at this inspection.<br>CAPT. A. HELLAWELL having proceeded to 35th. I.B.D is struck off the strength from this date.<br>2/LT. L. MARSH. having reported for duty, is posted to "Y" Coy. | |

1875 Wt. W593/826 1,000,000 4/15 J.B.C. & A. A.D.S.S./Forms/C. 2118.

Instructions regarding War Diaries and Intelligence Summaries are contained in F. S. Regs., Part II. and the Staff Manual respectively. Title Pages will be prepared in manuscript.

# WAR DIARY
*or*
# ~~INTELLIGENCE SUMMARY~~
*(Erase heading not required.)*

Army Form C. 2118

VOLUME IV. — MAY 1916.

| Place | Date | Hour | Summary of Events and Information | Remarks and references to Appendices |
|---|---|---|---|---|
| VIEILLE CHAPELLE. | MAY 18th. | 9.45 am. | The Battalion route marched in the following Order:- Signallers, Band, "X" Coy less 2 Sections, "Z" Coy, "W" Coy less 2 Sections, Battn. Hdqrs Machine Guns, Transport.<br>Dress. Skeleton Marching Order.<br>Route. Cross Roads R. 20.c.8.1 - Cross Roads Q.30.b.5.8 - Cross Roads R.25.c.5.2 - Road junction R.31.a.2.6 - LELOBES - ZELOBES.<br>Advance Guard. 2 Sections "X" Coy<br>Rear Guard. 2 Sections "W" Coy. | Ref Bethune Map (Sheet 36 A B Combined |
| VIEILLE CHAPELLE. | MAY 18th to MAY 22nd. | | The usual Divisional Reserve Programme was carried out during this period.<br>N.B. 1. The O.C. 35th Divisional Signal Coy., delivered a lecture to all the Signallers of the Brigade in the VIEILLE CHAPELLE CHURCH at 6.30 p.m. on May 20th<br>2. Second Lieut. J. H. S. SYKES joined for duty and posted to "X" Coy. from May 21st | |
| VIEILLE CHAPELLE to RICHEBOURG (Fme du Bois) SECTION. | MAY 22nd | | The Battalion marched to relieve the 19th Durham Light Infantry in the LEFT SUB-SECTION TRENCHES of the FERME DU BOIS Section.<br>Lewis Guns, Signallers, and Snipers were relieved by 8 am.<br>Companies moved in the following Order:- Headquarters, W, X, Z, Y.<br>Starting Time:- 7 p.m. Starting Point - Cross Roads R.28.d. Central<br>Route. Queen Mary's Road. | |

1875 Wt. W593/826 1,000,000 4/15 J.B.C. & A. A.D.S.S./Forms/C. 2118.

Instructions regarding War Diaries and Intelligence Summaries are contained in F. S. Regs., Part II. and the Staff Manual respectively. Title Pages will be prepared in manuscript.

# WAR DIARY

*or*

~~INTELLIGENCE SUMMARY~~

*(Erase heading not required.)*

Army Form C. 2118

| Place | Date | Hour | Summary of Events and Information — VOLUME IV. — MAY, 1916. | Remarks and references to Appendices |
|---|---|---|---|---|
| LEFT SUBSECTION TRENCHES. FERME DU BOIS SECTION | 22 MAY — to — 6 a.m. 23 MAY | 9.45 pm | OPERATIONS. The relief was carried out without incident and complete by 9.45 p.m. INTELLIGENCE. The enemy was very quiet during the night – officer's patrol, which went out from S.10.3 about 10.30 p.m. reported no enemy activity. Four of enemy in sap opposite S.10.4 attempted to get into conversation with our men – they themselves refused to be drawn into conversation by one of our officers. WORK. very little done. | BRIGADE TRENCH MAP AREA "H". |
| | MAY 23 — to — MAY 24 | 6 a.m. 6 a.m. | OPERATIONS. Enemy sap head at BOAR'S HEAD was bombed and at same time rifle grenades were fired into the sap itself. Subsequent reconnaissance of enemy's sap head showed that enemy had retired. INTELLIGENCE. Patrol went out during night to examine supposed gaps in enemy's wire at S.10.c.6.1. Two gaps were found. A large enemy working party, with a covering party was found there. Patrol returned at 1.55 a.m. and a L.G was immediately turned on the working party which was dispersed. WORK. Under R.E. supervision – constructing and strengthening of dug-outs. Revetting – repairing of our own wire. STRENGTH. CAPT. W. I. HANSON proceeded this day to 35th I.B.D ETAPLES. | |
| | MAY 24 — to — MAY 25 | 6 a.m. 6 a.m. | OPERATIONS. Enemy heads seen in sap opposite BOAR'S HEAD – rifle grenades fired into sap and on to front line – no retaliation. Our artillery bombardment of last night drew retaliation on GUARDS TRENCH, FACTORY POST and PLUM ST where one direct hit was obtained. Enemy also obtained a direct hit on FACTORY POST earlier on in the day and damaged a dug out. INTELLIGENCE. Old workings and ditch in front of S.10.2 and S.10.3 reconnoitred both by day and by night. It offers no facilities for passage of troops on broad front. Enemy appeared to be registering for barrage fire about 6 p.m when he put several shrapnel into the open country to the right of PALL MALL. Our bombardment of last night and intense darkness made enemy very nervous as he threw up more lights than usual. WORK Under R.E. supervision, strengthening of dug outs. Parapet, parados and duck boards repaired. CASUALTIES. 2 other ranks killed. | |

1875 Wt. W593/826 1,000,000 4/15 J.B.C. & A. A.D.S.S./Forms/C. 2118.

Army Form C. 2118

# WAR DIARY
*or*
# ~~INTELLIGENCE~~ SUMMARY
*(Erase heading not required.)*

Instructions regarding War Diaries and Intelligence Summaries are contained in F. S. Regs., Part II. and the Staff Manual respectively. Title Pages will be prepared in manuscript.

VOLUME IV — MAY 1916.

| Place | Date | Hour | Summary of Events and Information | Remarks and references to Appendices |
|---|---|---|---|---|
| LEFT SUBSECTION TRENCHES FERME DU BOIS SECTOR. | MAY 25 — to — MAY 26 | 6 a.m. — to — 6 a.m. | OPERATIONS:- Morning very quiet - our T.M bombarded enemy front line and rifle grenades were fired on enemys sap at BOAR'S HEAD. Retaliation consisted of L.H.V which fell short of our front line.<br>INTELLIGENCE. Enemy relief probably taken place opposite S.10.3 as he was abnormally quiet up to the time of our bombardment - his retaliation was rapid, short and snappy on our front line and near supports. Enemy retaliation for our T.M and rifle grenades on BOAR'S HEAD is unique. It is probable that he supposed it to be prelude to an attack on his sap here. Sentries report, that by aid of very lights, Germans opposite were wearing brightly polished helmets, possibly of steel.<br>WORK. Under R.E supervision, reinforcing dugouts, building parapet and parados etc.<br>CASUALTIES. 2 men killed and 3 wounded by enemy T.M. 1 man sniped at "Stand Down". | BRIGADE TRENCH MAP AREA "H." |
| | MAY 26 | 9.45 p.m. | Relieved by 18th Battn. Lancashire Fusiliers and moved to Reserve Billets at RICHEBOURG ST. VAAST. Relief complete by 9.45 p.m. without incident. Distribution of Battalion was as before. | |
| RICHEBOURG ST. VAAST. | MAY 24th to MAY 30th | | During this period, the Battalion supplied working parties by day and by night on the front line and various communication trenches.<br>NOTES. 2/Lt WATSON, G. was wounded on the 28th May by a piece of enemy anti-aircraft shrapnel. | |
| RICHEBOURG ST VAAST | MAY 30th | 7.20 pm 8.15 p.m. | An intense enemy bombardment took place on the front and support trenches of the Right subsection of the Brigade Sector on our left. Our front line and supports as well as our Reserve Billets were heavily shelled.<br>Owing to this the relief of the 18th Lancashire Fusiliers by this unit was delayed until the bombardment had died down.<br>The Battalion carried out all the various defensive measures as laid down, ready to reinforce or defend as was necessary. | |

1875 Wt. W593/826 1,000,000 4/15 J.B.C. & A. A.D.S.S./Forms/C. 2118.

Instructions regarding War Diaries and Intelligence Summaries are contained in F. S. Regs., Part II. and the Staff Manual respectively. Title Pages will be prepared in manuscript.

# WAR DIARY
*or*
# INTELLIGENCE SUMMARY
*(Erase heading not required.)*

Army Form C. 2118

VOLUME IV — MAY 1916.

| Place | Date | Hour | Summary of Events and Information | Remarks and references to Appendices |
|---|---|---|---|---|
| LEFT SUBSECTION TRENCHES — u — FERME DU BOIS SECTOR | MAY 30th to MAY 31st | 10.10 p.m. to 6 a.m. | OPERATIONS The bombardment showing signs of dying down the Battalion carried on with the relief which was completed by 2 am. — the relief was delayed almost 3 hours — Enemy bombardment breeched our parapet at S.10.3, S.10.4, S.10.5. (TRENCH SECTORS) — also 4 or 5 direct hits on COPSE ST. C.T., N.W of RUE DU BOIS. Our retaliation considerably damaged enemy parapet opposite S.10.3. 'Stand to' this morning very quiet — enemy took advantage of mist to try and examine his wire — this party was dispersed by M.G fire.<br>WORK on breeches in our line commenced immediately on relief — big efforts made to repair damaged portions of line on the right of Battn on our left. COPSE STREET cleared and communication again made possible.<br>CASUALTIES. 2/LT DERWENT F.R., and 2 other ranks wounded. | Bde TRENCH MAP AREA "H". |
| | MAY 31st — to — MAY 31st | 6 am 12 p.m. | OPERATIONS Nothing of importance — patrols and listening posts as usual — At "Stand to" this morning a suspected sniper's post among trees at S.16.A.6.1 was bombarded with rifle grenades. Enemy machine gun silenced by rifle grenade fire.<br>INTELLIGENCE Several of enemy seen behind their 2nd line — pigeon seen at 7.30 pm and 2.30 am flying low from enemy line. At "Stand to" in the morning an aeroplane was observed dropping white lights, apparently over LE TOURET or VIEILLE CHAPELLE.<br>WORK. Repair of parapet and parados etc damaged by during last enemy bombardment. Other work under R E supervision. | BDE TRENCH MAP AREA "H". |
| | | | 1/6/16. A. Mills Lt. Colonel, Commdg., 17th (Service) Battn. Lanc. Fus. S. E. L. | |

1875 Wt. W593/826 1,000,000 4/15 J.B.C. & A. A.D.S.S./Forms/C. 2118.

WAR DIARY. MAY 1916.

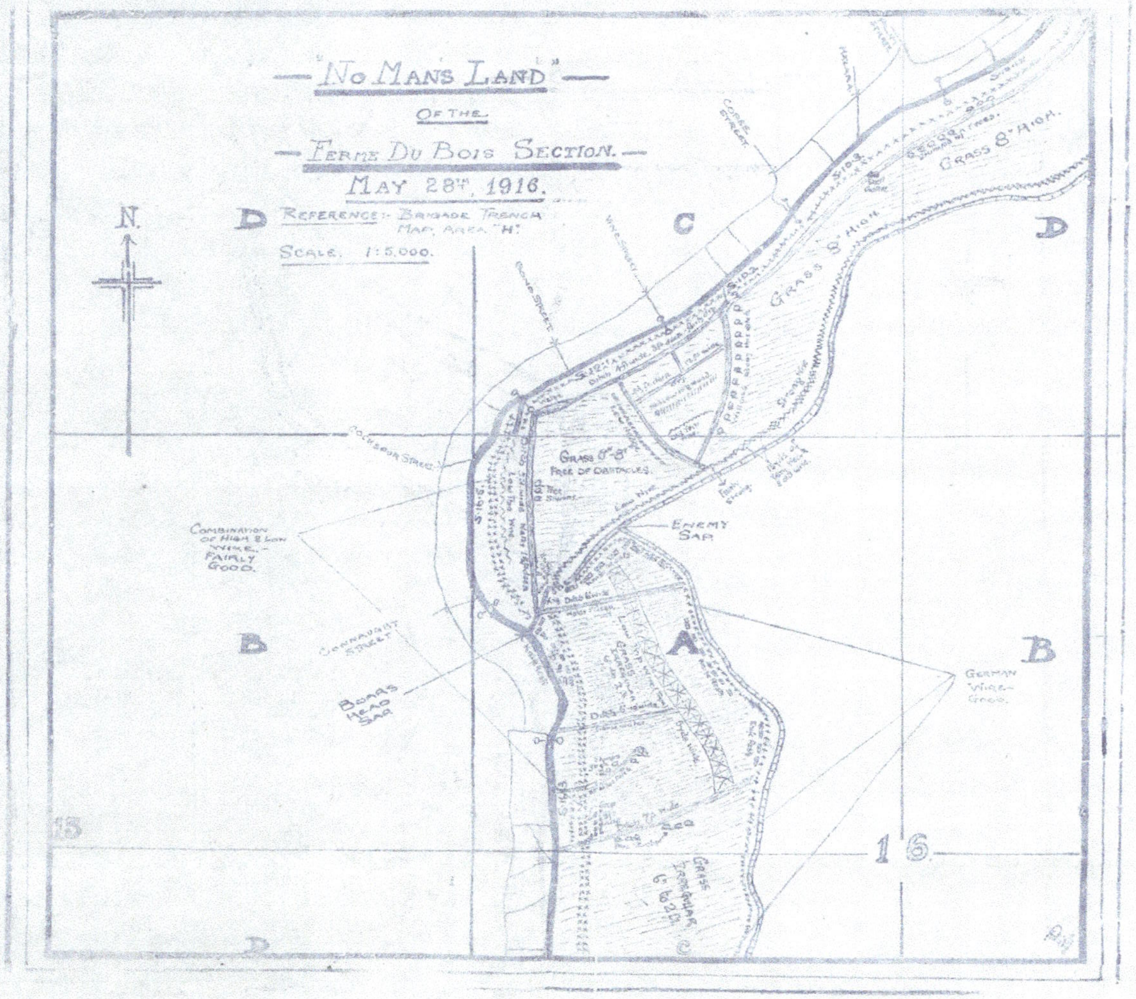

WAR DIARY. MAY 1916.

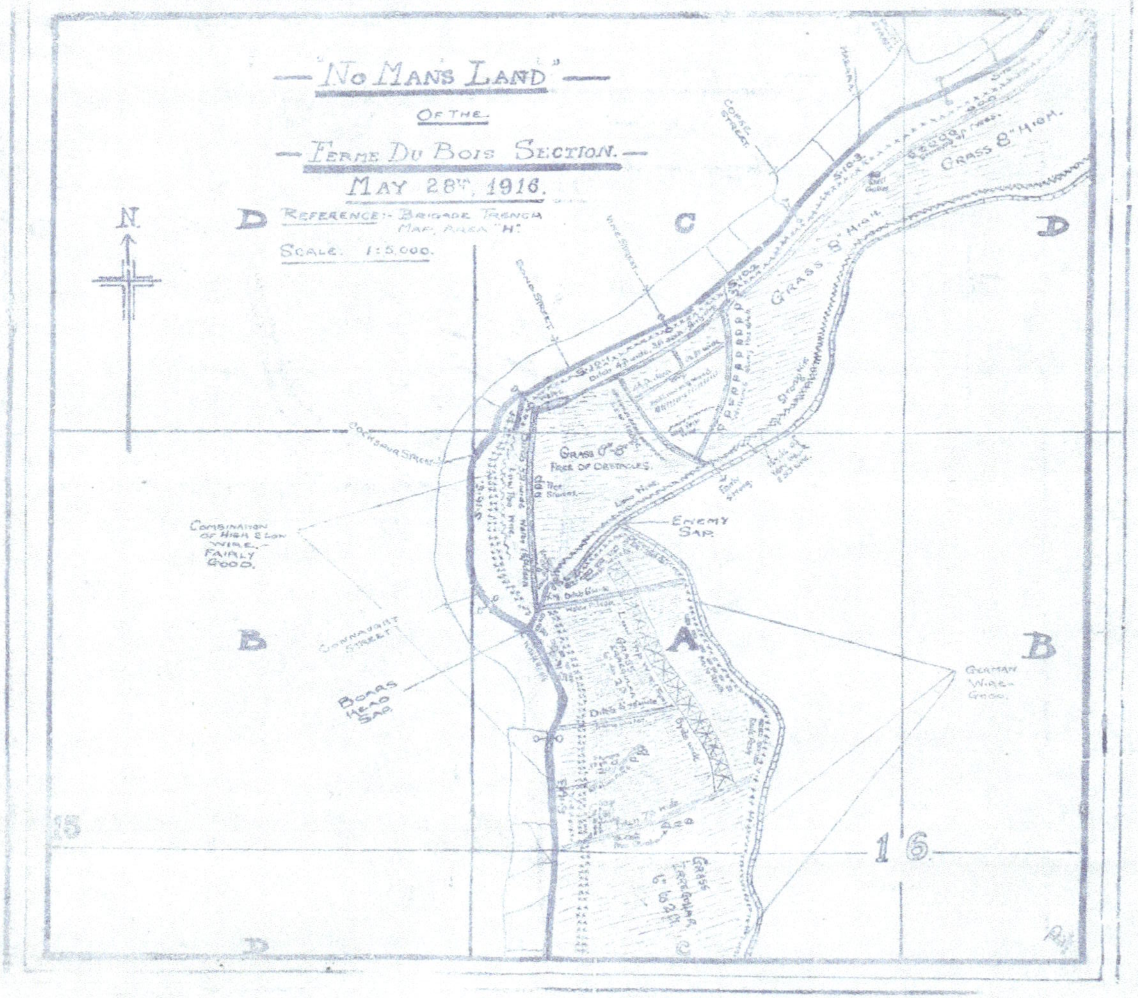

Vol 5.
17 Lan Fus
June

War Diary XXX

of

17th Service (1st S. [illegible]) Bn.,
Lancashire Fusiliers

1916

Volume V

June 1st — June 30th

5-V.
11 sheets

Instructions regarding War Diaries and Intelligence Summaries are contained in F. S. Regs., Part II. and the Staff Manual respectively. Title Pages will be prepared in manuscript.

# WAR DIARY
*or*
# ~~INTELLIGENCE SUMMARY~~
*(Erase heading not required.)*

Army Form C. 2118

| Place | Date 1916. | Hour | – VOLUME V – Summary of Events and Information – JUNE 1916. – | Remarks and references to Appendices |
|---|---|---|---|---|
| LEFT SUB SECTION TRENCHES FME DU BOIS SECTION –o– | June 1st to June 2nd | 7am<br>7am. | Operations. The day passed without incident – Artillery Tests asked for as usual – between 6 & 7 in the evening our Artillery (18 pdrs). destroyed a hostile M.G. emplacement about S.16.a.5.6. – number of rounds fired was 26. Patrols went out to cut off supposed enemy patrol – no trace of it found – An enemy Very light set fire to parapet at Bay 30. S.16.4. – enemy opened rapid and M.G. fire – fire was extinguished and we retaliated with rifle grenades.<br>Intelligence. Enemy nervous but very quiet – used large numbers of Very Lights. Enemy shelled spot over which aeroplane dropped lights on 31/5/16.<br>Work. Strengthening and heightening parados – under R.E. supervision.<br>Casualties. 1 man wounded.<br>A Coy. of 2/7th Worcesters was attached to the Battalion for instruction and distributed amongst the companies in the Front Line. | Reference Brigade Trench Map Area H. |
| –do– | June 2nd to June 3rd | 7am<br>7am. | Operations. Day quiet on the whole. – usual Artillery tests – considerable sniping activity on enemy's part checked by rifle grenades. Enemy working parties on parapet disturbed by rifle grenades and M.G. fire.<br>Intelligence. It is probable that enemy sap at BOARS HEAD is protected from our rifle grenades etc. by overhead wire netting – A German who was seen sniping at our Sap periscope was using a Mauser pistol.<br>Work. Parados and trench board work under R.E. supervision – night wiring – one party was out for 1½ hours.<br>Casualties. 2 men wounded.<br>Lieut Fitzgerald G.W.R. having been transferred to the General List is struck off the strength of the Battalion from this date | –do–<br><br>Authority 35/D/1888/A 1/6/16. |

1875 Wt. W593/826 1,000,000 4/15 J.B.C. & A. A.D.S.S./Forms/C. 2118.

Instructions regarding War Diaries and Intelligence Summaries are contained in F. S. Regs., Part II. and the Staff Manual respectively. Title Pages will be prepared in manuscript.

# WAR DIARY
*or*
# ~~INTELLIGENCE SUMMARY~~
*(Erase heading not required.)*

Army Form C. 2118

| Place | Date | Hour | Summary of Events and Information — VOLUME V. — JUNE 1916. | Remarks and references to Appendices |
|---|---|---|---|---|
| LEFT SUBSECTION TRENCHES -o- FERME DU BOIS SECTION. | June 3rd to June 4 | 7am 7am | The day was excentionally quiet. With the exception of the usual Artillery Tests and occasional odd enemy shrapnel rounds, there is nothing at all to report. Patrols went out as usual - some during the day to reconnoitre in the fairly long grass. The work done on this day was similar to that already referred to. Casualties - One man wounded - Since died of wounds. | Ref Bde. Trench Map Area "76" |
| | June 4th to June 5th | 7am | Operations Hostile T.M's registered on N end of PLUM ST - our "heavies" and T.M's registered on enemy wire opposite S.10.3 with good results. Enemy retaliated by shelling BUTE ST with L.H.V. and RUE DE BOIS, FACTORY CORNER. Intelligence Nil. Work continued under R.E. supervision. | |
| | | 9.30 pm | The Battalion was relieved by the 18th Battn. Lancashire Fusiliers and moved to Reserve Billets at RICHEBOURG St VAAST. A draft of 35 NCO's and men was distributed amongst the various Companies. | -do- |
| RICHEBOURG St VAAST. | June 6th to June 11th | | During this period the Battalion supplied working parties for the front, support and communication trenches. The demands of the Higher Command were so heavy that every available man had to be taken in order to carry out the urgent work. One man was mortally wounded on one of these parties. On June 8th/16. the 2/7th Worcesters left the Battalion and their place was taken by "B" Coy 2/6th Glosters. | -do- |

1875 Wt. W593/826 1,000,000 4/15 J.B.C. & A. A.D.S.S./Forms/C. 2118.

Instructions regarding War Diaries and Intelligence Summaries are contained in F. S. Regs., Part II. and the Staff Manual respectively. Title Pages will be prepared in manuscript.

# WAR DIARY
*or*
# ~~INTELLIGENCE~~ SUMMARY
*(Erase heading not required.)*

Army Form C. 2118

| Place | Date | Hour | Summary of Events and Information — VOLUME V — 1916 | Remarks and references to Appendices |
|---|---|---|---|---|
| LEFT SUBSECTION TRENCHES — o — THE DU BOIS SECTION | June 11th 1916 | 8.50 pm to 9.40 p.m. | The Battalion relieved the 18th Battn. Lancashire Fusiliers in the Left Subsection Trenches. The Companies took up positions as under:- LEFT COMPANY . . . . . "Z" Coy. RIGHT COMPANY . . . . "X" " CENTRE COMPANY . . . "Y" " SUPPORT COMPANY . . . "W" " Specialists relieved as under:- Snipers . . . . . by 10 a.m Lewis Guns . . . by 12 noon. Signallers . . . by 5 p.m The inter-Battalion relief was completed without incident by 9.40 p.m - the enemy was very quiet throughout the night. | Ref Bde. Trench Map Area "H". |
| -do- | June 11/16 to June 12th | 10pm to 7am | Operations Very quiet night except for bursts of rapid M.G fire after 1a.m. Patrols reported everything quiet and enemy using large number of Very Lights. Intelligence Enemy working opposite one of our listening posts - many of sandbags of "Z" Coy parapet were cut during the night - enemy probably has many fixed rifles on this part. Work Nil. Casualties - Nil | |
| -do | June 12/16 to June 13th | 7am to 7am. | Operations Exceptionally quiet day - During the night continuous rifle fire - M.Gs. active during the night. The usual Artillery tests were carried - an enemy patrol was reported to be out but a patrol which was sent out failed to find any trace. Enemy was using a rapid firing M.G from his second line at morning and evening "Stand To" - shooting was pretty accurate. Intelligence M.G. fire directed at several of enemy along road well behind enemy's line - they were dispersed, taking cover very quickly. Work [illegible] and dug out improvements under R.E. Casualties 1 O.R. killed whilst on Sentry / 1 O.R. accidentally Killed. | |

1875 Wt. W593/826 1,000,000 4/15 J.B.C. & A. A.D.S.S./Forms/C. 2118.

Instructions regarding War Diaries and Intelligence Summaries are contained in F. S. Regs., Part II. and the Staff Manual respectively. Title Pages will be prepared in manuscript.

# WAR DIARY
*or*
# INTELLIGENCE SUMMARY
*(Erase heading not required.)*

Army Form C. 2118

Volume V — June 1916.

| Place | Date | Hour | Summary of Events and Information | Remarks and references to Appendices |
|---|---|---|---|---|
| LEFT SUBSECTION TRENCHES FME DU BOIS | June 13th to June 14th | 7am / 7am | Operations Enemy very quiet - he sent over about 15 L H V during the day - no damage done as they fell behind our line about BOND ST Great deal of rifle fire during night - this was effectively silenced by three salvoes from Artillery. Hostile MG active during night<br>Intelligence: Very little as the day and night were very quiet - enemy keeps a constant fire along our wire.<br>Work Revetting and strengthening parapet along the line. - building parados - making Sally Ports under R. E.<br>Casualties Two men wounded whilst on Listening Post. | Ref Bde Trench map Area H. |
| SECTION. | June 14th to June 15th | 7am / 7am | Operations. Enemy artillery sent over about 16 H.E at STRAND POST and FACTORY KEEP. - 2 direct hits on former where he also breached the parapet. Our artillery silenced a hostile M.G which was very active at "Stand to". Enemy also lightly shelled area of COCKSPUR ST. but no damage was done<br>Intelligence Patrols reported that enemy fired a great number of his Very lights from just in front of his parapet - enemy very nervous - Smoke observed from S.10.3 probably from locomotive proceeding from ILLIES to AUBERS Officers patrol reports "No man's Land" to be in very bad state.<br>Work Completing Dugouts - drainage improved - clearing and relaying trench boards.<br>Casualties - Nil. | |

1875 Wt. W593/826 1,000,000 4/15 J.B.C. & A. A.D.S.S./Forms/C. 2118.

Instructions regarding War Diaries and Intelligence Summaries are contained in F. S. Regs., Part II. and the Staff Manual respectively. Title Pages will be prepared in manuscript.

# WAR DIARY
*or*
# ~~INTELLIGENCE SUMMARY~~
*(Erase heading not required.)*

Army Form C. 2118

Volume V — June 1916.

| Place | Date | Hour | Summary of Events and Information | Remarks and references to Appendices |
|---|---|---|---|---|
| LEFT SUBSECTION TRENCHES FME DU BOIS SECTION | June 15th to June 16th | 7am to 7am | Operations. The front line Coys. bombarded the enemy front line with rifle grenades. Germans retaliated with a salvo of shrapnel which burst short. An officer's patrol bombed an enemy wiring party at S 16. a. 6. 2½. Enemy apparently reserving his artillery as no retaliation followed our artillery's shelling his trenches during afternoon and evening. Intelligence. Patrol reported that a well beaten track lead from enemy line to ours through the long grass. Work done. Reveting and strengthening of parapet continued - raising duck boards to improve drainage. Casualties. 1 man killed and 1 "patrol" man wounded | Ref Bde French map Area "16". |
| — do. | June 16th | | The Battalion was relieved by the 13th Royal Sussex Regt. Companies moved out in the order, Centre Coy, Left Coy, Right Coy, Support Coy, Hdqrs. Coy. These concentrated at RICHEBOURG POST and marched independently ~~to~~ via LACOUTURE, VIEILLE CHAPELLE, road junction at ZELOBES, where the Battn formed up and proceeded to Billets at LES CAUDRONS via LOCON. The Battalion was billeted here at about 2 a.m 17/6/16. | MAP BETHUNE COMBINED SHEET |
| LES CAUDRONS | June 17th to June 19th | | The Battalion remained here until June 19th. | |
| — do — | June 19th | 9.30 a.m. | The Battalion was formed up as follows to march to FOUQUIERES Advanced Guard - 2 sections Y Coy. Band and main Body and Transport Rear Guard — 2 sections Z Coy. | — do — |

1875 Wt. W593/826 1,000,000 4/15 J.B.C. & A. A.D.S.S./Forms/C. 2118.

Instructions regarding War Diaries and Intelligence Summaries are contained in F. S. Regs., Part II. and the Staff Manual respectively. Title Pages will be prepared in manuscript.

# WAR DIARY
*or*
# INTELLIGENCE SUMMARY
*(Erase heading not required.)*

Army Form C. 2118

Volume V — June 1916.

| Place | 1916. Date | Hour | Summary of Events and Information | Remarks and references to Appendices |
|---|---|---|---|---|
| ES CAUDRONS | June 19th | 9.30 am. | The starting time was 9.30am and the Route was via the main road to BETHUNE. Just after moving off word came that the Billeting Area had been changed to CHOQUES. When about half way to the new destination the Billeting area was changed to BETHUNE. Consequently, a fresh billeting party was sent out and the Battalion had dinners in the field. Finally the Battalion was settled in Billets at COLLEGE DES JEUNES FILLES, BETHUNE at about 1.30 pm. | COMBINED SHEET BETHUNE. |
| BETHUNE | June 20th | | The Battalion was exercised in the ordinary drill routine in the morning. Games etc. took place in the afternoon. | |
| -do- | June 21st | | A miniature Rifle Range was constructed this day. Lieut. J.E. LAPES and two Corporals proceeded this day to the 35th I.B.D at ETAPLES as instructors. | |
| do | June 23rd & 24th. | 3.30 pm | The short range was used by Companies in rotation. In the afternoon a Horse Show was held at ANEZIN where one of our Travelling Field Kitchens ("W" Coy) took the 1st Prize for general cleanliness and smartness | |
| -do | June 24th | 10.15 am. | Brig-Gen J.W. Sandilands G.O.C 104th Inf Bde inspected the Battalion this morning and was highly pleased with the way in which the men turned out. After the inspection the G.O.C. delivered a lecture to all officers and N.C.Os. of the Battalion. | |

1875 Wt. W593/826 1,000,000 4/15 J.B.C. & A. A.D.S.S./Forms/C. 2118.

Army Form C. 2118

Instructions regarding War Diaries and Intelligence Summaries are contained in F. S. Regs., Part II. and the Staff Manual respectively. Title Pages will be prepared in manuscript.

# ~~WAR DIARY~~
*or*
# INTELLIGENCE ~~SUMMARY~~
*(Erase heading not required.)*

Volume V

June 1916.

| Place | 1916 Date | Hour | Summary of Events and Information | Remarks and references to Appendices |
|---|---|---|---|---|
| BETHUNE. | July 25th/16 | | The following Officers reported for duty this date, and were posted to Companies as follows:-<br>2/LIEUT. J. B. STRANG - - - - - - "W" Coy. 2/LIEUT. R.S HEAPE - - - - - } 2/LIEUT. H. MARSHALL - - - . } "Z" Coy | |
| -do- | July 26th | | The usual parades were held this morning - Football, cricket and parades to the Swimming Baths were held in the afternoon. | |
| -do- | July 27th | | The Battalion took part in a Brigade Route march this day.<br>ADVANCED GUARD: 2 Coys 17th LAN FUS - "Y" & "Z" Coys. under Command of Capt. CROOK. These Coys moved off at 8.45 a m. After passing the cross roads at E. 21 a.6.5 the Advanced Guard halted to allow the Battn to close up.<br>MAIN BODY: H Q 104th Bde; 17th Lan. Fus (less 2 Coys); 18th Lan Fus; 20th Lan. Fus.; 23rd Manchester Regt (less 1 Coy)<br>REAR GUARD. 1 Coy 23rd Manchr. Regt.<br>STARTING POINT & TIME:- Road junction E. 15. d 8. 3 at 9.30 a.m.<br>ROUTE. Road junction E. 22 c - VERQUIN - VAUDRICOURT - HESDIGNEUL - road junction E. 21. c. 0. 9 - thence shortest route to Bn. Billets.<br>DRESS. Light marching Order. - Bombers wore bomb jackets half full (5 bombs) and one S.A.A bandolier (no S A A in pouches)<br>TRANSPORT 1st Line Transport (less 2 S.A.A carts and pack animals which accompanied Battn - pack mules in rear of S.A.A Carts) was brigaded under T.O. 23rd Manchr. Rgt and marched in rear of main Body in corresponding order of march.<br>Dinners were cooked on the march. | BETHUNE COMBINED SHEET |

Instructions regarding War Diaries and Intelligence Summaries are contained in F. S. Regs., Part II. and the Staff Manual respectively. Title Pages will be prepared in manuscript.

# WAR DIARY
*or*
# INTELLIGENCE SUMMARY
*(Erase heading not required.)*

Army Form C. 2118

Volume V — June 1916.

| Place | Date 1916 | Hour | Summary of Events and Information | Remarks and references to Appendices |
|---|---|---|---|---|
| BETHUNE. | June 27th | | CAPT J.W. EVATT. O.C "X" Coy having proceeded to Bde Hdqrs. relinquishes Command and payment of "X" Coy. Lieut J.M. COWAN assumes Command and Payment of "X" Coy. Parades as usual this day. | |
| -do- | June 28th | | The usual parades were held this day. The Battn was under 3 hours notice to move from this date. | |
| -do- | June 29th & 30th | | Parades etc were held as usual. | |
| | | | ADDITIONS | |
| | | | The following congratulatory messages were received on June 14/16. | |
| | | | I To 104th Inf Bde. The Lieut General Commdg XIth Corps has read with much pleasure the mention received by the 17th Battalion Lancashire Fusiliers in the Commander-in-Chief's despatch of the 29th May and he desires that you will convey to the Battalion his congratulations and thanks. (Sd) A W B SPENCER Major for Lt Col. G.S. 35th Division | |
| | | | II To O.C. 17th Lan. Fus:- Please convey this message to your Battalion and add my own congratulations. (Sd) J.W. SANDILANDS Brig. Gen, Commdg 104th Inf Bde. | |

1875 Wt. W593/826 1,000,000 4/15 J.B.C. & A. A.D.S.S./Forms/C. 2118.

Instructions regarding War Diaries and Intelligence Summaries are contained in F. S. Regs., Part II. and the Staff Manual respectively. Title Pages will be prepared in manuscript.

# WAR DIARY
*or*
~~INTELLIGENCE SUMMARY~~
*(Erase heading not required.)*

Army Form C. 2118

Volume V — June 1916.

| Place | Date | Hour | Summary of Events and Information | Remarks and references to Appendices |
|---|---|---|---|---|
| | | | ADDITIONS (Contd). | |
| | | | The following promotions of Officers were received this month:- | |
| | | | CAPT. F.J.F. CROOK promoted MAJOR. | |
| | | | LIEUT. C.E. JEWELS " CAPTAIN and appointed ADJUTANT. | |
| | | | LIEUT. J.M. COWAN " CAPTAIN. | |
| | | | 2/LT H.J. BIRNSTINGL " LIEUT. | |
| | | | Medical Report The whole Battn. has been medically inspected, special attention being directed to the detection of cases of Scabies and Pedienti. The men have been found to be exceptionally clean. The Sanitary Squad have removed all refuse to the destructor. The latrines are in good order and the buckets have been emptied twice daily. [Sd. H.G. Parker, Lieut. R.A.M.C.] | |
| | | | 16-7-16 | |
| | | | [signature] Lieut. Colonel, Commdg. 17th Service (1st S.E.L.) Battn., Lancashire Fusiliers | |

1875 Wt. W593/826 1,000,000 4/15 J.B.C. & A. A.D.S.S./Forms/C. 2118.

104th Bde.
35th Div.

# WAR DIARY

17th BATTALION

LANCASHIRE FUSILIERS

1st to 31st JULY 1916.

104/35 35

July
LAN Fus
17 Manchester
VOL 6

Confidential

War Diary

of

14th Service (1st S.E.L.) Battalion, Lancashire Fusiliers

From July 1st 1916 To July 31st 1916

(Volume 6)

6.V
5 sheets

Instructions regarding War Diaries and Intelligence Summaries are contained in F. S. Regs., Part II. and the Staff Manual respectively. Title Pages will be prepared in manuscript.

# WAR DIARY
*or*
~~INTELLIGENCE SUMMARY~~
*(Erase heading not required.)*

Army Form C. 2118

| Place | Date | Hour | Summary of Events and Information | Remarks and references to Appendices |
|---|---|---|---|---|
| BETHUNE | July 1 | | The Battalion still in G. H. Q. Reserve. | |
| BETHUNE | July 2 | | Battalion marched to FOUQUEREUIL leaving BETHUNE at 9.45 p.m. and entrained at the former for BOUQUEMAISON. | |
| BOUQUEMAISON | July 3 | | Arrived at BOUQUEMAISON at 3 a.m. Battalion billeted here under orders to move at shortest possible notice. | |
| BOUQUEMAISON | July 6 | | Marched from BOUQUEMAISON to BUS-LES-ARTOIS arriving about midnight. Under orders to move at the shortest possible notice. | |
| BUS-LES-ARTOIS | July 9 | | Marched from BUS-LES-ARTOIS to LEALVILLERS. Received orders at about 11-30 p.m. to move to BOUZINCOURT. | |
| LEALVILLERS | July 10 | | About 3 a.m. the Battalion moved to BOUZINCOURT by Motor Lorries. On arrival, ordered to march to AVELUY WOOD, where Battalion was entrenched. Casualties in the wood 1 Man Killed & 3 men Wounded. | |
| AVELUY WOOD | July 13 | | Marched from AVELUY WOOD to MORLANCOURT, moving the same night to HAPPY VALLEY. Battalion under ½ hours notice to move. Here the attack was practiced. | |
| HAPPY VALLEY | July 14 | | 12 Men Accidentally Wounded by Bomb Explosion. | |
| HAPPY VALLEY | July 18 | | About 7 p.m. the Battalion marched from HAPPY VALLEY to MARICOURT. 1 Man Killed. | |
| MARICOURT | July 19 | | 5 Men wounded whilst at MARICOURT. In the afternoon the Battalion moved from MARICOURT to TALUS BOISE, where it was in Divisional Reserve. | |
| TALUS BOISE | July 20 | | About 8 p.m. the Battalion moved into the line relieving the 16TH CHESHIRE REGT in BERNAFAY WOOD. | |

1875 Wt. W593/826 1,000,000 4/15 J.B.C. & A. A.D.S.S./Forms/C. 2118.

Instructions regarding War Diaries and Intelligence Summaries are contained in F. S. Regs., Part II. and the Staff Manual respectively. Title Pages will be prepared in manuscript.

# WAR DIARY
*or*
~~INTELLIGENCE SUMMARY~~
*(Erase heading not required.)*

Army Form C. 2118

| Place | Date | Hour | Summary of Events and Information | Remarks and references to Appendices |
|---|---|---|---|---|
| BERNAFAY WOOD | July 21. | | Relieved 18TH BN. LAN. FUS. in the front line, holding a position from TRONES WOOD inclusive to MALTZ HORN FARM exclusive (extreme right of the British line). 3 Men Wounded in Action and 1 Transport Driver Wounded. | |
| FRONT LINE. | July 22 | | The Battalion still holding the front line which was subjected to heavy fire from hostile Artillery. Casualties as follows:-<br>OFFICERS. Killed — Nil<br>Wounded — LIEUT. COL. A.M. MILLS. LIEUT. H.J. BIRNSTINGL. 2/LT. S.R. CARTER.<br>OTHER RANKS. Killed — 8<br>Wounded. — 75. | |
| FRONT LINE. | July 23. | | The front line was again heavily shelled throughout the day. The Battalion was relieved by the 23RD BN. THE MANCHESTER REGIMENT at about 11 p.m. and proceeded to TALUS BOISE. Casualties during the day were as follows:-<br>OFFICERS. Killed — Nil.<br>Wounded — MAJOR SIR H.S.M. HAVELOCK-ALLAN. 2/LT. H. MARSHALL.<br>OTHER RANKS. Killed — 18<br>Wounded — 58 | |
| TALUS BOISE. | July 24 | | Relief Complete and Battalion in TALUS BOISE at about 2 a.m. Casualties during this day were as follows:-<br>OFFICERS. — NIL.<br>OTHER RANKS. Killed 6.<br>Wounded. 14.<br>Missing 2. | |

1875 Wt. W593/826 1,000,000 4/15 J.B.C. & A. A.D.S.S./Forms/C. 2118.

Army Form C. 2118

Instructions regarding War Diaries and Intelligence Summaries are contained in F. S. Regs., Part II. and the Staff Manual respectively. Title Pages will be prepared in manuscript.

# WAR DIARY
*or*
# ~~INTELLIGENCE SUMMARY~~
*(Erase heading not required.)*

| Place | Date | Hour | Summary of Events and Information | Remarks and references to Appendices |
|---|---|---|---|---|
| TALUS BOISE. | July 25 | | At about 8 p.m. the Battalion proceeded to and relieved the 18TH BN. LAN. FUS. in DUBLIN TRENCH. RELIEF complete by 8.30 p.m. No Casualties | |
| DUBLIN TRENCH | July 26 | | The 16TH BN. CHESHIRE REGT. relieved the Battalion in DUBLIN TRENCH, commencing at 10 a.m. The Battalion proceeded to MINDEN POST. No Casualties | |
| FRONT LINE. | July 29 & July 30. | | Parties as under proceeded to the line for attachment to Battalions (as shown) of the 89TH BRIGADE in the attack on GUILLEMONT.<br>No. — COY. — PARTY DETAILED. — BATTALION ATTACHED TO<br>1. — W. — 2 Offs. & 80 Other Ranks. — 19TH KINGS LIVERPOOL RGT.<br>2. — W. — 1 Off. & 40 Other Ranks. — 2ND BEDFORD RGT.<br>3. — X. — 2 Offs. & 80 Other Ranks. — 20TH KINGS LIVERPOOL RGT.<br>4. — X. — 1 Off. & 40 Other Ranks. — 2ND BEDFORD RGT.<br>5. — Y. — 1 Off. & 100 Other Ranks.<br>6. — Z. — 2 Offs. & 80 Other Ranks. — 17TH BN. KINGS LIVERPOOL RGT.<br>7. — Z. — 1 Off. & 40 Other Ranks. — 2ND BN. BEDFORD RGT.<br>These parties were employed as Carrying Parties & moved with the 4th Waves of the attacking force.<br>Casualties during this Operation.<br>OFFICERS. Killed — 2/Lt. J. B. STRANG.<br>WOUNDED — CAPT. W. T. TAYLOR. 2/Lt. W. H. ROBINSON.<br>OTHER RANKS. Killed — 2.<br>Wounded — 31.<br>Missing — 7. | |
| MINDEN POST. | July 31 | | The Battalion moved from MINDEN POST to HAPPY VALLEY arriving about 10.30 am. | |

[signature] Major
Commdg. 17th (S) Bn. Lancashire Fusiliers

1875 Wt. W593/826 1,000,000 4/15 J.B.C. & A. A.D.S.S./Forms/C. 2118.

35th Division.

104th Infantry Brigade.

---

1/17th BATTALION

LANCASHIRE FUSILIERS

AUGUST 1 9 1 6

3 Sketch maps attached.

Vol 7

— CONFIDENTIAL —

35th Divn
104th Bde.

War Diary

— of —

17TH SERVICE (1ST S.E.L.) BATTALION, LANCASHIRE FUSILIERS.

From:- 1st August, 1916, to:- 31st August, 1916

(VOLUME 7.)

7. V.
12 Marks

Instructions regarding War Diaries and Intelligence Summaries are contained in F. S. Regs., Part II. and the Staff Manual respectively. Title Pages will be prepared in manuscript.

# WAR DIARY

~~or~~

~~INTELLIGENCE SUMMARY~~

*(Erase heading not required.)*

Army. Form C. 2118

| Place | Date | Hour | Summary of Events and Information (SHEET 1) | Remarks and references to Appendices |
|---|---|---|---|---|
| HAPPY VALLEY. | August 1. | | Battalion in Bivouac in HAPPY VALLEY. MINDEN DAY was commemorated by a ceremonial parade of the Battalion in conjunction with the 18th & 20th Battalions Lancashire Fusiliers. Brigadier General J.W. Sandilands inspected and addressed the parade. | CSJ |
| HAPPY VALLEY. | August 2. | | The 104th Brigade Group will move to CORBIE Area on 2nd August as under:- Route:- Cross roads at K.6.d.9.8. - MORLANCOURT, - thence South-west through CRUCIFIX and back to K.13.d.6.2, - thence West down main road from BRAY to CORBIE. Starting Point:- Point where HAPPY VALLEY track meets main road from BRAY to ALBERT. Units with their 1st Line Transport will pass the Starting Point at the undermentioned times:- Unit:- 17th LANCASHIRE FUSILIERS: Time:- 6.0 p.m: Destination:- VAUX-sur-SOMME. - Reached there at 9.0 p.m | CSJ |
| VAUX-sur-SOMME. | August 3. | | Training was carried out by Company arrangements including Bathing and Swimming Parades in the SOMME. | CSJ |
| VAUX-sur-SOMME. | August 4. | | All 1st Line Transport, Baggage Wagons, and Horses, moved to VECQUEMONT, en route for MONTAGNE-LE-FAYEL. | CSJ |
| VAUX-sur-SOMME | August 5. | | The personnell of the Battalion, (less that which went in advance on the 4th instant) was ordered to move into billets in MONTAGNE-FAYEL. — Reference Map: Sheet Amiens 1/100,000. Operation Order dated 4th instant:- The Battalion will move tomorrow to MONTAGNE-LE-FAYEL, entraining at MERICOURT L'ABBE at 8.0 a.m. Battalion will reach the Station at 7.0 a.m. Starting point:- Battalion Headquarters, 5.30 a.m. Route:- Cross roads, North of O in VAUX-sur-SOMME: Church at MERICOURT STATION. Order of march:- Hd. Qrs., "X" Coy, "Z" Coy, "W" Coy, "Y" Coy, Lewis Gunners. Detraining Station:- probably AILLY. —— Detrained at SALEUX and marched to destination, via:- CLAIRY, PISSY, FLUY, BOUGAINVILLE and MOLLIENS VIDAME. Settled in billets at 8.0 p.m. — Despite the heat of the day, and the length of the march, the Battalion arrived intact, with the exception of 3 men, who did not report untill late in the night. | CSJ |
| MONTAGNE-LE-FAYEL | August 6. | | Was observed as a holiday after Church Parade. | |
| MONTAGNE-LE-FAYEL. | August 7. | | Commenced training of the Battalion in the attack. Operation was carried out on imaginary situation at FLOXICOURT. Musketry practice, Lewis Gun practice, and Bomb throwing from 6.0 p.m. to 7.0 p.m. | CSJ |
| MONTAGN-LE-FAYEL. | August 8. | | Battalion continued training: Much useful work done. | CSJ |

1875 Wt. W593/826 1,000,000 4/15 J.B.C. & A. A.D.S.S./Forms/C. 2118.

P.T.O.

Instructions regarding War Diaries and Intelligence Summaries are contained in F. S. Regs., Part II. and the Staff Manual respectively. Title Pages will be prepared in manuscript.

# WAR DIARY

~~or~~

~~INTELLIGENCE SUMMARY~~

*(Erase heading not required.)*

Army Form C. 2118

| Place | Date | Hour | Summary of Events and Information (SHEET 2) | Remarks and references to Appendices |
|---|---|---|---|---|
| MONTAGNE-LE-FAYEL. | August 9. | | Practised Battalion attack on & clearing of wood. Divisional Gas Officer lectured Companies. Transport ~~[illegible]~~ moved to VAUX-sur-SOMME. - Brigade Operation Order No 30, paras. 1 and 2:- 1. The 35th Division will move on August 9th and 10th by road and train into the XIII Corps Area. 2. All 1st Line Transport, Baggage wagons and horses of the 104th Brigade Group will move by road tomorrow, 9th August to VECQUEMONT and DAOURS as under:- Starting Point: Cross roads at M of MOLLIENS VIDAME: 6:30 a.m. | C.S./ |
| MONTAGNE-LE-FAYEL | August 10 | | Moved by road and train to XIII Corps Area. - Battalion Operation Order:- 1. The 104th Brigade Group will entrain on 10th August, as under:- 1st Train, 6a.m:- Bde H.Q., 17th Lancashire Fusiliers, 18th Lancashire Fusiliers, 203rd Field Coy. R.E., 104th M.G. Coy. 2. Ref: para 1. The Battalion will parade for march to AIRAINS as under:- Starting point:- Battalion Headquarters, 4.0a.m. Order of March:- Band, Headquarters, Lewis Gunners, "W" Coy, "Z" Coy, "Y" Coy, "X" Coy. Reveille will be at 3.a.m. 3. Detraining Station:- CORBIE. 4. On arrival at detraining station, the Battalion will march to VAUX, Companies taking over their former billets at that place. | C.S./ |
| VAUX-sur-SOMME | August 11 | | Standing by under orders to move to HAPPY VALLEY. | C.S./ |
| VAUX-sur-SOMME | August 12 | | Training carried out by Companies. Bathing parades in the SOMME were included. Instruction in wiring given by R.E. to party consisting of 2 Officers per Coy, 2 N.C.O's & 15 men per Platoon of the Battalion | C.S./ |
| VAUX-sur-SOMME | August 13 | | After Church Parade, observed as a holiday. In the afternoon, held informal Gala in the SOMME. | C.S./ |
| VAUX-sur-SOMME | August 14 | | Training in open warfare was continued. Throughout the day, by arrangements with the R.E., squads were given instructions in wiring. | C.S./ |
| VAUX-sur-SOMME | August 15 | | The Battalion was exercised in the attack: Operation Order for attack on WELLCOME WOOD - (Imaginary) (Ref: Map:- Sheet 62D.N.E. scale 1/20,000). 1. The 104th Brigade will attack & hold the German defences in WELLCOME WOOD. 2. The 17th LANCASHIRE FUSILIERS assault in the centre, with the 23rd MANCHESTER REGT on their right and the 18th LAN. FUS. on their left. 3. The Battalion will attack ~~& hold the~~ on a front of 200 yards, in 3 waves, each consisting of 4 Platoons:- "W" Company on the left and "X" Coy. on the right, form the first two waves. ½ of "Y" Coy. on the left, and ½ of "Z" Coy. on the right, form the 3rd wave:-<br>1st LINE: "W" Coy. — 1 Platoon. 1 Platoon. "X" Coy. — 1 Platoon. 1 Platoon. | C.S./ |

1875 Wt. W593/826 1,000,000 4/15 J.B.C. & A. A.D.S.S./Forms/C. 2118.

P.T.O.

Instructions regarding War Diaries and Intelligence Summaries are contained in F. S. Regs., Part II. and the Staff Manual respectively. Title Pages will be prepared in manuscript.

# WAR DIARY
or
# ~~INTELLIGENCE SUMMARY~~

*(Erase heading not required.)*

Army Form C. 2118

| Place | Date | Hour | Summary of Events and Information (SHEET 3.) | Remarks and references to Appendices |
|---|---|---|---|---|
| (cont^d) | August 15 | | (Attack on WELLCOME WOOD - cont^d) | C.J. |

2nd LINE: W Coy: 1 Platoon, 1 Platoon. X Coy: 1 Platoon. 1 Platoon.

3rd LINE: Y Coy: 1 Platoon. 1 Platoon. "Z" Coy: 1 Platoon. 1 Platoon.

2 Platoons each of "Y" & "Z" Coys: will act as Reserves or Carrying Parties for R.E. material.

4. The Battalion's objective will be the 1st & 2nd Lines of the German defences - (imaginary). The first wave will seize and hold the German ~~defence~~ trench for a length of 100 yards on each side - N. and S. - of the old Windmill. The Mill may be regarded as a strong point. The second wave will have as its objective the second line running along the Western edge of WELLCOME WOOD from the S.W. corner to a point about 200 yards N. where the hedge on the Wood front ends. The 3rd Line will consolidate the 1st position gained - i.e., the Mill line.

5. 4 Lewis Guns each will accompany the 2nd & 3rd Lines. A Lewis Gun & a bombing section will protect each flank of the 2nd Line. - 2 guns will be placed in the Mill until the 3rd Line arrives, when all four guns with the 3rd Line will be used for making the Mill a strong point & the 2nd Line guns will go forward. All rifle men will carry 100 rounds S.A.A. - Bombers, 6 bombs (dummies), & 50 rounds S.A.A. All 3rd Line men will carry either a pick or shovel.

7. Iron rations only will be carried on the man. - Waterbottles full.

8. Each Coy will tell off parties for S.A.A. and bombs, before the assault. These will go back for supplies as soon as their Coys. are established in the enemy lines. Battalion dump will be at junction of VAUX - SAILLY and WELLCOME WOOD roads, & will be moved forward if circumstances permit. Special parties will also be told off to deal with any live Germans in dugouts or cellars.

9. The first 3 Lines will assemble in the Trench - (imaginary) running N. & S. through the O in VAUX-sur-SOMME.

10. The attack will be on a bearing 64° true from this point.

11. All front line parties will advance together at ZERO and will be followed by the 2nd Line at an interval of 50 yards. 3rd Line will follow 2nd at an interval of 100 yards.

12. Zero time will be notified later.

13. Battalion Headquarters will be at ROAD JUNCTION ~~will be~~ - J.27.c.3.5. All reports to this point.

Before the final stages of the exercise had been completed, orders were received for the Battalion to stand by ready to move at short notice. At 3.30 p.m. the Battalion marched to HAPPY VALLEY, which was reached at about 8.15 p.m. — C.J.

1875 Wt. W593/826 1,000,000 4/15 J.B.C. & A. A.D.S.S./Forms/C. 2118.

P.T.O.

Instructions regarding War Diaries and Intelligence Summaries are contained in F. S. Regs., Part II. and the Staff Manual respectively. Title Pages will be prepared in manuscript.

# WAR DIARY
or
# INTELLIGENCE SUMMARY
*(Erase heading not required.)*

Army Form C. 2118

(SHEET 4)

| Place | Date | Hour | Summary of Events and Information | Remarks and references to Appendices |
|---|---|---|---|---|
| VAUX-sur-SOMME | August 15 (contd.) | | Operation Order: 1. The 104th Brigade Group will move today to HAPPY VALLEY. 2. Units with 1st Line Transport & Baggage Wagons will march independently to HAPPY VALLEY as under:- Route:- MORLANCOURT, thence EAST by road and track direct to HAPPY VALLEY. Starting Point of Battn: VAUX CHURCH, 3.30 p.m. 3. On arrival at HAPPY VALLEY, Units will bivouac at same place as before. 4. Ref. para 2: Battalion will concentrate on road running past Bn. Hdqrs. ready to move off at 3.30 p.m. Order of March: H.Q., Y Coy. less 1 Officer & 70 O.R., X Coy, Z Coy, W Coy, Lewis Gunners, Transport. 5. DRESS: Light-Marching Order, coats open, sleeves rolled up. 6. All Transport will be loaded up by 3 p.m. Cookers move behind Companies. 7. O's. C. Companies and detachments will take steps at once to have all billets thoroughly cleaned. Reports that this has been done to head of column by 3.25 p.m. | C.S.J. |
| HAPPY VALLEY | August 16 | | In bivouac in HAPPY VALLEY. Companies were exercised independently in the attack. | C.S.J. |
| HAPPY VALLEY | August 17 | | Battalion training continued. | C.S.J. |
| HAPPY VALLEY | August 18 | | At 6 p.m. orders were received for the Battalion to move to TALUS BOISE. The Battalion Depot, including re-organising details remained at HAPPY VALLEY. TALUS BOISE was reached about 9.30 p.m. | C.S.J. |
| TALUS BOISE | August 19 | | Having bivouaced for the night at TALUS BOISE, the Battalion (less Depot), marched to DUBLIN TRENCH, and occupied trenches in the vicinity of the main line. - Casualties:- 1 O.R. killed | C.S.J. |
| DUBLIN TRENCH | August 20 | | Remained in Brigade Reserve in DUBLIN TRENCH area. - Casualties:- 1 O.R. wounded. | C.S.J. |
| DUBLIN TRENCH. | August 21 | | Remained in Brigade Reserve in DUBLIN TRENCH area. - Casualties:- NIL. | C.S.J. |
| DUBLIN TRENCH. | August 22 | | Took over from the French the front line system in ANGLE WOOD sector. Operation Order: 1. The Battalion will take over the front tonight from 43rd & 127th FRENCH I. REGts. 2. Distribution:- Coy. fronts will be as under:-<br>FRONT SYSTEM: "Y" Coy: approx. — B.2.c.4.3. (right) — B.1.d.9.9. (left)<br>"X" " " Post B.1.d.8.9½ (right) — B.1.d.3.6½ (left) with other Posts at B.1.d.0.9½ and B.1.d.6.5<br>SUPPORT: "Z" & "W" Coys. " "Z" Coy: right on B.7.b.3.8 "W" " left " B.1.c.2.6<br>3. Battalion Headquarters will probably be at- (approx:) A.12.b.7.5½. | C.S.J. |

1875 Wt. W593/826 1,000,000 4/15 J.B.C. & A. A.D.S.S./Forms/C. 2118.

P.T.O.

Instructions regarding War Diaries and Intelligence Summaries are contained in F. S. Regs., Part II. and the Staff Manual respectively. Title Pages will be prepared in manuscript.

# WAR DIARY
or
~~INTELLIGENCE SUMMARY~~
*(Erase heading not required.)*

Army Form C. 2118

(SHEET 5)

| Place | Date | Hour | Summary of Events and Information | Remarks and references to Appendices |
|---|---|---|---|---|
| (contd) | August 22 | | 4. The L.G.O. will detail detachments to Coys. as under:- "Y" Coy. - 3 guns: "X" Coy. - 3 guns: "Z" Coy. - 1 gun, "W" Coy. - 1 gun. 5. O's C. "Z" Coy. & "W" Coy. will each draw 4000 rounds S.A.A. for use of L.G. detachment in their sector. They will detail party to carry this up from STANLEY DUMP where it will be handed over by the R.S.M. 6. Order of March:- "Y", "X", "Z", "W", H.Q., by Platoons at 100 yards interval. The leading Coy. will pass Bde. H.Q. at 9.0 p.m. that hour. (Additional guides will be provided at the probable Bn. H.Q. to conduct Coys. into positions in the line. Guides will be at Bde. H.Q. at 7. Dress: Trench Marching Order; Gas-helmets worn in "gas-alert" positions; water bottles filled. 8. All necessary precautions must be taken to guard against Platoons or sections losing touch, and Coys. will move into line at a slow pace. 9. The water supply is a matter of great difficulty; there is no water in the line and all water has to be carried from about Bde. H.Q. at night. Men must therefore be warned that one bottle of water has to last them for the whole 24 hours, and must accordingly be used very sparingly. 10. There must be the absolute minimum of movement during the day & no work whatever will be done then. Consequently the greatest possible amount of work will be done ~~then~~ during the dark to make the front line continuous and to improve existing trenches. (a) O.C. "Y" Coy. will work to the left to link up with X. (b) O.C. "X" Coy. will work to the left to link up with Post at B.1.d. 0.9½ and left Battn. (c) O's C. "W" & "Z" Coys. will do all that is possible to improve their line, or such other work as is detailed. 11. Reports of relief complete to Bn. H.Q. without delay. 12. Acknowledge receipt of move order & destroy before moving into line. | CS |
| TRENCHES. | August 23 | | The relief though carried out under heavy hostile shelling, was entirely satisfactory and completed, with only 4 casualties, by 4 a.m. on the 23rd. The distribution of the Battn. was then as shown on the accompanying sketch. "Y" Coy. was established in shell-holes in the approximate alignment shown. "X" Coy. held the Posts indicated. TALUS TRENCH was occupied by 2 platoons of "W" Coy. & 2 platoons "Z" Coy. The Balance of these Coys. was held in Reserve in trenches near Battn. H.Q. During the early hours, whilst darkness yet permitted, "Y" Coy. & "X" Coy. did excellent work in consolidating their positions, and digging with a view to linking up the respective Coy. fronts. During the day both the front & support lines were subjected to intermittent heavy hostile shelling. Approximate casualties:- O.R., 13. (Killed & wounded) 2 Officers wounded (2/Lt. G.E. CONDLFFE & 2/Lt. RAWLINSON) | Appendix 1. CS |
| TRENCHES | August 24 | | During the early hours of the morning the Battalion was concentrated for the attack in shell holes E. of ANGLE WOOD. The Battalion was detailed to push forward the British right, in conjunction with the forward movement of the French on our immediate right. | Appendix 2. CS |

1875 Wt. W593/826 1,000,000 4/15 J.B.C. & A. A.D.S.S./Forms/C. 2118.

P.T.O.

Instructions regarding War Diaries and Intelligence Summaries are contained in F. S. Regs., Part II. and the Staff Manual respectively. Title Pages will be prepared in manuscript.

# WAR DIARY
or
~~INTELLIGENCE SUMMARY~~
(Erase heading not required.)

Army Form C. 2118

| Place | Date | Hour | Summary of Events and Information (SHEET 6) | Remarks and references to Appendices |
|---|---|---|---|---|
| (contd.) | August 24 | | Bde. Operation Order: B.M. 820. - 17th L.F. :- "Your Battalion will push forward the right flank to keep in touch with the French left. AAA The French left flank will rest on point 48 and will not go further than that AAA ----". The rôle of the Battn. was thus to cover the French left flank in their attack. At 5.45 p.m. the attack was launched, & the Battn. was disposed with 3 Companies in the front line and 1 in reserve. The right Company moved forward a distance of a little over 300 yards and established immediate touch with the French left. The other two Coys. in front line established themselves in immediate echelon back to the N.E. corner of ANGLE WOOD, where touch was maintained with the British troops on the left. On this new alignment the Battalion dug in and a trench was established after a few hours steady work carried out under heavy hostile Artillery fire. - Following message received from Brigadier:- "Congratulate you on your success up to date AAA".<br>Approximate Casualties:- 2 Officers (wounded). O.R. 4 killed, 16 wounded. | Appendix 3<br>Officers wounded:- LIEUT. E.M. SCHILL 2/LT. J.J. FLOWER. |
| TRENCHES | August 25. | | A returning strong patrol which had been pushed out from our left, encountered & engaged the enemy at FALFEMONT FARM. This position was found to be strongly held by the enemy. At 6 a.m., as a result of outpost encounter mentioned the enemy placed a heavy barrage on ANGLE WOOD and our new advanced line. Heavy shelling continued throughout the remainder of the day & culminated in an intense bombardment of our position from 8.15 p.m. - 9.30 p.m. Towards midnight the shelling became intermittent. The following message was received from G.O.C. Division:- "Major Crook, 17 Lancs. Fusrs. - Congratulate you and 17 Lancs. Fusiliers on your good work. Maj. Gen. PINNEY."<br>Relieved by the 20th Lancashire Fus: & moved into reserve in CASEMENT TRENCH. - (Operation Order, A114)- 1. Bn. will be relieved tonight by DEFIANCE & will proceed to CASEMENT TRENCH. 2. Only 2 Platoons of DEFIANCE will relieve each Coy. as a whole, the relieving Platoons taking over the front line. 3. Platoons will move out as relieved. O's. C. Coys. will take steps to have support & reserve platoons collected after dusk so that the will be able to follow out after the second platoon relieved thus ensuring that the Company moves intact. "X" Coy will move out last. The first two Companies relieved will move into CASEMENT TRENCH on the West of BRIQUETERIE ROAD. Hdqrs. & remaining 2 Coys. on EAST side.<br>Approximate Casualties:- Officers 1 (wounded) O.R. 64 (Killed & wounded). Missing:- 2 Officers, 31 O.R. | Officer wounded:- LIEUT. W.E.M. CURNOCK.<br>Officers missing:- CAPT. J.M. COWAN 2/LT. J.E. SANDERS |

1875 Wt. W593/826 1,000,000 4/15 J.B.C. & A. A.D.S.S./Forms/C. 2118.

P.T.O.

# WAR DIARY
or
~~INTELLIGENCE SUMMARY~~
*(Erase heading not required.)*

Army Form C. 2118

| Place | Date | Hour | Summary of Events and Information (SHEET 7.) | Remarks and references to Appendices |
|---|---|---|---|---|
| CASEMENT TRENCH | August 26 | | Settled in CASEMENT TRENCH by 5.30 a.m. About 1 p.m. relieved by 14th WARWICKS and moved to CITADEL.<br>Bde. Operation Order: B.M 856. - "After relief this morning by 14TH WARWICKS you will move to CITADEL area where the Brigade will be accommodated in Huts and Tents AAA." | |
| CITADEL | August 27 | | Battalion under canvas at CITADEL. | |
| CITADEL | August 28 | | G.O.C. 35TH DIVISION addressed the Battalion | |
| CITADEL | August 29 | | Officers & N.C.O's of the Battalion were addressed by Brigadier General J.W. SANDILANDS. CMG DSO Battalion Transport marched to CANDAS. - Operation Order 32 - 1. The 35th Division (less Artillery) will be transferred from XIV Corps to 3rd Army (VI Corps) from midnight 29th/30th August. All Transport will move by road on the 29th instant. Infantry and dismounted personnels of R.E. and R.A.M.C. will proceed by train on the 30th instant. 2. All Transport, horses and bicycles of the 104TH BRIGADE GROUP will march to ALLONVILLE: Starting point CITADEL, 11 a.m: Route - BRAY - road junction I.35.b.6.7. (to be passed at 3.35 p.m.) - LA NEUVILLE - BUSSY-LES-DAOURS - road junction H.25.a.3.9. - ALLONVILLE. 4. On 30th August the Transport will continue the march to the new area under orders which will be issued by Capt. Kerr, leaving ALLONVILLE at 10 a.m. - Route: RAINVILLE - VILLERS-BOCAGE - road junction on main AMIENS road ½ mile N.N.W. of VILLERS BOCAGE (to be passed at 12.30 p.m.) - FLESELLES - HAVERNES - CANAPLES - MONTRELET. From MONTRELET, the transport of units will proceed by the shortest route to billeting areas. 5. Billeting areas are allotted to units as under :- 17TH LAN. FUS. - CANDAS.<br>Weather conditions bad; very heavy rain, & thunderstorms were experienced in the afternoon & evening. | |
| CITADEL | August 30 | | Operation Order F.R 56. - 1. Units will entrain tomorrow, as under. - Entraining station, HEILLY (Ref. Sheet, AMIENS.) 1st Train. Departs 5-0 p.m. - 104 th. Bde. H.Q., 17th Lan. Fus. ..... 2. Route to entraining station :- MEAULTE, - A of DERNANCOURT - TREUX - HEILLY Station (HALTE about one mile South-West of HEILLY.) 3. Units will march to HEILLY, entrain, detrain, and march to destinations, under orders of O.C. trains, leaving camp at the following times :- 1st Train Units :- 12 noon.<br>At 12 noon the dismounted personnel of the Battalion left CITADEL and marched to HEILLY STATION which was reached at 4.40 p.m. Almost throughout the march heavy rain fell. On the whole roads were good taking into consideration the weather. The train conveying the Battalion left HEILLY | |

Instructions regarding War Diaries and Intelligence Summaries are contained in F. S. Regs., Part II. and the Staff Manual respectively. Title Pages will be prepared in manuscript.

# WAR DIARY

or

~~INTELLIGENCE SUMMARY~~

*(Erase heading not required.)*

Army Form C. 2118

| Place | Date | Hour | Summary of Events and Information (SHEET 8). | Remarks and references to Appendices |
|---|---|---|---|---|
| (contd.) | August 30. | | at 5.10pm. and reached CANDAS at 11.40pm. In the latter place the Battalion was billeted for a few hours. | C.E.J. |
| CANDAS. | August 31. | | Marched with Transport complete to IVERGNY. – (Bde. Opn. Ord. 33) 1. The Brigade will march to-morrow to the IVERGNY area, as under:- Route: DOULLENS – HAUTE VISEE. Starting point: Crossroads at N.E exit of CANDAS. Units will pass the Starting point as under, and march independently to their destinations:-<br>UNIT. 17TH LAN. FUS. TIME. 5.10 a.m. DESTINATION. IVERGNY.<br>2. 1st Line Transport ~~will~~ and Baggage Wagons will accompany Units. Lewis Gun Carts of 17th Lancashire Fusiliers will also be taken.<br>The roads were good and weather fine. Just WEST of DOULLENS a halt was made to enable the men to have breakfast.<br>IVERGNY was reached at 12.45 p.m. | C.E.J. |
| | | | Total Casualties from 19TH August, 1916, to 26TH August, 1916, – (period in line) :–<br>OFFICERS:- Killed: – Wounded: 5. Missing: 2.<br>OTHER RANKS:- Killed: 11. Wounded: 105. Missing: 31.<br>[signature] Major.<br>Commanding, 17th (S) Battn, Lancashire Fusiliers | |

1875 Wt. W593/826 1,000,000 4/15 J.B.C. & A. A.D.S.S./Forms/C. 2118.

## APPENDIX 1.

Extract from TRENCH MAP 62c N.W.1.

Scale 1/10,000

Disposition on Aug. 23rd 1916.

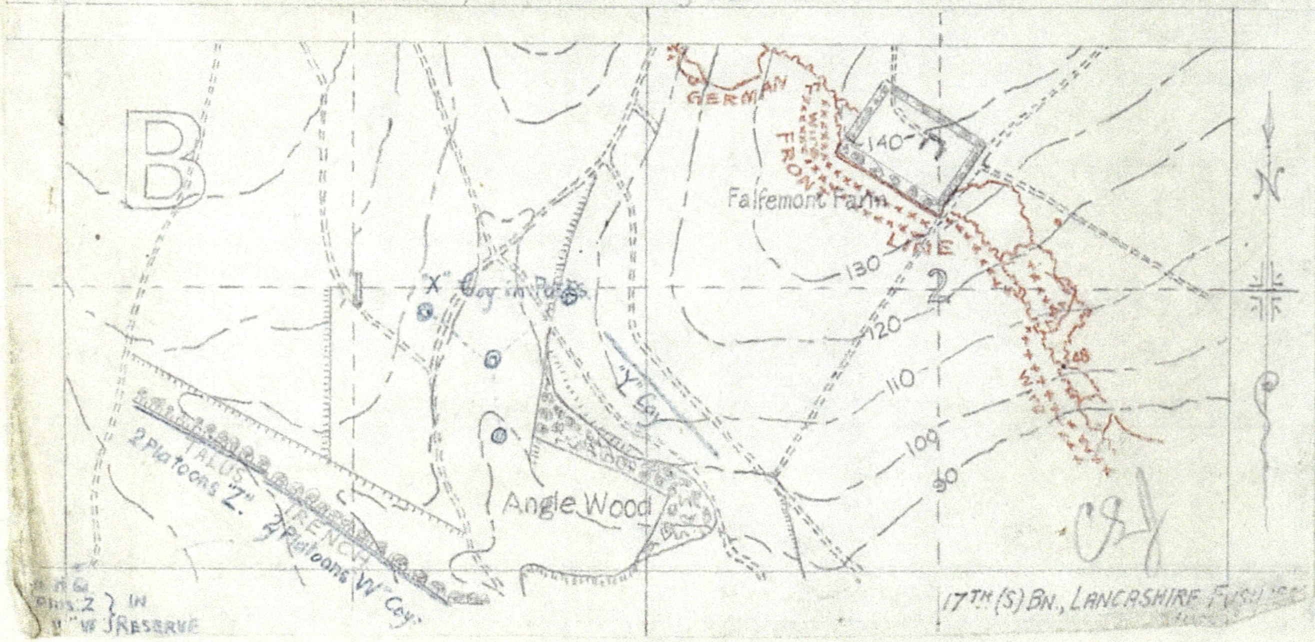

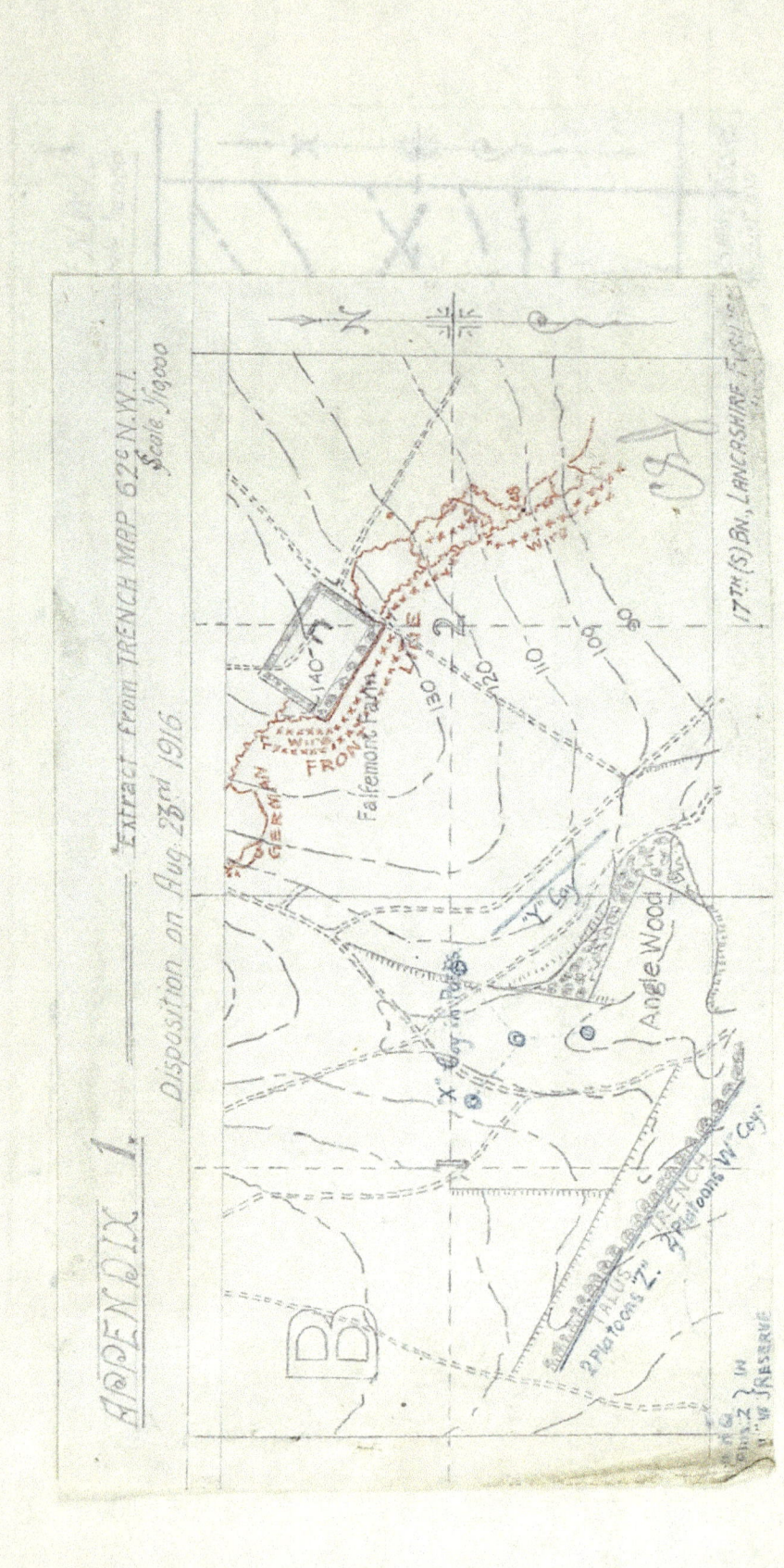

## Appendix 2

Sketch from Trench Map 62c N.W.1.

Disposition on Aug. 24th 1916, before forward movement

Scale 1/10,000

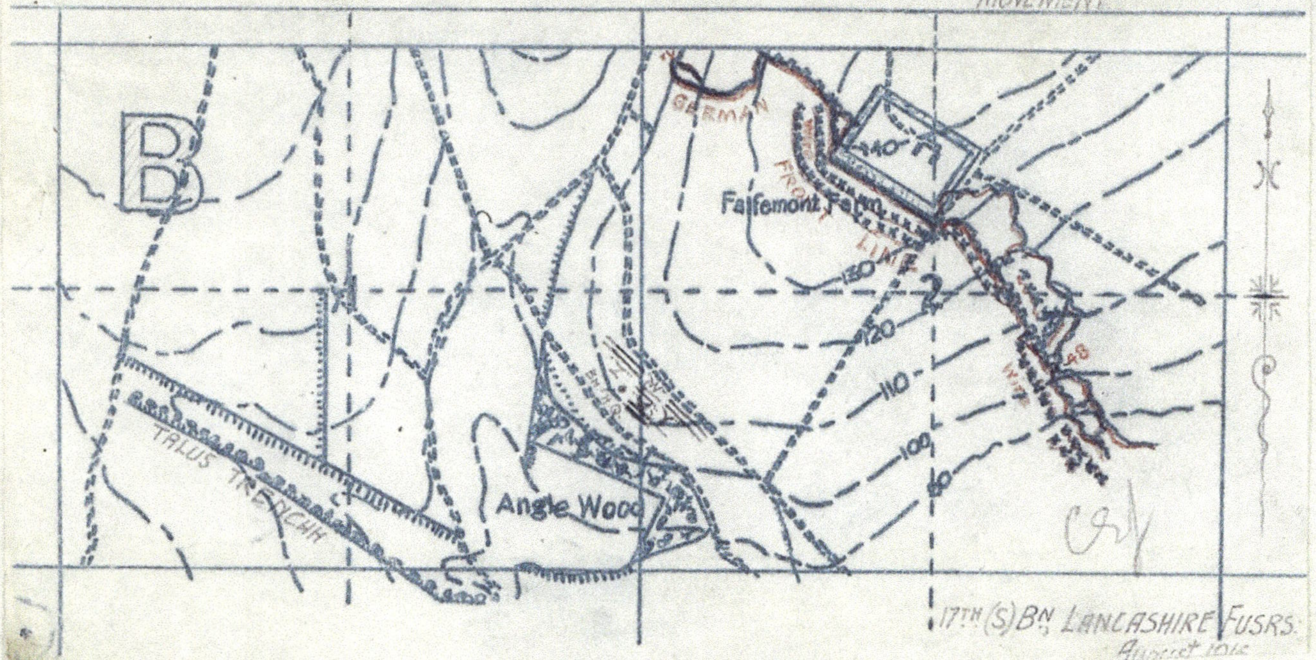


17th (S) Bn. Lancashire Fusrs.
August 1916

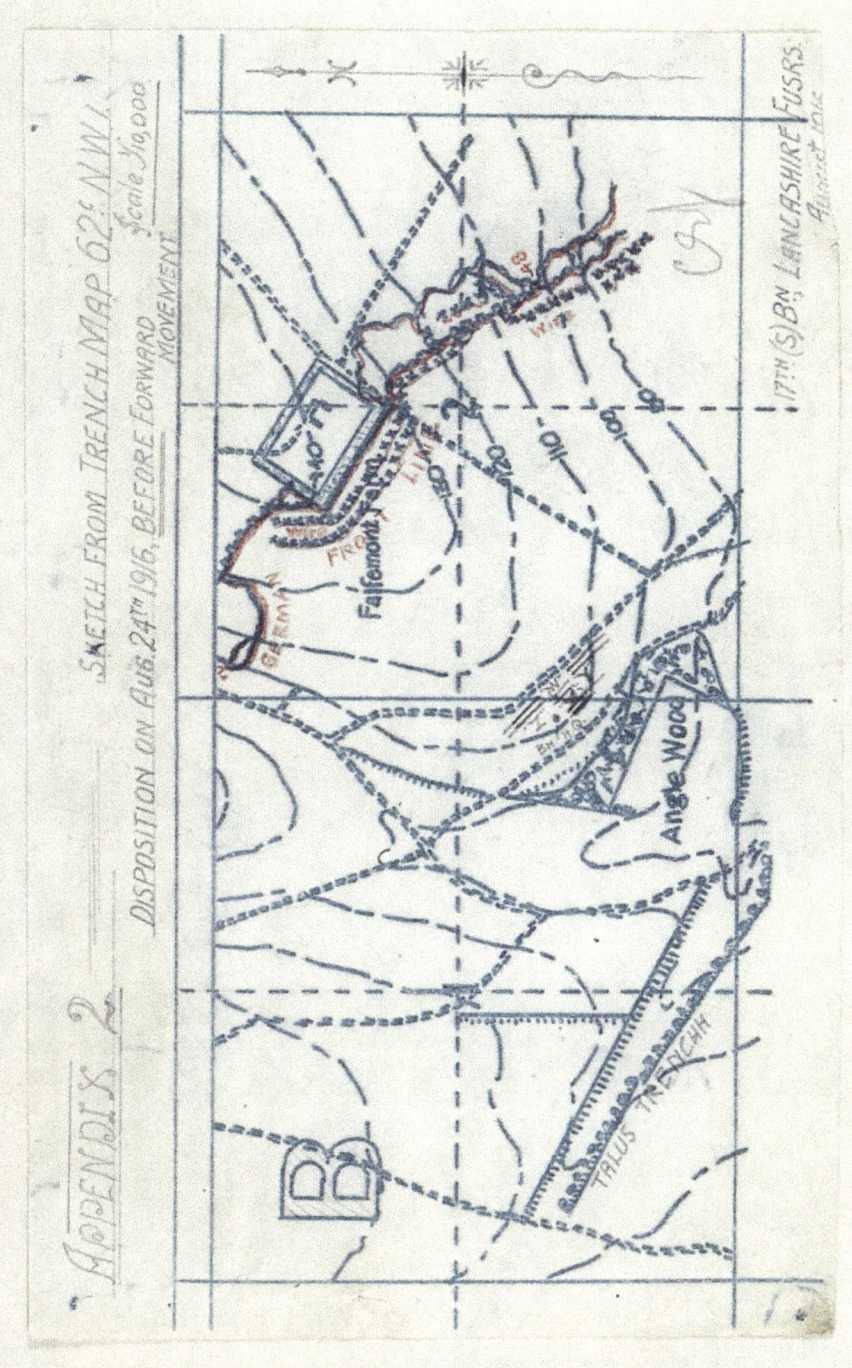

## APPENDIX 3.

SKETCH FROM TRENCH MAP 62C N.W. 1.

DISPOSITION ON AUG 24TH 1916. AFTER FORWARD MOVEMENT. Scale 1/10.000

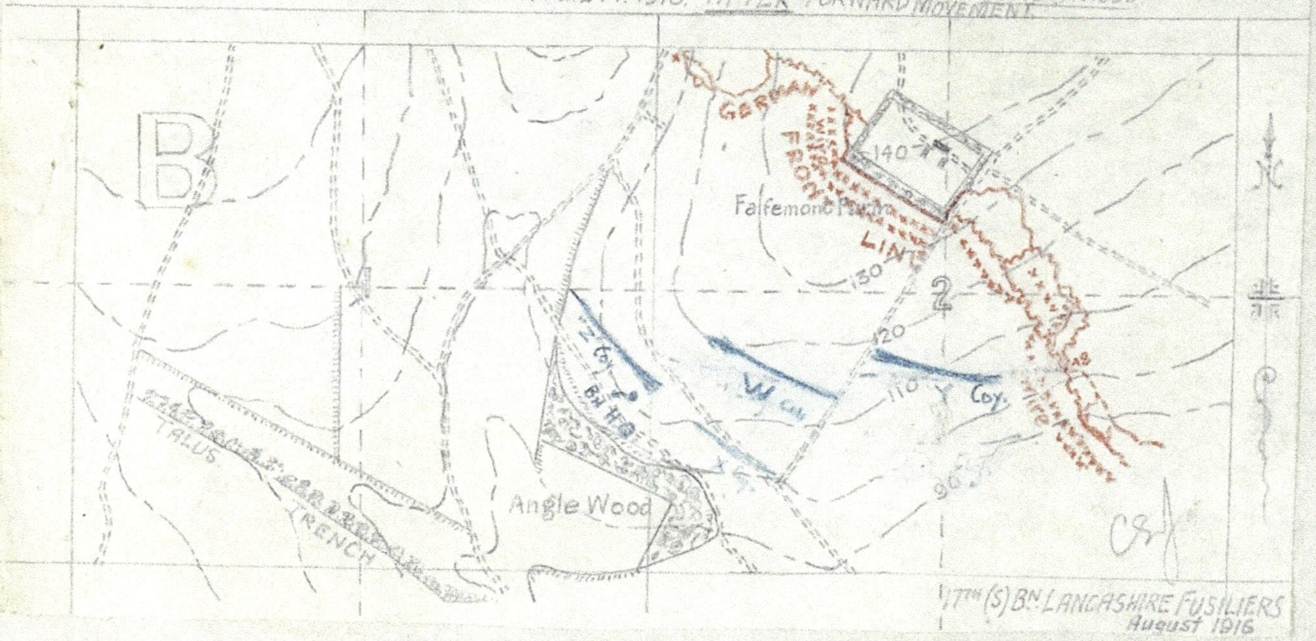

17/20 LANCS FUSILIERS

Army Form C. 2118

VOL 8

SEPT 1916

104/35

Instructions regarding War Diaries and Intelligence Summaries are contained in F. S. Regs., Part II. and the Staff Manual respectively. Title Pages will be prepared in manuscript.

# WAR DIARY

or

~~INTELLIGENCE SUMMARY~~

*(Erase heading not required.)*

(SHEET 1.)

| Place | Date | Hour | Summary of Events and Information | Remarks and references to Appendices |
|---|---|---|---|---|
| [..]ERGNY | Septr. 1st | | Battalion with first line Transport marched to GRAND RULLECOURT - Operation Order, dated 31st August 1916:- 1. Battalion and first line Transport will move tomorrow by route march to GRAND RULLECOURT. 2 Starting point, - "W" Coy's billet; 10.30 a.m. 3. Order of March - Band H.Q. "W","X","Y","Z" Coys., Lewis Gunners, Transport. The Battalion was settled in the new area about midday, and billeted till the next day | CS |
| [G]RAND RULLE-COURT | Septr. 2nd | | Battalion with first line Transport marched to FOSSEAUX - Operation Order No. C.4, dated 1-9-16 - 1. The Battalion with Transport will march to FOSSEAUX via SOMBRIN - BARLY tomorrow. Starting point, "Y" Coy: No. 75 Billet at 9.15 a.m. 2. Companies will concentrate on "Y" Coy. ready to move off at 9.15 a.m. Order of March - Band, H.Q., "Y", "Z", "X", "W", - Coys. Lewis Gunners, Transport. 3. The Battalion will billet in FOSSEAUX and proceed by road to DAINVILLE on the 3rd instant. | CS |
| FOSSEAUX | Septr. 3rd | | Transport moved to AGNEZ-les-DUISANS, leaving FOSSEAUX at 3 p.m. Battalion, less Transport moved to DAINVILLE. - Operation Order No. C.5. - 1. The Battalion will march to DAINVILLE tonight. Starting point "Z" Coy's Billet. Companies will concentrate on "Z" Coy. Column will be ready to move off at 7.15 p.m. 2. Order of March. - Hdqrs, "Z" - "X" - "W" - "Y" Coys; Lewis Gunners. 3 Men will not be allowed to smoke or strike matches East of WARLUS. The Battalion was settled in billets by 11 p.m. | CS |
| DAINVILLE. | Septr. 4-5-6-7. | | Battalion remained in Divisional Reserve. Owing to movement restrictions during the hours of daylight no outdoor training was done. Lectures & inspections were held in the respective Company billets, and theoretical instruction given to the specialists in training. | CS |
| DAINVILLE. | Septr. 8 | | Preparatory to taking over the right subsector of the Brigade front, the Battalion moved to ARRAS where billets where allotted for the night - Operation Order No. C.6. - 1. The Battalion will move to ARRAS tonight. Starting point: "Z" Coy. Billets 8 p.m. 2 Order of March - H.Q, "Z" - "Y" - "X" - "W" Coys; by Companies at 100 yards interval. Especial care must be taken that touch is not lost marching through ARRAS, the streets of which will be probably full of traffic of all sorts. 3 Dress: - Full Marching Order: Steel Helmets will be worn. | CS |
| ARRAS | Septr. 9 | | Relieved the 18th Lancs: Fusiliers in the right subsector "I.1" of front line system: Operation Order No. C.7. - 1 The Battalion will take over the front line, subsector I.1 tonight from GLUE. 2 Companies will be disposed in the line as follows:- Right Coy "Z"; Centre Coy. "X"; Left Coy. "W"; Reserve Coy. "Y". 3. Relief will leave the present area at 4.30 p.m. Companies will move out in above order by half-platoons at 100 yards interval. N.C.O's must be carefully informed as to which part of the line their respective Companies are taking over. (contd. on next SHEET) | CS |

1875 Wt. W593/826 1,000,000 4/15 J.B.C. & A. A.D.S.S./Forms/C. 2118.

P.T.O.

8 V.

Instructions regarding War Diaries and Intelligence Summaries are contained in F. S. Regs., Part II. and the Staff Manual respectively. Title Pages will be prepared in manuscript.

# WAR DIARY
or
# ~~INTELLIGENCE SUMMARY~~
*(Erase heading not required.)*

Army Form C. 2118

| Place | Date | Hour | Summary of Events and Information (SHEET 2) | Remarks and references to Appendices |
|---|---|---|---|---|
| ARRAS | Septr 9 | (contd.) | The relief was completed by 6.5 p.m. The subsector taken over extended northwards from FIFTEENTH ST. to INFANTRY SAP inclusive, the main line of resistance being the line of saps pushed out from the I.S. line. This and the saps were held by 3 Companies, and Lewis Gunners. The Support Company were accomodated in ruins on the road, shown in 29C. The normal rôle of the Support Company was the supply of all fatigues; meals were cooked ~~near~~ by the Support Company and carried up to the front line by fatigues from that Company. Wiring of the I.B. line was part of the duty of the Support Company | C.S. |
| TRENCHES | Septr. 9 to Septr. 10 | 6.5 pm 2.0 p.m. | Operations on this front were confined to a light hostile bombardment of our front line with aerial torpedoes and Trench Mortars. Intelligence - Practically nil. The enemy opposite this front does not show himself. | C.S. |
| TRENCHES. | Septr. 10 to Septr. 11 | 2.0 pm 2.0 pm | Our patrols were very active during darkness. Enemy working party harassed and dispersed. Enemy were found to be very strong and distributed in fair depth. Much work done in trench improvement | C.S. |
| TRENCHES. | Septr. 11. to Septr. 12 | 2.0 pm 2.0 pm | Enemy sent over a large number of T.M. bombs, particularly on right Company's front about Saps 15, 16, & 17, & shelled generally with L.H.V. saps & I.S. line. - Little damage done. Our retaliation with Stokes' Gun effectively silenced him. Our patrols again active; - succeeded in an encounter in driving hostile patrol back to their line. Much work done on our wire. | C.S. |
| TRENCHES | Septr. 12 to Septr 13 | 2.0 p.m 2.0 p.m. | The usual trench mortar & rifle grenade exchanges took place. Patrols succeeded in locating hostile saps which were occupied as distinct from those not used. Patrols reported our wire, particularly opposite the left Company, in a poor condition. The work of repair and construction of new entanglements was put in hand at once | C.S. |
| TRENCHES. | Septr 13 to Septr 14 | 2.0 p.m. 2.0 pm | A very quiet period. Patrols examined old trench approximately connecting sap heads along our front. The trench was found to be full of wire and barricaded at intervals. Work was done in the construction of bomb proof shelters. in the saps, and in general trench repair and improvement. | C.S. |
| TRENCHES | Septr 14 to Septr. 15 | 2.0 p.m 2.0 pm | We bombarded enemy saps and line with rifle grenades to which he made feeble reply. Apart from this the day was quiet. A good deal of wiring was done, and wire on the left Company front now provides a substantial obstacle. Much work done in improvement of saps and raising of fire-steps in I.S. line | C.S. |

1875 Wt. W593/826 1,000,000 4/15 J.B.C. & A. A.D.S.S./Forms/C. 2118.

Instructions regarding War Diaries and Intelligence Summaries are contained in F. S. Regs., Part II. and the Staff Manual respectively. Title Pages will be prepared in manuscript.

# WAR DIARY

or

## ~~INTELLIGENCE SUMMARY~~

(Erase heading not required.)

Army Form C. 2118

(SHEET 3)

| Place | Date | Hour | Summary of Events and Information | Remarks and references to Appendices |
|---|---|---|---|---|
| TRENCHES | Septr. 15 | 6.30 pm | The Battalion was relieved in the line by the 18th Lancashire Fusiliers: - Operation Order C.8:- 1. The Battalion will be relieved by the 18th Lancs. Fusiliers, relief commencing about 4.30 p.m. 2. After being relieved the Battalion will take over the billets in ARRAS vacated by the 18th Lancs. Fusiliers, and will proceed to DAINVILLE when it is dark. 3. Companies will move out in order of relief and will march to billets in parties of half-platoons at 100 yards interval. | CS |
| ARRAS. | Septr. 15 | 8.15 pm | Battalion moved to Divisional Reserve billets at DAINVILLE. | CS |
| DAINVILLE. | Septr. 16 | to 20. | Remained in Divisional Reserve. The usual inspections and theoretical instruction within billets took place | CS |
| DAINVILLE. | Septr. 21 | 10.20 pm | Took over right subsector "I" of front line system from 18th Lancashire Fusiliers: - Operation Order C.9:- 1. The Battalion will relieve the 18th Lancs. Fus. on Sept. 21st 1916. 2. The usual advance parties will be detailed and will leave DAINVILLE for the trenches after breakfast, but they must adhere strictly to the rules laid down for traffic by day. 3. Unless otherwise ordered the Battalion will leave DAINVILLE at dark (7.30 p.m.). Order of March:- "Z"-"X"-"Y"-"W". 4. "Y"-"X"-"Z" will occupy the front line from left to right; "W" Company will occupy the Reserve billets and find all ration and carrying parties etc. | CS |
| TRENCHES. | Septr. 21 to Septr. 22 | 10.20 pm to 2.0 p.m | The relief was completed without incident and the period passed very quietly. A new work begun by enemy opposite INDIA SAP was destroyed. | |
| TRENCHES. | Septr. 22 to Septr. 23 | 2.0 p.m. 2.0 p.m | Hostile bombardment of our position was carried out intermittently with T.M. bombs and aerial torpedoes. Our Stokes' Guns were able on each occasion to silence the enemy. Systematic wire-cutting operations evoked no retaliation from enemy. Enemy working parties were discerned and dispersed by Lewis Gun fire. Much wiring was done and much work throughout the sector on improvement of saps and I.S. and I.B. lines. | CS |
| TRENCHES | Septr. 23 to Septr. 24 | 2.0 p.m. 2.0 p.m | Artillery and Trench Mortars ~~again~~ registered again on enemy wire. His front line was bombarded intermittently with rifle grenades and by Stokes' Gun. Enemy absolutely passive. He is distinctly nervous and appears anxious to avoid combat in any form. A hostile sniper's post was demolished. Trench improvement steadily continued. Wire strengthened, particularly between INFANTRY and IODINE and between ITALY and IDEAL. Work was commenced on clearing of wire and obstacles from trench, approximately connecting sap-heads, which was examined by patrols on night of 13-14 instant. | CS |

Instructions regarding War Diaries and Intelligence Summaries are contained in F. S. Regs., Part II. and the Staff Manual respectively. Title Pages will be prepared in manuscript.

# WAR DIARY

~~or~~

~~INTELLIGENCE SUMMARY~~

*(Erase heading not required.)*

Army Form C. 2118

(SHEET 4.)

| Place | Date | Hour | Summary of Events and Information | Remarks and references to Appendices |
|---|---|---|---|---|
| TRENCHES. | Septr. 24 to Septr. 25 | 2.0p.m. 2.0p.m. | Enemy positions were freely treated with rifle grenades and Trench Mortar bombs, evoking a very feeble reply from the enemy. I.S. line lightly shelled with L.H.V. by hostile Artillery. No damage whatever was done. The enemy was extremely careful in expenditure of Artillery ammunition, and it is the exception for his Artillery to fire. He appears to be very short of guns and ammunition opposite this front. Hostile Transport appears to come quite close to forward positions. Machine-gun fire was brought to bear on roads behind enemy lines. Work was commenced in construction of protected look-outs for Company Commanders, and in making of shelters in saps. Clearing of the old line was continued. | CS |
| TRENCHES. | Septr. 25 to Septr. 26 | 2.0pm 2.0pm | An uneventful period. The enemy positions were bombarded with rifle grenades and T.M. bombs. Our patrols were active; no enemy patrols or working parties were discerned. Work continued on Saps and the construction of shelters. Work of clearing wire from old line progressed favourably. | CS |
| TRENCHES | Septr. 26 to Septr. 27. | 2.0pm 2.0pm | Apart from our usual bombardment of enemy positions with rifle grenades and Trench Mortar bombs, there were no operations. Hostile fire negligible. Hostile working parties were located and dispersed by grenades and machine-gun fire. Shelters for bombs and S.A.A. were considerably improved and dug-outs in saps were made. The old trench was by this time cleared from Lee Street to 20th Street inclusive. | CS |
| TRENCHES | Septr. 27 to Septr. 28 | 2.0pm 2.0pm 10.15pm | Apart from a successful bombing operation by one of our Patrols, operations were NIL. Our wire was strengthened in various places. The Battalion was relieved in the line by the 18TH LANCS FUSILIERS and proceeded to billets in ARRAS. - Operation Order, C10:- 1. The Battalion will be relieved by 18th Lancs. Fusiliers in the line tomorrow, Thursday 28th Septr., 1916. 3. The relief will commence as soon as it is dark. 3. On relief the Battalion will return to billets at ARRAS. Companies will move out independently as relieved. | CS |

Instructions regarding War Diaries and Intelligence Summaries are contained in F. S. Regs., Part II. and the Staff Manual respectively: Title Pages will be prepared in manuscript.

# WAR DIARY

or

~~INTELLIGENCE SUMMARY~~

(Erase heading not required.)

Army Form C. 2118

| Place | Date | Hour | Summary of Events and Information (SHEET 5). | Remarks and references to Appendices |
|---|---|---|---|---|
| ARRAS | Septr. 29 | 2.0 p.m. | Whilst in Reserve in ARRAS the Battalion supplied large Working Parties. Two reliefs of parties consisting of 2 Officers and 100 Other Ranks worked during the day on the clearing of the old front line already referred to. Considerable progress was made. The following Bathing parades were held for the Battalion:— Battalion Order No. 284 dated 28th September:- Baths. RUE DE LILLE are allotted to Companies as under:- Friday, Septr, 29th - "Z" Coy: 7-9.30 a.m: "X" Coy: 9.30 a.m. - 12 noon. Saturday Sept. 30th "W" Coy: 7-9.30 a.m: "Y" Coy: 9.30 a.m. - 12 noon. Men with Hdqrs, Lewis Gunners etc. will bathe with their Companies. Parties must arrive at the Baths 5 minutes before time allotted. The Town Orders, ARRAS, regarding movement of troops in daylight must be strictly complied with. | C.S. |
| ARRAS. | Septr. 30 | | Further working parties were supplied for the work in front line system; - in all 3 Officers - 150 Other Ranks | C.S. |
| | | | Casualties during month:- 1 Officer wounded: 2/Lt. R.S. HEAPE (23rd) | C.S. |
| | | | Honours and Awards - (see Appendix 2) | |
| | | | [signature] Major. Commanding: 17th (S) Battalion, Lancashire Fusiliers. | |

1875 Wt. W593/826 1,000,000 4/15 J.B.C. & A. A.D.S.S./Forms/C. 2118.

Appendix 2

# 17TH (S) BATTALION, LANCASHIRE FUSILIERS.

## HONOURS & REWARDS. No 1

BRIGADE ORDER No 180 dated 28·9·16:—

"The G.O.C. in C., under authority granted by H.M. the KING, has awarded decorations to the undermentioned Officers and men. (Authority Fourth Army No 62/277 A.M.S., dated 23/9/16).
The G.O.C. XIV Corps congratulates the recipients:-

(I). DISTINGUISHED SERVICE ORDER

MAJOR E.J.F. CROOK, 17TH LANCASHIRE FUSILIERS."

With reference to the above award the Commanding Officer wishes it to be understood that he regards this as a Battalion honour as much as a personal award, and takes this opportunity of congratulating all ranks on the success of the operation on the 24-5 August and of thanking them for the manner in which they upheld the traditions of the Lancashire Fusiliers. The admirable behaviour of all ranks on this occasion made the task of singling out any particular individuals for especial notice, almost impossible, a fact which reflects the greatest possible credit on the Battalion.

(II). MILITARY CROSS.

CAPTAIN W. RENNISON, 17TH LANCASHIRE FUSILIERS.

(III) DISTINGUISHED CONDUCT MEDAL.

19418, PTE. J.H. BIRTWELL, 17TH LANCASHIRE FUSILIERS.

"Did specially good work acting as runner between Coy: and Bn. H.Q: during 3 days he carried messages, usually under heavy shell-fire. When the new line had been reached, he crossed the open under Machine-Gun fire on 3 occasions and delivered messages to his Company Commander.
It was largely due to his work as runner that communication was kept with the right Company, and so with the French on the right of the Battalion.

25360, PTE. S. WALL, 17TH LANCASHIRE FUSILIERS.

"Did excellent work as runner between Battn. H.Q. and his Company, and between Battn. H.Q. and Advanced Signals Station. He carried messages under very heavy shell-fire, (see above)
He was wounded just before the Battn. was relieved when acting as guide to the Officer relieving the right Company, - work for which he volunteered, though the right Company's line was being heavily shelled at the time."

C. E. Jewels. Capt.

29th Septr. 1916. Adjutant, 17th (S) Battn. Lancs. Fusiliers

Extract from Battalion Orders dated 20th Sept. 1916.

HONOURS & AWARDS: The XIV Corps Commander has awarded the MILITARY MEDAL to the undermentioned men:- No. 14668, PTE. G. WRIGHT. No. 18292, PTE. B. TAYLOR. } 17TH LANCASHIRE FUSILIERS

"These two men did splendid work as Runners between Battn. H.Q. and advanced Signal Station. On three or four occasions they went through enemy barrage with messages. During the Operations in which the Battalion took part on the 24th August, 1916, their work was invaluable and it was due to their efforts that the Higher Command were kept in touch with the situation." C. E. Jewels

**BATTALION** 17 Lancashire Fusiliers **DATE** 28/9/1916

**COMPANY** X Company.

**OBJECT** To bomb garrison of enemy sap-head at G.30.d.1880.

**STRENGTH** 1 Officer 1 Cpl. + 4 Privates.

**PATROL LEADER** 2Lt C.MACKERETH.

Cpl. WATTS (W Company)

26433 Pte GOLDING. P. }
32725 " MINSHALL J. } "X" Company.
22077 " BRIGGS J E }
14409 " HILL G }

**POINT OF EXIT** INFERIOR SAP **TIME** 11.10 PM 27/9/1916

**POINT OF RETURN** ______ **TIME** 12.45 AM. 28/9/1916

**RESULT.** The patrol consisting of 2 bayonets + 4 bombers left INFERIOR SAP at 11.10pm. moved in the direction E.S.E. reached a point due north of enemy sap at G.30.d.1880. – from this point it would be possible to enfilade sap-head. The patrol lay down to await a favourable opportunity – the German sentry was clearly seen and appeared unsuspecting.

At about 2.30 am sounds of men approaching along sap were heard – followed by a whispered conversation; there seemed to be 3 men engaged.

Deeming this a suitable moment the bombers were moved up to enemy's wire – we were then less than 20 yards from sap-head. Sentry, who seemed suspicious stood well up + looked round, not apparently satisfied he raised himself on to the parapet into a kneeling position. Four bombs were thrown by us from standing position. 2 Bombs burst in the air about 2ft from ground both within a yard of man on parapet who must

Signature [illegible]

Rank & Regt.

P.T.O.

have been severely mutilated — he fell back into trench. 2 bombs burst in sap head + probably wounded if not killed the other men in sap who had been whispering just prior to the explosion.

The patrol being in very exposed ground pushed to cover obtained by fold of ground + after rifle fire had died down somewhat, returned to INFERIOR SAP all safe at 12.45 P.M.

— —

No reply was made from Sap-head after explosion. From the enemy's front line, N. of sap, a burst of rapid rifle fire was given — I should estimate from not more than a dozen rifles. Also a short burst of M.G from N. Enemy wire in front of sap — very thick + strong.

G. Machirith
2/Lieut
17 Lancashire Fusiliers

PATROL REPORT

Appendix 1.

"Secret"

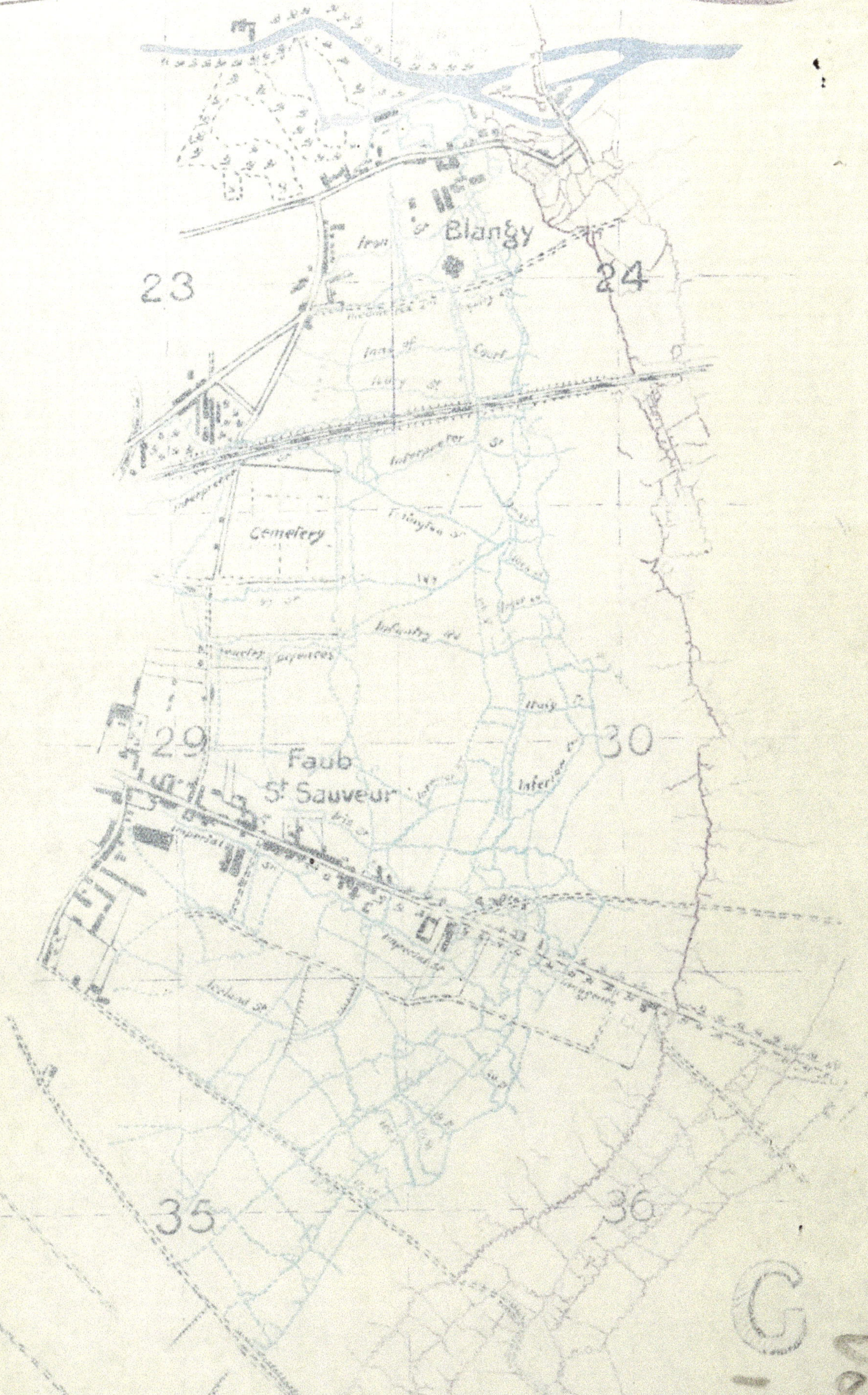


scale $\frac{1}{10,000}$: "I" SECTOR

V009

Confidential

— War Diary —

— of —

17th Service (1st S.E.L.) Battalion, Lancashire Fusiliers

FROM:- 1st October, 1916 ——— To:- 31st October, 1916

(Volume 9)

9. V.

12 sheets

Instructions regarding War Diaries and Intelligence Summaries are contained in F. S. Regs., Part II. and the Staff Manual respectively. Title Pages will be prepared in manuscript.

# WAR DIARY

~~or~~

~~INTELLIGENCE SUMMARY~~

*(Erase heading not required.)*

Army Form C. 2118

(SHEET 1)

| Place | Date | Hour | Summary of Events and Information | Remarks and references to Appendices |
|---|---|---|---|---|
| ARRAS. | October 1 to October 4 | | Battalion remained in Divisional Reserve in ARRAS. During this time working parties (an average of 3 Officers and 100 Other Ranks per diem) were found daily for work in the front line, I (1) Subsector and for special work under Royal Engineers. | C.S. |
| ARRAS. | October 5. | | Relieved without incident 18th Lancashire Fusiliers in I (1) Subsector – Operation Order:- "1. The Battalion will relieve the 18th Lan. Fus. in the line on the 5th instant. 2. Coys will move out by half-Platoons at 100 yards interval, in the following order:- "W" Coy: right subsector Battn front: "X" Coy central Coy. Battn. front: "Y" Coy. left subsector Battn. front: "Z" Coy. Support Coy: The head of "W" Coy will leave the Battn billet at 2.0 p.m. 3. Specialists will proceed to the line during the morning in time to complete reliefs by 12 noon. | C.S. |
| TRENCHES | 5/10/16 to 11/10/16. | 3.20 pm | Throughout the tour in the trenches the enemy's main line and saps were vigorously bombarded by STOKES GUN, 2" TRENCH MORTARS, and with Rifle Grenades. Wire-cutting operations were successfully carried out South of the CAMBRAI ROAD and at G.30.b.33.40, whilst a machine-gun emplacement at G.30.d.15.70 was demolished by 4 direct hits from 2" Trench Mortars. Hostile working parties were occasionally harassed and dispersed, with the result that his work in repair of his damaged positions progressed very slowly. Gas was discharged with good results from Subsector I (2) immediately to North of Subsector held by the Battalion. A strong patrol was sent out from our sector 2 hours after Zero, to obtain if possible an identification and to investigate the effects of the gas on the enemy. The floatation occasioned considerable confusion in the enemy lines; a great deal of excited shouting was heard, and red & green rockets were fired apparently for barrage ~~for~~ hostile retaliation which was, however distinctly weak and apparently feeble. The reconnoitring patrol discovered that the enemy front line was strongly held 2 hours after the discharge, and that all gaps which had been cut in his wire were covered by Machine Guns and Bombing parties, rendering entry into his line a matter of considerable difficulty.<br>OPERATION ORDER C12 dated 5/10/16<br>1. A Gas attack will be carried out on the 35th Division front from I (2) Subsector (trenching 60 to 75) and from K (2) Subsector (Trenches 117 to 125). 2. All preparations for floating will be completed by 10 p.m. on 5th October and the gas will be discharged with unrestricted jets sometime between 10 p.m. | C.S. |

1875 Wt. W593/826 1,000,000 4/15 J.B.C. & A. A.D.S.S./Forms/C. 2118.

(cont'd over)

Army Form C. 2118

Instructions regarding War Diaries and Intelligence Summaries are contained in F. S. Regs., Part II. and the Staff Manual respectively. Title Pages will be prepared in manuscript.

# WAR DIARY
or
# ~~INTELLIGENCE~~ SUMMARY
*(Erase heading not required.)*

| Place | Date | Hour | Summary of Events and Information (SHEET 2) | Remarks and references to Appendices |
|---|---|---|---|---|

Operation Order C.12 (contd)
and 5 a. m; on the first favourable opportunity after the preparations are completed. This means that if the wind is favourable the gas will be discharged sometime between 10 p.m. & 5 a. m. on the night of the 5th/6th October. 3. If the wind appears to be in a suitable quarter, a warning order will be issued two hours before the time selected for Zero. If, after this order is issued it becomes necessary to postpone the gas attack, the recipients of the above order will be informed. The following code will be used in sending the above message:- "Gas to be discharged" (Zero) - "DUNCAN" (Hour)
"Gas discharge cancelled" "JACK"

4. The following arrangements will be made by O's C. Coys:-
(a) All men in the front line trenches will have on their gas helmets from zero hour till the discharge of gas is finished
(b) All men within 500 yards of the front line will wear their Gas Helmets in the "Alert position"
(c) All anti-gas blankets will be lowered. Dug-outs in the front line will not be occupied for at least four hours after zero.
(d) In anticipation of enemy retaliation, steps will be taken to get all ranks under cover as far as possible - without making use of dug-outs
(e) The Reserve Company will be ready for instant action, in case required, from zero hour
5. The discharge of gas from I subsector will be accompanied by an artillery bombardment. All artillery fire will cease at Zero + 30 minutes.
6. At Zero + 2 hours the enemy trenches will be raided at G.30.b.3.2 according to special orders being issued
7. Battn. Hdqrs will move to Left Coy. Hdqrs at time to be notified later.
8. All ranks must be warned that the greatest secrecy must be observed concerning the discharge of gas and under no circumstance will any reference be made to it on the telephone or by telegraph.

OPERATION ORDER No C.13. dated 5/10/16:
1. At Zero + 2 hours 2/Lt. KITCHEN with 10 Other Ranks will raid the enemy line at G.30.b.3.2
2. The raiders will start from IDEAL SAP.

(contd over)

1875 Wt. W593/826 1,000,000 4/15 J.B.C. & A. A.D.S.S./Forms/C. 2118.

Army Form C. 2118

Instructions regarding War Diaries and Intelligence Summaries are contained in F. S. Regs., Part II. and the Staff Manual respectively. Title Pages will be prepared in manuscript.

# WAR DIARY
~~or~~
# ~~INTELLIGENCE SUMMARY~~

*(Erase heading not required.)*

(SHEET 3)

| Place | Date | Hour | Summary of Events and Information | Remarks and references to Appendices |
|---|---|---|---|---|
| | | | Operation Order C.13 (contd)<br>3. 2/LT. MACKERETH with 10 Other Ranks, will act as covering party, with the necessary connecting files to the head of IDEAL SAP<br>4. At Zero, plus two hours, the raiding party consisting of 4 Bombers and 6 Bayonet-men led by 2/LT KITCHIN will pass through our own wire to the spot where the enemy wire is damaged<br>5. One Bomber and 2 Bayonet-men of this party will block each flank, while the rest of the party enters the enemy trench in search of any available identification<br>6. The covering party will move to a position some 50 yards from the enemy wire, paying particular attention to the left flank where there is reported to be an enemy sap<br>7. The raiding party will not stay in the enemy trenches longer than five (5) minutes and on the sound of 2/LT. KITCHIN'S whistle will at once retire on to the covering party<br>8. No hostile dug-outs will be entered on any account as gas may lurk therein.<br>9. (a) Bombers will carry at least six bombs each<br>(b) Bayonet-men will carry rifle & bayonet and two clips ammunition in each side pocket<br>(c) Gas Helmets will be worn in the "Gas Alert" position.<br>(d) All ranks in the raid will wear a white band round each arm.<br>(e) Equipment will NOT be worn<br>10. Reports to Left Coy. Headquarters. | C.S. |
| TRENCHES | 5/10/16 to 11/10/16 | (contd) | Work in the line was almost entirely confined to the improvement of the reclaimed fire-trench, and strengthening of wire. | C.S. |
| TRENCHES | 11/10/16 | 8.30pm | Battalion was relieved in the line by 18th Lancashire Fusiliers, and proceeded to billets (Ecole de Jeunes Filles), ARRAS – Operation Order:– 1. The Battn. will be relieved in the line by 18th Lan Fus on Wednesday, 11th October 1916. 2. The relief will take place probably about 7 p.m. 4. The Battn will move into the usual billets in ARRAS. | C.S. |

1875 Wt. W593/826 1,000,000 4/15 J.B.C. & A. A.D.S.S./Forms/C. 2118.

Army Form C. 2118

Instructions regarding War Diaries and Intelligence Summaries are contained in F. S. Regs., Part II. and the Staff Manual respectively. Title Pages will be prepared in manuscript.

# WAR DIARY
~~or~~
# ~~INTELLIGENCE SUMMARY~~
*(Erase heading not required.)*

(SHEET 4)

| Place | Date | Hour | Summary of Events and Information | Remarks and references to Appendices |
|---|---|---|---|---|
| ARRAS | 13/10/16 to 17/10/16 | | Battalion remained in Divisional Reserve in ARRAS.<br>The rôle of the Battalion (apart from its tactical use as Reserve to the Division in case of emergency) was the provision of working and carrying parties, principally in the right (I.1) subsector | |
| | 12th to 14th | | On nights of 12th, 13th & 14th the entire Battalion was employed in carrying out from the front line empty gas cylinders. | |
| | 15th to 16th | | Working parties were found for duty under R.E, and under O.C. "I(1)" for work in repair of reclaimed fire trench.<br>Generally for about 8 hours a day (on an average) Companies were at the disposal of the Battn. Commander. During these hours bathing parades were held; Specialists were trained and lectures were given to N.C.O's | |
| ARRAS. | 17/10/16 | | Battalion relieved 18th Lancashire Fusiliers in I(1) line. - <u>Operation Order:-</u> 1. The Battn will relieve the 18th Bn. Lan. Fus. in the line on the 17th inst. 2. Coys will take over as under - "W" Coy. Right Subsector<br>"Z" " Centre —"—<br>"Y" " Left —"—<br>"X" " Support Line.<br>3. Coys. will move off in above order by half. Platoons at 100 yards interval commencing at 5 pm<br>4. Lewis Gunners, Bombers, Snipers and Signallers will relieve during the morning. Reliefs to be complete by 12 noon.<br>5. All Bombers will carry two bombs in each pouch and 10 rounds S.A.A in each side pocket | |
| TRENCHES. | 17/10/16 to 23/10/16 | 8.0 pm | Our Stokes Guns and 2" Trench Mortars carried out during the period a general bombardment of enemy saps and front line; certain selected points received particular attention:- Gap in enemy wire at G.30.b.3.4, G.36.c.30.95 - wire at both sides of CAMBRAI ROAD, and saps at G.36.a.4.1, G.36.c.3.9 & G.36.c.35.95. A rifle grenade emplacement at G.30.c.34.95 was demolished. (contd) | |

1875 Wt. W593/826 1,000,000 4/15 J.B.C. & A. A.D.S.S./Forms/C. 2118.

Instructions regarding War Diaries and Intelligence Summaries are contained in F. S. Regs., Part II. and the Staff Manual respectively. Title Pages will be prepared in manuscript.

# WAR DIARY
or
# ~~INTELLIGENCE SUMMARY~~
(Erase heading not required.)

Army Form C. 2118

(SHEET 5)

| Place | Date | Hour | Summary of Events and Information | Remarks and references to Appendices |
|---|---|---|---|---|
| TRENCHES. | 17-23/10/16 | | (contd) On one occasion in the wire-cutting operations on G.30.b.3.4. and bombardment of G.36.c.30.95, 6" Howitzers co-operated. Enemy positions were considerably damaged. Hostile retaliation was for the most part feeble, & principally confined to a light bombardment of our forward positions with aerial torpedoes, Trench Mortars, & occasionally L.H.V. On three occasions his retaliation took the form of a light shelling of ARRAS with 5.9's.<br>The Stokes' Gun has proved itself an effective weapon in silencing hostile T.M. & A.T. activity.<br>Inclement weather hindered work on a few occasions, but despite it considerable improvement was made in the reclaimed fire-trench. Revetting & duck-boarding & construction of fire-step progressed favourably.<br>An old sap running out from 20 STREET was reclaimed. | CR/ |
| TRENCHES. | 23/10/16 | | Battalion was relieved in the line by 18th Lancashire Fusiliers, and moved into billets in Divisional Reserve in ARRAS. + Operation Order:- "1. The Battn will be relieved in the line on the 23rd instant by the 18th Lan. Fus. 2. The relief will leave ARRAS as soon as it is dark. 3. Coys will move out independently as they are relieved and will proceed to the billets last occupied by the Battn when in ARRAS. 4. Lewis Gunners, Bombers, etc will be relieved during the day." | CR/ |
| ARRAS | 24-25/10/16 | | Remained in Divisional Reserve in ARRAS, providing usual working parties for front line, I(1), and for special work under R.E. | CR/ |
| ARRAS | 26/10/16 | | Moved into Brigade Reserve in ARRAS, holding ST SAUVEUR and CEMETERY DEFENCES respectively with one Company in each. The Battn - (less garrisons of above defences) constituted the Mobile Brigade Reserve and was billeted in ARRAS near PORTE DE BAUDIMONT (see Operation Order over) | CR/ |

1875 Wt. W593/826 1,000,000 4/15 J.B.C. & A. A.D.S.S./Forms/C. 2118.

Instructions regarding War Diaries and Intelligence Summaries are contained in F. S. Regs., Part II. and the Staff Manual respectively. Title Pages will be prepared in manuscript.

# WAR DIARY
*or*
# ~~INTELLIGENCE SUMMARY~~
*(Erase heading not required.)*

Army Form C. 2118

(SHEET 6)

| Place | Date | Hour | Summary of Events and Information | Remarks and references to Appendices |
|---|---|---|---|---|
| ARRAS | 26/10/16 | (contd) | Operation Order:- 1. On Thursday 26/10/16. "X and "Z" Coys will take over CEMETERY and ST. SAUVEUR DEFENCES respectively from the 23rd Manchester Regiment. 2. The Lewis Gun Officer will detail guns with their detachments to Companies as under - "Z" Coy. - 3 guns: "X" Coy. - 2 guns. 3. Movement will commence at 4 pm starting with "X" Coy. The rules for traffic must be strictly complied with and parties must not be stronger than 9. Battalion remained in Brigade Reserve in ARRAS until the evening of 29th October. Special working parties were provided for work on gas-cylinder emplacements in I.(3) line, and in carrying gas into the line. | C.S. |
| ARRAS. | 29/10/16 | | Relieved 18th Lancashire Fusiliers in Right Subsector I(1). - Operation Order - 1. The Battalion will relieve the 18th Lan. Fus. in the line tomorrow the 29th instant. 2. Lewis Gunners, Bombers and Signallers will take over during the day; reliefs to be complete by 3 pm. Companies will be disposed in the line as under:- Right Sector - "W" Coy: Centre Sector - "Z" Coy; Left Sector - "X" Coy. Support Coy. - "Y" Coy. 4. "X" and "Z" Coys will move to their positions in the line after dinner on 29th instant. 5. The Battn. (less "X" and "Z" Coys. and 5 detachments Lewis Gunners) will proceed to line in order: H.Q., "W" Coy: "Y" Coy; by half platoons at 100 yards interval. | C.S. |
| TRENCHES | 29/10/16 to 31/10/16 | 6.20 pm | Despite a good deal of very wet weather our patrols were very active and much useful work was done. Operations were confined to the usual exchanges of T.M's and aerial torpedoes on the one hand, and 2" T.M's., Stokes' Gun and rifle grenades on the other. Gas had been installed in the front of Battn. on our immediate left (I.(3)) & was to be discharged on the first favourable opportunity after the 30th instant. (see Operation Order No C.20 dated 30/10/16, - over) | C.S. |

1875 Wt. W593/826 1,000,000 4/15 J.B.C. & A. A.D.S.S./Forms/C. 2118.

Instructions regarding War Diaries and Intelligence Summaries are contained in F. S. Regs., Part II. and the Staff Manual respectively. Title Pages will be prepared in manuscript.

# WAR DIARY
or
# ~~INTELLIGENCE SUMMARY~~
*(Erase heading not required.)*

Army Form C. 2118

(SHEET 7)

| Place | Date | Hour | Summary of Events and Information | Remarks and references to Appendices |
|---|---|---|---|---|
| | | | OPERATION ORDER No C.20 dated 30/10/16 | |
| | | | 1. There will be a discharge of Gas from I.(3) at the first opportunity after 6 p.m. Oct 30th between 6 p.m. and 4 a.m. when the wind is favourable. | |
| | | | 2. Warning order will be issued under code word "RUBBER" followed by Zero time of discharge. This will be sent from Battn. Hdqrs by runner. | |
| | | | 3. Postponement of gas attack will be wired from Battn. Hdqrs by the code word "GRAVEL". | |
| | | | 4. All men will take cover as much as possible in case of retaliation. | |
| | | | 5. The Gas Helmet will be worn in the "alert position" by all ranks in advance of Battn. Hdqrs from "Stand to" at night until "Stand to" in the morning until further orders whether there be "gas alert" or not. | |
| | | | 6. All anti-gas blankets will be lowered on the night of the flotation. | |
| | | | 7. Coys which have out patrols or working parties will arrange to have them warned when warning is sent from Battn. Hdqrs. This could be arranged by a special very light signal - say 3 very lights fired in quick succession from any prearranged point in Coy front. | |
| | | | 8. When the wind is favourable, no patrols will be sent out N. of the CAMBRIA RD. | |
| | | | 9. Watches will be synchronised daily at 5 p.m. | C.S./ |
| | | | Casualties during month. - Other Ranks. - Killed in Action:- 1. Wounded in Action:- 4. Accidentally wounded:- 2. | C.S./ |

A. McMills
Lt. Col.
Commdg 17th (S) Bn Lan Fus.

BATTALION 17 Lancashire Fusiliers DATE 6/10/1916

COMPANY "X"

OBJECT Examine gap in enemy wire at G.30.b.3.3.

STRENGTH 1 Officer, 1 N.C.O and 3 men.

PATROL LEADER 2 Lt G MACKERETH.

| | | |
|---|---|---|
| 18279 | L/Cpl | MILLS. H. |
| 22130 | Pte | BRADBURY. J. |
| 32997 | " | DOGHERTY. R. |
| 15516 | " | SIMPSON. W. B. |

POINT OF EXIT INFANTRY SAP TIME 8.5 P.M.

POINT OF RETURN INFANTRY SAP TIME 9.35 PM

RESULT There is no gap at G.30.b.3.3. At G.30.b.3.4. there are 2 gaps separated by 3 yards of thick wire. The north gap is about 15 feet wide, the south gap is about 10 feet wide. In these places there is no thick high wire, but near parapet there is a very narrow stretch of low trip wire. Entry into enemy trench should not be difficult here. Two enemy sentries were observed – one about 20 yards to north of gaps the other about 30 yards south. No talking or movement noticed in enemy lines. Enemy sap to South is very strongly wired.

Patrol returned safely.

Good

Signed G. Mackereth, 2/Lieut.

Rank & Regt. 17 Lancashire Fusiliers

BATTALION 17th Lancs. Fus. DATE 8-10-16

COMPANY X

**OBJECT**

To strongly reconnoitre enemy's line at point G.30. b.3.4 with a view to entering it & finding the effect of our Gas Attack.

**STRENGTH.** 1 Officer & 10 other ranks.

PATROL LEADER 2nd Lt. Kitchin.

POINT OF EXIT. Infantry Sap TIME 10.45 pm

POINT OF RETURN Infantry Sap TIME 12.10 a.m.

**RESULT.**

Ref. G.30 b.3.4

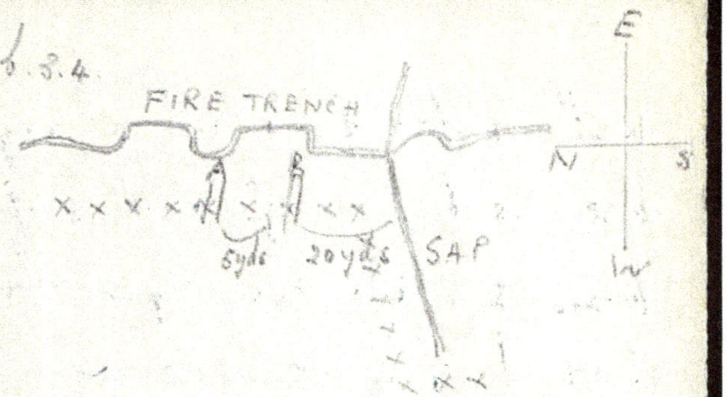


By previous reconnaissance, on night of 6th/7th 2 gaps had been located at point G.30.b.3.4, the right gap (B) being about 20 yards from sap on right and the left gap (A) being about 15 feet from right gap (B).

My patrol left Infantry Sap at 10.45 pm with a covering party of 10 men under 2nd Lt. MacKerett protecting the right flank, and advanced up to enemy's wire at point G 30 b.3.4. Finding that gap A in the meantime had been closed with knife-rests, my patrol moved to entrance of gap B, where it was bombed from the right from the junction of the sap & firing line. After exchanging bombs with the enemy, the patrol withdrew. The junction of sap & firing trench was strongly held, & enemy's sentries were very active.

Signed L. Kitchin, 2nd Lt.

Rank & Regt. 17th Lancs. Fus.

with rifle fire all along our front, & there seemed to be a fixed rifle on Sap B. There was no machine gun fire. Talking & the sound of a whistle were heard apparently in their support line.

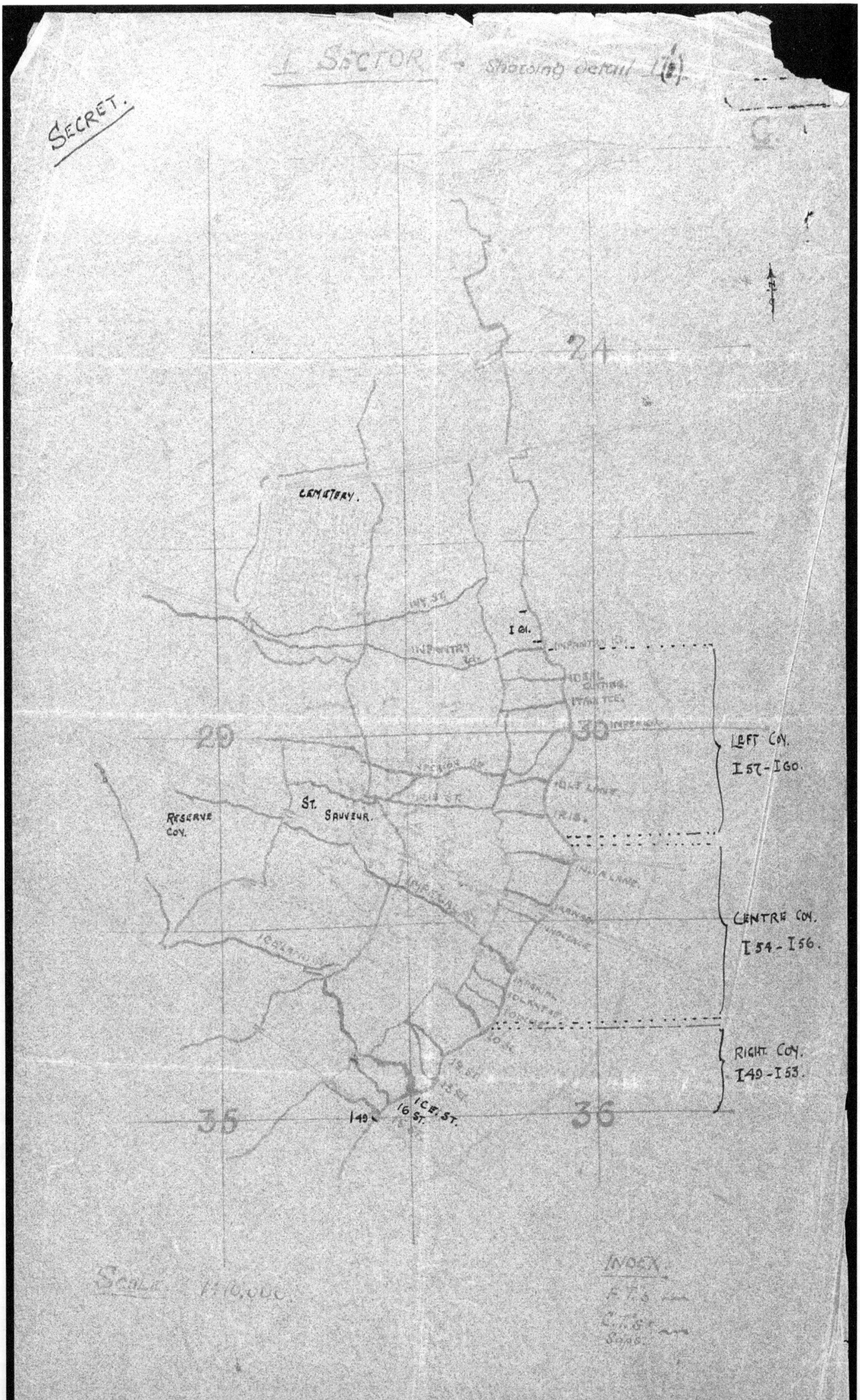
SECRET.
SECTOR
CEMETERY.
I 61.
INFANTRY
24
29
30
35
36
RESERVE COY.
ST. SAUVEUR.
LEFT COY.
I 57 - I 60.
CENTRE COY.
I 54 - I 56.
RIGHT COY.
I 49 - I 53.
I 49
16 ST.
ICE ST.
SCALE
INDEX

Vol 10

Confidential.

# War Diary

— of —

## 17th Service (1st S.E.L.) Battalion, Lancashire Fusiliers

FROM:- 1ST NOVEMBER, 1916, —— TO:- 30TH NOVEMBER, 1916.

(Volume 10.)

10. V.
5 sheets

Instructions regarding War Diaries and Intelligence Summaries are contained in F. S. Regs., Part II. and the Staff Manual respectively. Title Pages will be prepared in manuscript.

# WAR DIARY

~~or~~

~~INTELLIGENCE SUMMARY~~

(Erase heading not required.)

Army Form C. 2118

| Place | Date | Hour | Summary of Events and Information (SHEET 1.) | Remarks and references to Appendices |
|---|---|---|---|---|
| TRENCHES. | 1-11-16. to 4-11-16. | | Our Trench Mortars and Stokes' Guns were very active during this period, and much damage was done to selected points of enemy's line and to his wire. Hostile retaliation took the form of light bombardment of our line with medium T.M's. and Aerial Torpedoes. | |
| ARRAS. | 4-11-16. to 10-11-16. | | The Battalion was relieved by the 18th Lancashire Fusiliers and proceeded to ARRAS as Brigade Reserve, less 2 Companies - "W" and "Y", in St Sauveur and Cemetery Defences respectively:- OPERATION ORDER:- "1. The Battalion will be relieved in I.1. Sector by the 18th Bn. Lan. Fus. on Saturday, the 4th November 1916. 2. "W" Coy. and "X" Coy. will be relieved after dinner by "W" Coy. and "X" Coy. respectively of 18th Bn. Lan. Fus. 3. On relief "W" Coy. will proceed to St. Sauveur's Defences, and "X" Coy. to Reserve Coy. billets. 4. "Y" Coy. will move into Cemetery Defences after dinner. 5. The Lewis Gun Officer will detail guns with detachments to Companies in the Defences, as under:-<br>"W" Coy:- 3 Lewis Guns.<br>"Y" " :- 2 Lewis Guns.<br>7 Specialists will be relieved during the morning under mutual arrangements by Officers concerned."<br>The usual working parties were furnished, and the training of Specialists proceeded with on usual lines. | |
| TRENCHES. | 10-11-16 to 16-11-16. | | OPERATION ORDER:- "1. The Battalion will take over Subsector I.1. from 18th Bn. Lan. Fus., on Friday, 10th November 1916. 2. Lewis Gunners, Bombers and Signallers will take over during the day; reliefs to be complete by 3.0 p.m. Disposition of Companies in the line will be as under:-<br>Right Sector:- Z Coy.<br>Centre " Y "<br>Left " X "<br>Support ":- W " | |

(Contd. over)

1875 Wt. W593/826 1,000,000 4/15 J.B.C. & A. A.D.S.S./Forms/C. 2118.

Instructions regarding War Diaries and Intelligence Summaries are contained in F. S. Regs., Part II. and the Staff Manual respectively. Title Pages will be prepared in manuscript.

# WAR DIARY

~~or~~

~~INTELLIGENCE SUMMARY~~

(Erase heading not required.)

Army Form C. 2118

| Place | Date | Hour | Summary of Events and Information (SHEET 2) | Remarks and references to Appendices |
|---|---|---|---|---|
| | (contd) | | 4. "W" Coy. and "Y" Coy. will move to their positions in line after dinner on the 10th instant. 5. The Battalion, (less W. & Y. Coys. and 5 detachments of Lewis Gunners) will proceed to line in order:- H.Q., "Z" Coy., "X" Coy: 6. All Bombers will carry 2 bombs in each pouch." <br> Organised fire of 2" T.M's. and Stokes Guns was carried out daily, and much damage was done to enemy's line and wire. There was considerable hostile retaliation, especially on Right-Company front, where a very heavy T.M. was used by the enemy. | |
| ARRAS. | 16:11:16 to 22:11:16. | | OPERATION ORDER:- "1. The Battalion will be relieved in I.1. by 18th Bn. Lan. Fus. on Thursday, 16th November, 1916. 2. "Z" and "X" Companies will be relieved after dinner by "Z" and "Y" Companies, respectively, of 18th Bn. Lan. Fus. 3. On relief "Z" Coy. will proceed to St. Sauveur Defences and "X" Coy. to CEMETERY DEFENCES. 4. The Lewis Gun Officer will detail guns with detachments to the Companies in DEFENCES as under:- <br> Z Coy:- 3 Lewis Guns. <br> X " :- 2 Lewis Guns." <br> The usual working parties were provided, and the training of Specialists carried on. | |
| TRENCHES | 22:11:16 to 26:11:16. | | OPERATION ORDER:- "1. The Battalion will take over Subsector I.1. from 18th Bn. Lan. Fus. on Wednesday, 22nd November, 1916. 2. Lewis-Gunners, Bombers and Signallers will take over during the day, reliefs to be complete by 3.0 p.m. 3. Disposition of Companies in the line will be as under:- <br> Right Sector:- "W" Coy: <br> Centre " :- "Y" " <br> Left " :- "X" " <br> Support :- "Z" " <br> (contd: over) | |

1875 Wt. W593/826 1,000,000 4/15 J.B.C. & A. A.D.S.S./Forms/C. 2118.

Instructions regarding War Diaries and Intelligence Summaries are contained in F. S. Regs., Part II. and the Staff Manual respectively. Title Pages will be prepared in manuscript.

# WAR DIARY

~~or~~

~~INTELLIGENCE SUMMARY~~

*(Erase heading not required.)*

Army Form C. 2118

| Place | Date | Hour | Summary of Events and Information (SHEET 3.) | Remarks and references to Appendices |
|---|---|---|---|---|
| | (continued). | | 4. "X" Coy will move to its position in the line after dinner on 22nd instant. 5. "Z" Coy will relieve the Centre Coy: (W Coy) of 18th Lan. Fus. after dinner on 22nd, and will remain in the Line until relieved by "Y" Coy. 17th Lan. Fus. on evening of same day." | |
| | | | Heavy hostile bombardment of our Right Coy. front with medium & heavy T.M's, and Aerial Torpedoes, took place. Our trenches here were very badly damaged and the wire in front cut. At 2·20 am. on the 26th instant the enemy raided our trenches in strength, and succeeding in inflicting the following severe casualties:- Killed, 2 Other Ranks; Wounded, 6 O.R.; "Missing," 25 O.R. In addition 10 O.R. were killed, and 6 wounded during the several days intermittent bombardment which preceded the raid. | |
| | | | At 2·30 a.m. on the 26th instant, the flotation of Gas was successfully carried out from Subsector I.2. | |
| ARRAS. | 26:11:16. to 30:11:16. | | The Battalion was relieved in I.1. Subsector by the 18th Bn. Lan. Fus, and moved into Brigade Reserve in ARRAS, less 2 Companies - "W." & Y." - holding CEMETERY and St. SAUVEUR'S DEFENCES respectively. | |
| | | | The usual working parties were found, and the training of Specialists carried on as heretofore. | |
| | | | Total Casualties for month of November:- KILLED: WOUNDED: MISSING. OFFICERS:- NIL: OTHER RANKS:- 12. 15. 25. | |

A. Whitts
Lieut. Colonel.
Commanding, 17th (S) Battn. Lancashire Fusiliers:

1875 Wt. W593/826 1,000,000 4/15 J.B.C. & A. A.D.S.S./Forms/C. 2118.

Vol XI

# Confidential
# War Diary
# of

## 17th Service (1st S.E.L.) Battalion, Lancashire Fusiliers.

FROM:- 1st Decr., 1916. —— TO:- 31st Decr., 1916.

(Volume 11.)

11. V.
7 sheets

Instructions regarding War Diaries and Intelligence Summaries are contained in F. S. Regs., Part II. and the Staff Manual respectively. Title pages will be prepared in manuscript.

# WAR DIARY
~~or~~
~~INTELLIGENCE SUMMARY.~~

(Erase heading not required.)

Army Form C. 2118.

| Place | Date | Hour | Summary of Events and Information SHEET I. | Remarks and references to Appendices |
|---|---|---|---|---|
| ARRAS. | 1·12·16. | | Battalion in ARRAS disposed with 2 Companies and Headquarters in Mobile Brigade Reserve in ARRAS, and two companies in CEMETERY & ST SAUVEUR DEFENCES. | C.E.J. |
| ARRAS. | 2·12·16. | | Battalion with "W" Coy: 20th Lancashire Fusiliers relieved 18th Lancashire Fusiliers in Subsector I(1):- OPERATION ORDER:- 1. The Battn. & 1 Coy. of 20th Lancs. Fus. will relieve 18th Bn. Lancs. Fusiliers in Subsector I.(1) on Saturday, 2nd inst. 2. The Bn. front will extend from IRIS ST. to 15 ST. according to detailed instructions already issued to O's. C. Coys. 3. Coys. will be disposed in the line as under:-<br>RIGHT COY: - 19 ST. exclusive, to 15 ST. inclusive - Z COY.<br>CENTRE COY: - IMPERIAL ST. " to 19 ST. " - Y "<br>LEFT COY: - IRIS ST. inclusive, to IMPERIAL ST. inclusive, W "<br>ONE COY: 20TH L.F. IRIS ST. exclusive to INFANTRY RD. "<br>SUPPORT COY: - - - - - - - - - - - - - X "<br>4. Specialists will proceed to the line after dinner so as to complete relief by 3 p.m. 5. Coys. in ARRAS will move out in order:- H.Q., Z COY., X COY. Starting time 4·0 p.m. 6. W Coy. and Y Coy. respectively will proceed to their places in the line on 2nd inst., moving from the DEFENCES at 4 p.m. | C.E.J. |
| TRENCHES. | 3-4·12·16. | | This period in Line was uneventful. | C.E.J. |
| TRENCHES. | 4·12·16. | | Relieved in the Line by 8TH BLACK WATCH. OPERATION ORDER:- 1. The Battalion will be relieved by the 8th BLACK WATCH on the evening of 4th December. 2. On completion of relief Coys. will move out & march independently to DAINVILLE. If necessary, Coys will move out at 100x interval. ROUTE:- ARRAS RLY. STATION, BOULEVARD CARNOT, RUE DE L'ARSENAL, RUE D'AMIENS, DAINVILLE. The Route will be picquetted by the Pioneer Platoon. 3. On relief W COY, 20th LANCS. FUSRS, will move out & rejoin their Battn. at the ECOLE DES JEUNES FILLES. 4. O's. C. Coys. will report personally ~~when~~ at Battn. H.Q. when their respective Coys. are clear of the Line. 5. Billeting party consisting of 2 N.C.O's per Coy., 1 N.C.O. for Hdqrs. and 1 N.C.O. for Pioneer Platoon, under command of 2/Lt. MARSH, will proceed to DAINVILLE on the morning of the 4th Decr., leaving Battn. H.Q. at 9·30 a.m. | C.E.J. |
| | | | | |

1577 Wt. W10791/1773 500,000 1/15 D. D. & L. A.D.S.S./Forms/C. 2118.

Instructions regarding War Diaries and Intelligence Summaries are contained in F. S. Regs., Part II. and the Staff Manual respectively. Title pages will be prepared in manuscript.

# WAR DIARY

~~or~~

~~INTELLIGENCE SUMMARY.~~

(Erase heading not required.)

Army Form C. 2118.

| Place | Date | Hour | Summary of Events and Information (SHEET 2) | Remarks and references to Appendices |
|---|---|---|---|---|
| DAINVILLE | 4·12·16 to 28·12·16 | | Battalion in billets at DAINVILLE.<br>Whilst in DAINVILLE the instruction of Bombers, Grenadiers, Lewis-Gunners & Signallers was carried on. With the exception of these, and Guards for billets & their reliefs under instruction, and Regtl. employed men, the whole of Battn. at DAINVILLE was employed on working parties throughout the period:-<br>BATTN. ORDER 628 - WORKING PARTIES:<br>The following working parties will be found by Coys. daily from 8th inst. inclusive until further orders:-<br>"W" Coy: Work for O.C. VI Corps Park – 30 men for Sgt. Hodder at G.14.c.8.8.<br>20 " " Cpl. at G.7.c.6.2. (2 Officers & approximately 50 men).<br>"X" Coy: Will report to Capt. Buchanan, R.E., O.C. VI Corps Park at 8·30 a.m. on Friday 8th instant and onwards. They may proceed to DUISANS by platoons, passing behind DAINVILLE WOOD on to level crossing and hence follow behind embankment to CORPS PARK. (2 Offs. & approximately 50 men).<br>"Y" Coy: 20 men to report to Cpl. Monk at new position G.13.b. central.<br>20 " " " " L/c. James " " (G.7.d.6.1.)<br>10 " " " " Cpl. Harrison at "Belgian Bty: (L.35.c.0.3.) (2 Officers & approximately 50 men).<br>"Z" Coy: 20 men to report to Cpl. Tomkiss. P.67, 68 & 69 (L.30.b.5.5.)<br>6 " " " " L/c. Carroll (G.22.d.8.2.)<br>6 " " " " Cpl. Shearing (G.34.d.6.6.)<br>6 " " " " Cpl. Lishman (G.29.d.7.7.)<br>12 " " " " L/c. Drury, AGNY MILL. (2 Officers and approximately 50 men).<br>Map locations given are of jobs. Parties are to parade at R.E. Coy: A.2 at 8·30 am. each morning. On 8th inst. Parties will parade 2 hours after scheduled time; on succeeding days, at times stated. All ranks will carry Haversack rations.<br>The greatest care must be taken to see that men turn out for these duties <u>clean & smart</u> and that they are <u>marched</u> to the rendezvous and as far as possible to their work. Parties from W.Y. & Z Coys. will parade by Coys. at No. 12 Rue de WARLUS, for tools, on night of 7th inst., starting with W Coy. at 4·30 p.m. | C.E.J. |
| | | | During the period Battn. was in this area, frequent inspections of the Battn. were held, with a view to eliminating men incapable of performing the ordinary duties of a normal infantryman | C.E.J. |

1577 Wt. W10791/1773 500,000 1/15 D. D. & L. A.D.S.S./Forms/C. 2118.

Instructions regarding War Diaries and Intelligence Summaries are contained in F. S. Regs., Part II. and the Staff Manual respectively. Title pages will be prepared in manuscript.

# WAR DIARY

~~or~~

~~INTELLIGENCE SUMMARY.~~

(Erase heading not required.)

Army Form C. 2118.

| Place | Date | Hour | Summary of Events and Information SHEET 3. | Remarks and references to Appendices |
|---|---|---|---|---|
| DAINVILLE | 12:12:16. | | The Battalion was inspected by A.D.M.S., 35th DIVISION:- Battn: Order No 657. - MEDICAL INSPECTION:- The A.D.M.S. will inspect the Battn. tomorrow, 12th inst., starting with "W" Coy. at 10:0 am. ~~tom~~ and followed by X. Y. & Z Coys. The inspection will be held in Y Coy. billets (Schoolrooms), the Western room being reserved for use of A.D.M.S. The men will be paraded by Platoons at full strength. DRESS:- Great-coat over shirt sleeves, trousers, etc. Puttees will not be worn. The Coy. Officer, Platoon Officer and C.S.M. will attend with each Platoon. Platoons parade in Eastern Room & O's. C. Coys will arrange mutually so that no time whatever is lost in the sequence of men. The first Platoon of "W" Coy. will be ready in the room by 9.55 a.m. Nominal rolls are not required. O's. C. Coys. will submit to Orderly Room after the inspection a nominal roll of men of their Coy: who will not have been inspected stating where these men are employed etc.<br>29 men were rejected as unfit on medical grounds. | C.E. |
| | 19:12:16. | | Battalion was inspected by VI Corp Commander:- Battn. Order No 698 - INSPECTION - 1. The whole Battn. less cooks, Orderly Room Staff and men actually on guard will be paraded as under:-<br>(a) Men ~~will be~~ rejected by A.D.M.S. & C.O. will be paraded in Schoolrooms, Y Coy. billets; those found unfit by A.D.M.S. in Western Room; those selected as unfit by C.O. in Eastern room.<br>(b) Battn., (less (a), cooks, Orderly Room Staff & men actually on guard), will be formed up in mass at a place to be notified later. This information will be sent to Coys. early tomorrow morning.<br>2. Dress will be clean fatigue with steel helmets for both 1(a) and 1(b). O's. C. Coys. must see that men are turned out thoroughly cleaned and smart. Buttons will be properly cleaned, & all mud stains etc. removed from the clothing and puttees; steel helmets will be washed where necessary. Only one gas helmet will be worn, & satchel must be clean. Care must be taken to ensure that guards are smart in every respect.<br>3. The Corps Commander will inspect parades 1(a) and 1(b) starting at 9.45 am. O's. C. Coys. and Medical Officer will attend at both parades. 4. The C.O. will inspect men for parades 1(a) & 1(b) at 9.15 a.m. Markers for 1(b) will report to R.S.M. at Bn. H.Q. at 8.55 a.m. Coys. will fall in on markers independently ready for inspection at 9.15 a.m.<br>5. All working parties for tomorrow are cancelled.<br>(contd over) | C.E. |

1577 Wt. W10791/1773 500,000 1/15 D. D. & L. A.D.S.S./Forms/C. 2118.

Army Form C. 2118.

Instructions regarding War Diaries and Intelligence Summaries are contained in F. S. Regs., Part II. and the Staff Manual respectively. Title pages will be prepared in manuscript.

# WAR DIARY

~~or~~

~~INTELLIGENCE SUMMARY.~~

(*Erase heading not required.*)

SHEET 4.

| Place | Date | Hour | Summary of Events and Information | Remarks and references to Appendices |
|---|---|---|---|---|
| DAINVILLE. | 19:12:16. | (contd). | 6. All billets and immediate surroundings must be thoroughly cleaned. This applies particularly to billet & out buildings of billet occupied by Y Coy. 140 men rejected as unfit to perform duties of normal infantryman. | CS |
| AGNEZ. | 21:12:16. | | Transport & Qr. Mr. Stores moved to Lines at BERNEVILLE. | CS |
| DAINVILLE. | 27:12:16. | | Men selected as unsuitable for work of normal infantryman were inspected at AGNEZ by the Army Commander:- Orderly Room No. 2371:- 1. The Army Commander will inspect the following on Wednesday Dec. 27th at DUISANS:- (a) All men selected as unsuitable by C.O's: (b) all men rejected by the Corps Commander. Men passed as unfit by A.D.M.S. are not required to attend the parade. 2. Men will parade by Coys. at 8 a.m.: Starting point:- Cross-roads West of Y.M.C.A. Hut. 8.15 a.m. Route:- via WARLUS & AGNEZ-LES-DUISANS: Coys. will march by Platoons, i.e. 20 men at 200x interval, as far as WARLUS, in following order:- W.X.Y.Z. Head of W Coy. will halt at the Northern exit of WARLUS to allow the rear of column to close up. 3. Dress:- Clean fatigue with Steel Helmets. Greatcoats to be carried En Bandrole. (These must be thoroughly cleaned. 4. Coy. Comdrs: & C.S.M's. will parade with each Coy. 5. One marker from each Coy; & a Bugler to be detailed by the Band Sgt., will report to LT. SYKES at Bn. H.Q. Mess at 7.45 a.m. This party will report to Bde. Major on the parade ground (L.7.c.5.8.) (the field opposite Balloon Kite Section), at 10.45 a.m. 6. Haversack Rations will be carried. 7. Each Coy. Comdr: must know his men & must be able to answer any questions as to reasons for rejection. | CS |
| —DO:— | 4:12:16. to 28:12:16. | | For tactical purposes the Battalion was under the orders of 9TH DIVISION in whose area it was working:- DIV: LETTER 127(G):- "The working parties at ---- DAINVILLE will be available to reinforce ---- 9TH DIVN in case of necessity but will not be moved without orders from VI Corps." | CS |
| | 28:12:16. | | Battalion was relieved in Forward Area by 15TH SHERWOOD FORESTERS & marched to MANIN. (See Operation Order over leaf.) | CS |

1577 Wt. W10791/1773 500,000 1/15 D. D. & L. A.D.S.S./Forms/C. 2118.

Instructions regarding War Diaries and Intelligence Summaries are contained in F. S. Regs., Part II. and the Staff Manual respectively. Title pages will be prepared in manuscript.

# WAR DIARY
~~or~~
~~INTELLIGENCE SUMMARY.~~
(Erase heading not required.)

Army Form C. 2118.

| Place | Date | Hour | Summary of Events and Information (SHEET 5.) | Remarks and references to Appendices |
|---|---|---|---|---|
| DAINVILLE | 28.12.16 | (contd.) | OPERATION ORDER:- 1. The Battn. will be relieved on the 28th inst. by the 15th SHERWOOD FORESTERS, and will move to MANIN. 2. Starting Point:- cross roads W. of Y.M.C.A. Hut at 9 a.m. Route:- WARLUS, WAQUETIN, LATTRE, NOVELLE-VION. East of WARLUS movement will be by Platoons at 200x interval. On getting clear of WARLUS each Coy. will close up on its head & will then move on until it catches the Coy. in front. Order of March:- Band, Hdqrs., W. X. Y. Z. Coys, followed by Cookers, Water Cart, Maltese & Mess Carts. O.C. W Coy. will furnish an Advanced Guard of 2 Sections under an Officer. O.C. Z Coy. will furnish a Rear-Guard of 2 Sections under an Officer & to march in rear of Transport. 4. Dress:- Fighting Order. | |
| MANIN. | 28.12.16. | | Whilst Battn. was at MANIN a working party was detailed for duty at WAQUETIN. – BATTn. ORDER No. 755 – WORKING PARTY:- 1. The Bn. will provide in the new area a Working Party of 2 Officers & 80 Other Ranks (exclusive of supervising N.C.O's. etc.) for work with 278th Field Coy. R.E. at WANQUETIN. 2. The party will be made up as follows:- (a) 2/Lt. Stenholm & 2/Lt. Stenholm: (b) O.C. W Coy. will detail 2 N.C.O's & 20 men, and 1 Cook. (c) O.C. X Coy will detail 2 N.C.O's & 20 men & 1 man for sanitary duties. (d) O.C. Y Coy will detail 2 N.C.O's & 20 men & 1 Cook. (e) O.C. Z Coy will detail 2 N.C.O's & 20 men and 1 man for sanitary duties. 3. N.C.O's. & men for this work will be selected from those who have been rejected as unfit for the duties of an ordinary infantry man. 4. The working party detailed will proceed to WANQUETIN tomorrow, the 28th inst. in parties of 20 at 200x interval, (as far as WARLUS) leaving DAINVILLE at 2.0 p.m. | |
| MANIN. | 29-30 & 31.12.16. | | Devoted to cleaning up and refitting, and inspections by O's. C. Coys. and C.O. | |
| | | | Casualties for month:- 3 Other Ranks wounded. | |

Lieut. Colonel.
Commdg: 17th (S) Bn. Lancs. Fusiliers

1577 Wt. W10791/1773 500,000 1/15 D. D. & L.

Vol 12

CONFIDENTIAL

# WAR DIARY

OF

17TH (S) BATTALION, LANCASHIRE FUSILIERS.

FROM 1ST JANUARY 1917 TO 31ST JANUARY 1917.

— VOLUME 12 —

12. V.

Instructions regarding War Diaries and Intelligence Summaries are contained in F. S. Regs., Part II. and the Staff Manual respectively. Title pages will be prepared in manuscript.

# WAR DIARY

*or*

~~INTELLIGENCE~~ SUMMARY.

(*Erase heading not required.*)

Army Form C. 2118.

| Place | Date | Hour | Summary of Events and Information | Remarks and references to Appendices |
|---|---|---|---|---|
| MANIN | 1 – 5th Jany | | Battalion in training. | |

| Coy. | January 1st. | January 2nd | January 3rd | January 4th | January 5th. |
|---|---|---|---|---|---|
| W | 8.45 – 9.0 a.m. Inspection by O.C. Coy.<br>9.0 – 9.45 a.m. Inspection by C.O.<br>9.45 – 10.30 am. Physical training<br>10.30 – 11.45 a.m. Bolt drill with rapid loading practice (dummy cartridges)<br>11.15 – 12 noon Handling of arms & close order drill. | 9.0 am – 12 noon Musketry. | 9.0 – 12 noon Bayonet Fighting<br>Squads not being instructed in Bayonet Fighting will be exercised in:–<br>(a) Close order drill<br>(b) Handling of arms.<br>(c) Dummy bomb throwing | 9.0 am. Lecture by Divisional Gas Officer to all officers & N.C.Os.<br>10.0 am. Fitting & testing of Respirators | (a) Bathing parade.<br>(b) Inspection of rifles by Armourer Sergt.<br>(c) Inoculation of 50 men of Y Coy. |
| X | 8.45 – 9.0 am Inspection by O.C. Coy.<br>9.0 – 9.45 am Handling of arms & close order drill<br>9.45 – 10.30 am Inspection by C.O.<br>10.30 – 11.15 am Physical training<br>11.15 – 12 noon Bolt drill & rapid loading practice with dummy cartridge | 9.0 am – 12 noon Bayonet Fighting<br>Squads not being instructed in Bayonet Fighting were exercised in:–<br>(a) Close order drill<br>(b) Handling of arms<br>(c) Dummy Bomb Throwing | 9.0 am – 12 noon Musketry. | | |
| Y | 8.45 – 9.0 am Inspection by O.C. Coy.<br>9.0 – 9.45 am Bolt drill & rapid loading practice with dummy cartridges<br>9.45 – 10.30 am Handling of arms & close order drill<br>10.30 – 11.15 am Inspection by C.O.<br>11.15 – 12 noon Physical training | 9 – 10 am Physical Training<br>10 – 11 am Instruction in Wiring<br>11 – 12 noon Close order drill and Handling of arms | 9 – 10 am Physical Training<br>10 – 11 am Instruction in Wiring<br>11 – 12 noon Close order drill and handling of arms. | | |
| Z | 8.45 – 9.0 am Inspection by O.C. Coy.<br>9.0 – 9.45 am Physical training<br>9.45 – 10.30 am Bolt drill & rapid loading practice with dummy cartridges.<br>10.30 – 11.15 am Handling of arms & close order drill.<br>11.15 – 12 noon Inspection by C.O. | 9 – 10 am Physical Training<br>10 – 11 am Close order drill and Handling of arms<br>11 – 12 noon Instruction in wiring. | 9 – 10 am Physical Training<br>10 – 11 am Close order drill & Handling of arms.<br>11 – 12 noon Instruction in wiring. | | |
| Extra for all Coys. | Jan 2nd (a) Lecture by G.O.C. 10th Bde at 12.45 pm to all offrs. N.C.Os of Bn.<br>(b) All Cpls will report to R.S.M. at Bn. HQ. for communication drill.<br>(c) 3 N.C.Os from each Coy will report to S.M. SMITH at Bn HQ. at 9 am for instruction in Bayonet Fighting | Jan 3rd. (a) All Platoon N.C.Os. will report to R.S.M. at Bn HQ. at 11 am for Communication Drill.<br>(b) All officers & Lewis Gunners (with revolvers) of W & X Coys. will report to the Adjt. on range at 12 noon for revolver practice. | | | |

A5834 Wt. W4973/M687 750,000 8/16 D. D. & L. Ltd. Forms/C.2118/13.

7.

Instructions regarding War Diaries and Intelligence Summaries are contained in F. S. Regs., Part II. and the Staff Manual respectively. Title pages will be prepared in manuscript.

# WAR DIARY
*or*
~~INTELLIGENCE SUMMARY.~~

*(Erase heading not required.)*

Army Form C. 2118.

| Place | Date | Hour | Summary of Events and Information | Remarks and references to Appendices |
|---|---|---|---|---|
| | 1 - 5th Jany. | | During this period a Working Party of 2 officers & 108 other ranks, including Other Ranks necessary for administration were detached on working party at WANQUETIN - under the orders of O.C. 278th Field Coy. R.E. | C.S.J. |
| | 6th | 2 p.m. | Transport marched to AGNEZ-LES-DUISANS and occupied Transport Lines there vacated by 20th Lan. Fus. | |
| | | 3 pm. | Battalion (less Transport & Working Party detached at WANQUETIN) moved by 23 motor lorries to ARRAS in relief of 20 L.F. Operation Order No 51. (1) The Bn (less working party at WANQUETIN) will proceed to ARRAS tomorrow, 6th January 1917. (2) The move will be carried out in lorries the distribution of which will be notified later. (3) Coys. will concentrate with heads at the five-cross-roads near Bn. HQ at 2.50 pm. Dress Full marching order, each man will carry his two blankets rolled in ground-sheets on top of his pack (4) The Transport will move independently to Transport Lines of 20th Lan. Fus at AGNEZ starting from road junction mentioned, at 2 pm. | |
| | | 6.30 pm. | Battalion was settled in Billets disposed :- HQ Coy, W Coy & X Coy in SEMINAIRE near PORTE BAUDIMONT. Y Coy & Z Coy at 27 RUE D'AMIENS. | C.S.J. |
| | 7th | | Church services held in Billets as under :- 10 am. W, X & H.Q Coys. 10.45 am. Y & Z Coys. | C.S.J. |
| | | 4 pm. | Working Party detached at WANQUETIN moved by 4 motor lorries and rejoined Battalion. | |
| | 9th | 10.45 am | G.O.C. 104 Bde inspected at SEMINAIRE, 58 other ranks selected by C.O. 17 L.F. as unable to perform duties of normal infantryman on active service. | C.S.J. |
| | 16th | 11.30 a.m. | IIIrd Army Commander inspected at AGNEZ in field opposite Kite balloon section, 58 other ranks who had been rejected by 104 Bde Commander and C.O. as unsuitable as infantry soldiers on active service. | C.S.J. |
| | 8 - 31st | | Bn. in ARRAS found working parties daily for A.D.A.S. Men were employed in digging cable trenches and laying cable between DAINVILLE and ARRAS, at ACHICOURT STN. and at factory at G.28 b 87.85 - about 500 yds E of N. of ARRAS railway station. During this period when men returned from working parties classes of instruction in bombing and Lewis Gun and revolver practices for Lewis Gunners and officers were held. | C.S.J. |
| | 12/13 - 31st | | Draft of 128 other ranks untrained were under training at Divisional Depot at AVERDOINGT. | C.S.J. |
| | 18 - 31st | | Untrained drafts of 106 and 100 other ranks at IZEL were trained under officers and N.C.Os specially detailed from the Bn. for the purpose. | C.S.J. |
| | | | Total casualties during the month - 1 other rank - wounded. | |

C.S. Jewels Capt
for Lieut. Colonel
Commdg. 17th (S) Bn. Lancashire Fusiliers.

A5834 Wt. W4973/M687 750,000 8/16 D. D. & L. Ltd. Forms/C.2118/13.

Vol 13

CONFIDENTIAL

# WAR DIARY

OF

17TH (S.) BATTALION, LANCASHIRE FUSILIERS.

FROM 1ST FEBRUARY 1917 TO 31ST FEBRUARY 1917.

(VOLUME 13.)

Instructions regarding War Diaries and Intelligence Summaries are contained in F. S. Regs., Part II. and the Staff Manual respectively. Title pages will be prepared in manuscript.

# WAR DIARY
*or*
# INTELLIGENCE SUMMARY.
*(Erase heading not required.)*

Army Form C. 2118.

| Place | Date | Hour | Summary of Events and Information | Remarks and references to Appendices |
|---|---|---|---|---|
| Arras. | 1·2·17 | | Battalion in ARRAS provided Working parties for Cable Trenches. | |
| ARRAS. | 2·2·17 | | Battalion moved to WANQUETIN enroute to LIENCOURT where concentration of Working party and new drafts with Battalion would take place. OPERATION ORDER – 1. The Bn. in ARRAS will march to WANQUETIN tomorrow 2nd February 1917. ROUTE:– DAINVILLE – WARLUS | |
| WANQUETIN | 3·2·17 | | Battalion moved to LIENCOURT. Operation Order:– The Bn. will march from WANQUETIN to LIENCOURT on Feb. 3rd 1917. ROUTE:– HAUTEVILLE – AVESNES. Starting point:– [illegible] Road Junction K.31 B | |
| LIENCOURT. | 4·2·17 | | Drafts which had been training at IZEL – LES – HAMEAU are posted to Companies. Inspections occupied the rest of the day. | |
| LIENCOURT | 5·2·17 | | A.D.M.S. rejected several more men who joined a party already marked down as unfit making a total of 47 Other Ranks. These proceeded to BOULOGNE. | |
| LIENCOURT. | 6·2·17 | | Battalion moved to RANSART and rested the night. Operation Order:– 1. The Bn. will march to RANSART (1½ miles N.W. of DOULLENS) on 6th instant. 2. Order of March:– Band. Hdqrs., Y Coy, X Coy, Z Coy, W Coy, Cookers, Transport & pack animals, L.G. Detachments with HANDCARTS under 2/Lt. WALLIS. Starting point:– Cross Roads, LIENCOURT. Route:– GRAND RULLECOURT – SUS-ST. LEGER – IVERGNY – LE SOUICH – BONNE MAISON – RANSART. | |
| RANSART | 7·2·17 | | Battalion moved to BEAUVAL via DOULLENS and rested there for the night. | |
| BEAUVAL | 8·2·17 | | Battalion moved from BEAUVAL to NAOURS. | |
| NAOURS | 9·2·17 to 15·2·17 | | Battalion in NAOURS. Training by Companies carried out. Platoons being reorganized under the new French method, providing that Specialists be abolished and every man be capable of using effectively, every Infantry Weapon. | |
| NAOURS. | 16·2·17 | | Transport moved to AUBIGNY and halted there the night. Battalion occupied cleaning equipment &c. | |

A5834 Wt. W4973/M687 750,000 8/16 D. D. & L. Ltd. Forms/C.2118/13.

Instructions regarding War Diaries and Intelligence Summaries are contained in F. S. Regs., Part II. and the Staff Manual respectively. Title pages will be prepared in manuscript.

# WAR DIARY
*or*
# INTELLIGENCE SUMMARY.
*(Erase heading not required.)*

Army Form C. 2118.

| Place | Date | Hour | Summary of Events and Information | Remarks and references to Appendices |
|---|---|---|---|---|
| | 17·2·17 | | Transport proceeded by Road to WIENCOURT. Battalion less Transport marched to FLESSELLES to entrain for MARCELCAVE. Train journey of 2 hours and a march of 3 Kilometres brought us to WIENCOURT CAMP. Operation Order. 1. The Battalion will move to the new area as under:- (I) Transport by Route march to AUBIGNY under Staff Captain, 104TH Brigade. (II) Battalion (less Transport) by Tactical Train entraining at FLESSELLES and detraining at MARCELCAVE. 2. All Transport of Battalion including Cookers will march to AUBIGNY on 16TH inst & will rendezvous at Cross Roads N of S in TALMAS at 10·2 a.m. on that date. ROUTE:- VILLERS BOCAGE – COISY – ALLONVILLE – BUSSY. 5. The Battalion (less Transport) will march to entraining Station on 17TH inst. Starting point:- NAOURS – TALMAS – FLESSELLES Cross Roads. | |
| WIENCOURT | 18·2·17. | | Battalion at WIENCOURT CAMP. Church Service in morning. Concert was held in the evening in conjunction with the 23rd Manchesters. | |
| ROSIERES. | 19·2·17. | | Battalion marched to ROSIERES. Operation Order:- 1. Battalion will march to ROSIERES tomorrow 19TH inst. Route:- WIENCOURT – GUILLAUCOURT – CAIX. Transport stopped at CAIX. At night Battn provided carrying party of 8 Officers + 400 other Ranks to carry up ammunition and bombs into the new line being taken over from the French. | |
| ROSIERES. | 20-2-17 TO 22-2-17. | | Battalion in ROSIERES. Spent in cleaning up Billets and lectures by Platoon Commanders on Trench Duties etc. Working parties provided each night carrying Munitions & making Dumps. | |
| ROSIERES. | 23·2·17. | | W. Y & Z Coys. of Battalion moved up line to relieve one Coy. of 23rd Manchesters 20TH Lan. Fus. and 18TH Lan. Fus. respectively. Operation Order. 1. Tomorrow Feby. 23rd the following Coys. will carry on reliefs in the line as under. Y. Coy. will relieve one Coy of 20TH Lan. Fus., W. Coy. will relieve one Coy. of 23rd Manchester Regt. Z. Coy. will relieve one Coy of 18TH Lan. Fus. Trenches are exceedingly bad, going being difficult. Relief completed finally at 10 a.m. on 24TH inst. During the relief the enemy heavily shelled the line. We suffered the following casualties:- 4 O.R. KILLED and 5 O.R. WOUNDED. | |

A5834 Wt. W4973/M687 750,000 8/16 D. D. & L. Ltd. Forms/C.2118/13.

Instructions regarding War Diaries and Intelligence Summaries are contained in F. S. Regs., Part II. and the Staff Manual respectively. Title pages will be prepared in manuscript.

# WAR DIARY
*or*
# INTELLIGENCE SUMMARY.

*(Erase heading not required.)*

Army Form C. 2118.

| Place | Date | Hour | Summary of Events and Information | Remarks and references to Appendices |
|---|---|---|---|---|
| ROSIERES. | 24-2-17. | | Battalion less 3 Coys. in ROSIERES. Casualties 1 O.R. WOUNDED IN ACTION. | [illegible] |
| ROSIERES. | 25-2-17 | | Working parties provided for line at night. Working party attached to Div. Pioneer Battn., (19TH NORTHUMBERLAND FUSILIERS) for duty. | [illegible] |
| ROSIERES. | 26-2-17 | | Battalion less 3 Coys. moved from ROSIERES to CAMP DECAUVILLE VIA CAIX. The 3 Coys attached to the Battalions in the line were relieved under arrangements made by their respective C.O.s as follows:— W+Y Coys by 16TH H.L.I. and Z Coy. by 17TH ROYAL SCOTS. As each Coy. was relieved, it marched back to ROSIERES and there rested the night. | [illegible] |
| CAMP DECAUVILLE | 27-2-17 | | Battalion less 3 Coys. at Camp DECAUVILLE. The 3 Coys. relieved last night marched from ROSIERES to Camp DECAUVILLE. | [illegible] |
| CAMP DECAUVILLE | 28-2-17 | | Battalion at Camp DECAUVILLE. Day spent in cleaning up and kit inspections | [illegible] |

[illegible signature] Lieut. Colonel
Commdg 17TH (S) Batt., Lancs. Fusrs.

A5834 Wt. W4973/M687 750,000 8/16 D. D. & L. Ltd. Forms/C.2118/13.

(Confidential)

# War Diary

of

17th Service (1st S.E.L.) Battalion, Lancashire Fusiliers.

From:- 1st March, 1917 — To:- 31st March, 1917.

(Volume 14)

Army Form C. 2118.

# WAR DIARY

or

~~INTELLIGENCE SUMMARY.~~

(Erase heading not required.)

Instructions regarding War Diaries and Intelligence Summaries are contained in F. S. Regs., Part II. and the Staff Manual respectively. Title pages will be prepared in manuscript.

| Place | Date | Hour | Summary of Events and Information | Remarks and references to Appendices |
|---|---|---|---|---|
| CAMP DECAUVILLE | 1·3·17. TO 5·3·17. | | Battalion at CAMP DECAUVILLE NEAR CAIX. Training carried out. | |
| TRENCHES | 6·3·17. | | Battalion moved to CHILLY SECTOR to relieve 15TH SHERWOOD FORESTERS - Operation Order No. 59- | APPENDIX 1. |
| Do. | 7 to 9·3·17. | | In the line. - Nothing to report. - 2/Lt. W. W. SPROSON Wounded in Action 8·3·17. (Remained at duty)<br>2 Other Ranks Wounded in Action 8·3·17.<br>1 " " " " " 9·3·17 (Remained at duty) | |
| SUPPORT TRENCHES | 10 to 13·3·17. | | Relieved in Front Line by 20TH LANCASHIRE FUSILIERS and moved to Support Line. Carrying parties provided nightly for urgent wiring work.<br>Casualty Return:- 1 Other Rank Wounded in Action - 13·3·17.<br>2 Other Ranks Accidentally Wounded 12·3·17. | |
| TRENCHES. | 14·3·17 to 16·3·17. | | In the Front Line - Nothing to report during relief. - Enemy very quiet. 2 Other Ranks Wounded in Action 15·3·17. | |
| Do. | 17·3·17. | | Patrols reported that the enemy line was not held. Report received from Division on our right had occupied enemy Front Line. Battalion moved forward & occupied enemy Front Line without opposition. Patrols were pushed forward to PONCHY but contact with enemy was not gained. | |
| | 18·3·17. | | 18TH LANCASHIRE FUSILIERS moved ahead and the Battalion moved forward in support of 18TH LAN. FUS. Op. Order S.14. occupying positions from 11·0AM to 6·0PM at HALLU moving to BELLE AIR FARM arriving at 8·0PM. | APPENDIX 2. |
| FOUQUESCOURT | 19·3·17. | | Battalion moves to FOUQUESCOURT. | |
| Do. | 19-27·3·17. | | Battalion in FOUQUESCOURT working on repair of roads across old Trench System and up to HATTENCOURT. | |
| Do. | 28·3·17. | | Battalion moved to ETALON. | |

A5834 Wt. W4973/M687 750,000 8/16 D. D. & L. Ltd. Forms/C.2118/13.

Army Form C. 2118.

Instructions regarding War Diaries and Intelligence Summaries are contained in F. S. Regs., Part II. and the Staff Manual respectively. Title pages will be prepared in manuscript.

# WAR DIARY

~~or~~

~~INTELLIGENCE SUMMARY.~~

*(Erase heading not required.)*

(SHEET 2)

| Place | Date | Hour | Summary of Events and Information | Remarks and references to Appendices |
|---|---|---|---|---|
| ETALON. | 29:3:17. | | Battalion moved to BACQUENCOURT. | |
| BACQUENCOURT | 30/31:3:17. | | Battalion in BACQUENCOURT. Working Parties were provided for road repair at OFFOY and on main roads. | |

K. M. Mills.
Lieut Colonel.
Commanding 17th (S) Battalion,
Lancashire Fusiliers

A5834 Wt. W4973/M687 750,000 8/16 D. D. & L. Ltd. Forms/C.2118/13.

APPENDIX I.

SECRET.

COPY No 16

17th (S) Battalion. Lancashire Fusiliers

# OPERATION ORDER No 59.

BY

Lt. Col. A. M. Mills. D.S.O. Commanding.

Headquarters: 5th March, 1917.

1. The Battn. will relieve the 15th Sherwood Forresters in the Right Sub-section. CHILLY Sector on night of March 6th/7th.

2. (a) Coys. will be disposed in the Line as under:-

| | | |
|---|---|---|
| RIGHT COY. FRONT | - | Z COY. |
| CENTRE " " | - | X " |
| LEFT " " | - | Y " |
| SUPPORT COY. | - | W " |

(b) Coy. fronts will in the first place be taken over as at present held by the 15th Sherwood Forrs.

(c) The Working Platoon under 2/Lt. STENHOLM will be accommodated probably in the neighbourhood of Battn. Hd. Qrs.

3. The Battn. will march from DECAUVILLE CAMP to VRELY tomorrow, 6th inst, via CAIX.

STARTING POINT:- Track leading into Camp from road E. of Camp, distinguished by Notice Board bearing name of Camp.

TIME:- Coys. will be in position ready to move off by 10:30 a.m.

ORDER OF MARCH:- W - Z - X - H.Q. - WKG. PLN. - Y - TRANSPORT. - Cookers will follow their Coys. Transport Officer will arrange necessary transport

DRESS:- Fighting Order: Jerkins will be worn, & ground sheets rolled on Haversack.

4. Movement E. of CAIX will be by Platoons at 200x interval.

5. Dinners will be cooked on the road.

6. Officers' valises, blankets rolled in bundles of 10, spare mess kits, packs etc. will be dumped in the Canteen Hut. (at the end remote from the Canteen) by 8 a.m. tomorrow, the 6th. inst.
The guard for stores so dumped will report to the Quartermaster at 8 a.m. tomorrow.

7. 2/Lt. STENHOLM & billeting party of 1 N.C.O. per Coy. will proceed in advance to VRELY to take over billets allotted by the Staff Captain.
Party will leave Camp not later than 8:30 a.m. tomorrow.

8. Coys. will move into the Line after tea in order given in para 3, starting with W Coy: at 5:30 p.m.
Guides will report at VRELY.

9. O's. C. Coys. must ensure that all precautions are taken against Trench Foot.

10. Trench Stores will be taken over carefully, receipts being rendered to Bn. H.Q. at 1 p.m. on 7th. inst.

11. Completion of relief will be reported to Bn. H.Q. without delay under code word "WIENCOURT."

12. Acknowledge.

G. Mackereth. 2/Lt.
A/Adjt. 17th Lancs. Fusrs.

COPIES TO:-

1. C.O.
2. 2 i/c.
3. O.C. H.Q. COY.
4. " W "
5. " X "
6. " Y "
7. " Z "
8. " T.O. "
9. M.O.
10. Q.M.
11. INTLGCE. OFF.
12. 2/LT. STENHOLM.
13. R.S.M.
14. FILE.
15. 15TH SHERWOODS.
16. WAR DIARY.

Confidential.

— War Diary —

of

17th (S) (1st S.E.L.) Battalion, Lancashire Fusiliers.

From:- 1st April, 1917. To:- 30th April, 1917.

(Volume 15)

Vol 15

15-V.
8 sheets

Instructions regarding War Diaries and Intelligence Summaries are contained in F. S. Regs., Part II. and the Staff Manual respectively. Title pages will be prepared in manuscript.

# WAR DIARY

or

~~INTELLIGENCE SUMMARY.~~

(Erase heading not required.)

17th Lancs Fus.

Army Form C. 2118.

104/35

| Place | Date | Hour | Summary of Events and Information — SHEET 1. | Remarks and references to Appendices |
|---|---|---|---|---|
| BACQUENCOURT: | APRIL - 1. | | Battalion moved to TOULLE. Strength of Battalion 1:4:17:- OFFS. 39 · O.R. 807. | |
| TOULLE. | 2. | | Battalion moved to GERMAINE. | |
| GERMAINE. | 3-5. | | Battalion in GERMAINE - Working Parties provided on roads and craters. | |
| GERMAINE. | 6. | | Battalion moved to UGNY and LANCHY - HD. QRS. X & Y COYS. billeted in UGNY and W & Z COYS. in LANCHY. | |
| UGNY & LANCHY: | 7-9. | | Battalion in UGNY & LANCHY, repairing roads. | |
| UGNY & LANCHY: | 10. | | Battalion moved to MARTEVILLE, & relieved the 2/7TH WARWICKS in Brigade Reserve. | |
| MARTEVILLE. | 11. | | Battalion relieved the 2/5TH WARWICKS in the Line at FRESNOY-LE-PETIT - (OPERATION ORDER No. S. 20. - LIEUT. H.G. LEAVER wounded whilst taking over. | APPENDIX "A") |
| LINE. (FRESNOY-LE PETIT) | 12+13. | | In the Line - 2/LTS. H.H. VALE & A. BELL and 3 Other Ranks wounded in action. 2 Other Ranks "Missing" - believed Prisoners of War. | |
| LINE. (FRESNOY-LE PETIT) | 14. | | In the Line - Enemy strong point raided at 6·0 a.m. 4 of enemy killed & several wounded. At 2·30 p.m. strong point threatened on two sides surrendered - garrison of 46 captured. The protective post on GRICOURT having fallen, GRICOURT was attacked, (TACTICAL PROGRESS REPORT - 53 Prisoners taken, 4 Granatenwerfers captured. Our casualties amounted to:- 13 Other Ranks killed; 1 Officer (2/LT. J.H. KIRKBY) & 34 Other Ranks wounded. | APPENDIX "B") |
| LINE (GRICOURT) | 14. | | Battalion relieved at night by 18TH LANCASHIRE FUSILIERS, & moved into Brigade Reserve around FRESNOY-LE-PETIT. | |
| FRESNOY-LE-PETIT. | 15. | | In Brigade Reserve. | |

1577 Wt. W10791/1773 500,000 1/15 D. D. & L. A.D.S.S./Forms/C. 2118.

Instructions regarding War Diaries and Intelligence Summaries are contained in F. S. Regs., Part II. and the Staff Manual respectively. Title pages will be prepared in manuscript.

Army Form C. 2118.

# WAR DIARY
~~or~~
~~INTELLIGENCE SUMMARY.~~
(Erase heading not required.)

| Place | Date | Hour | Summary of Events and Information SHEET 2. | Remarks and references to Appendices |
|---|---|---|---|---|
| FRESNOY-LE-PETIT. | APRIL. 15. | | Battalion relieved by 15TH SHERWOOD FORESTERS and moved to TREFCON. | |
| TREFCON. | 16. | | Battalion billeted in TREFCON. Working Parties provided on roads. | |
| TREFCON. | 17-22. | | Battalion in TREFCON. Working Parties provided daily on BEAUVOIS-MARTEVILLE road. | |
| TREFCON. | 23. | | Battalion moves to MAISSEMY & relieves 17TH ROYAL SCOTS on the front opposite BELLENGLISE. – "Y" Coy. Left front; "W" Coy. Right front; "X" Support Coy; "Z" Reserve Coy; Relief completed 11.50 P.M. | |
| LINE. (MAISSEMY) | 24. | | Battalion in line at MAISSEMY. – The village of PONTRUET was raided by a force of 5 Offs. and 100 Other Ranks provided from "W" & "Y" Companies. Artillery bombarded PONTRUET for 15 minutes; raiding party entered village under cover of BOX Barrage: No enemy seen or encountered. | |
| LINE. | 25. | | Battalion in line. | |
| LINE. | 26. | | Battalion in line. – Patrol inspected bridge over River L'OMIGNON which causes road from PONTRUET to STE HELENE; it was found to be substantial – brick and stone construction. | |
| LINE. | 27. | | Battalion relieved by 18TH LANCASHIRE FUSILIERS and moves to VILLECHOLES. | |
| VILLECHOLLES. | 28. | | Battalion in VILLECHOLLES. | |
| VILLECHOLLES. | 29 & 30. | | Battalion in VILLECHOLLES. Working party of 200 men found nightly digging BROWN LINE of defence. | |
| | | | Strength of Battalion 30.4.17.– OFFS: 33 · O.R. 744. | |

A. Mills. Lieut Colonel.
Commdg. 17th (S) Bn. Lancs. Fusiliers.

17th Service (1st S.E.L.) Battalion, Lancashire Fusiliers.

APPENDIX "B" to War Diary (Volume 15) for April, 1917.

Ref. attached Plan & 62.B.S.W. 1/20.000.

6.0 A.M. Two Officers Patrols were sent forward to reconnoitre GRICOURT and to occupy it should it prove to be lightly held. The enemy post in the FRESNOY CEMETERY opposed the passage of the left patrol & a sharp fight took place in which 4 enemy were killed. The right patrol, after establishing a post in the QUADRILATERAL reached the outskirts of GRICOURT and found the village was strongly held. The enemy in Cemetery Post attempted to cut our right patrol off but this was unsuccessful.

1.5 P.M. About this time, as attack of 32nd Division was developing, the enemy made several attempts to reinforce his threatened front at M.28.d.6.1. The manoeuvre was completely defeated by two Lewis Guns which had been posted at M.28.C.5.6. Again about 15 minutes later, the enemy being caught by the 32nd Division's Barrage endeavoured to retire to GRICOURT. Our two Lewis Guns prevented them & 3 enemy were killed & the ~~remai~~ remainder surrendered to the 32nd Division.

2.30 P.M. A patrol was pushed out towards Cemetery strong point from our post at M.21.a.8.3. This enemy post having its retirement threatened by our post at QUADRILATERAL trench, surrendered to our left patrol.

2.40 P.M. The left company ("Z") was ordered to establish a position E. of CEMETERY. This was completed by 7.45 p.m. The enemy put down a heavy barrage E. of FRESNOY. "W" & "Y" Companies - in reserve & support respectively were ordered up towards FRESNOY.

3.0 P.M. "X" Coy. on the right & "Z" Coy. on the left were ordered to push on towards GRICOURT at 3.30 p.m. A footing was obtained on the outskirts of GRICOURT; the flanks were moved round with the intention of enveloping the village. The left flank being under heavy enfilade fire could not advance further than GRICOURT-PONTRUET road where it established itself. Meanwhile the right flank managed to get well round & the enemy retreated in a N.E. direction leaving behind sniping posts.

Patrols were then pushed through the village, and after some fighting killed or captured the enemy who remained. Enemy Artillery & enfilade M-G. fire was very severe. The environs of GRICOURT, lying at the bottom of a shallow basin, did not provide a suitable position upon which to consolidate, moreover the left flank was very much exposed owing to the unit on our left not advancing in conjunction. Therefore the line shown in red was ordered to be taken up & consolidated at dusk leaving posts as shown.

This was carried out and consolidation begun at 7.45 pm. & continued until relieved by 18th Lancashire Fusiliers at 12.45 a.m. 15th April 1917.

During the operation an enemy aeroplane flying very low & directing Artillery was brought down by concentrated L-G. fire by support company ("Y")

53 Prisoners of 453rd Regt. and 4 Granatenwerfers and ammunition were captured & many casualties were inflicted on the enemy.

---

For this action the following rewards were granted:

2nd Lt G. Mackereth – Military Cross.

Temp: 2nd Lt W. M. Holden. " "

No. Pte Booth. Military Medal –

" Pte Walker – " "

" Pte Chisnall – " "

A. Whitmills [signature]

Lieut Colonel.

Commdg. 17th (S) Bn. Lancs. Fusiliers.

SITUATION AT. 3·30 PM.

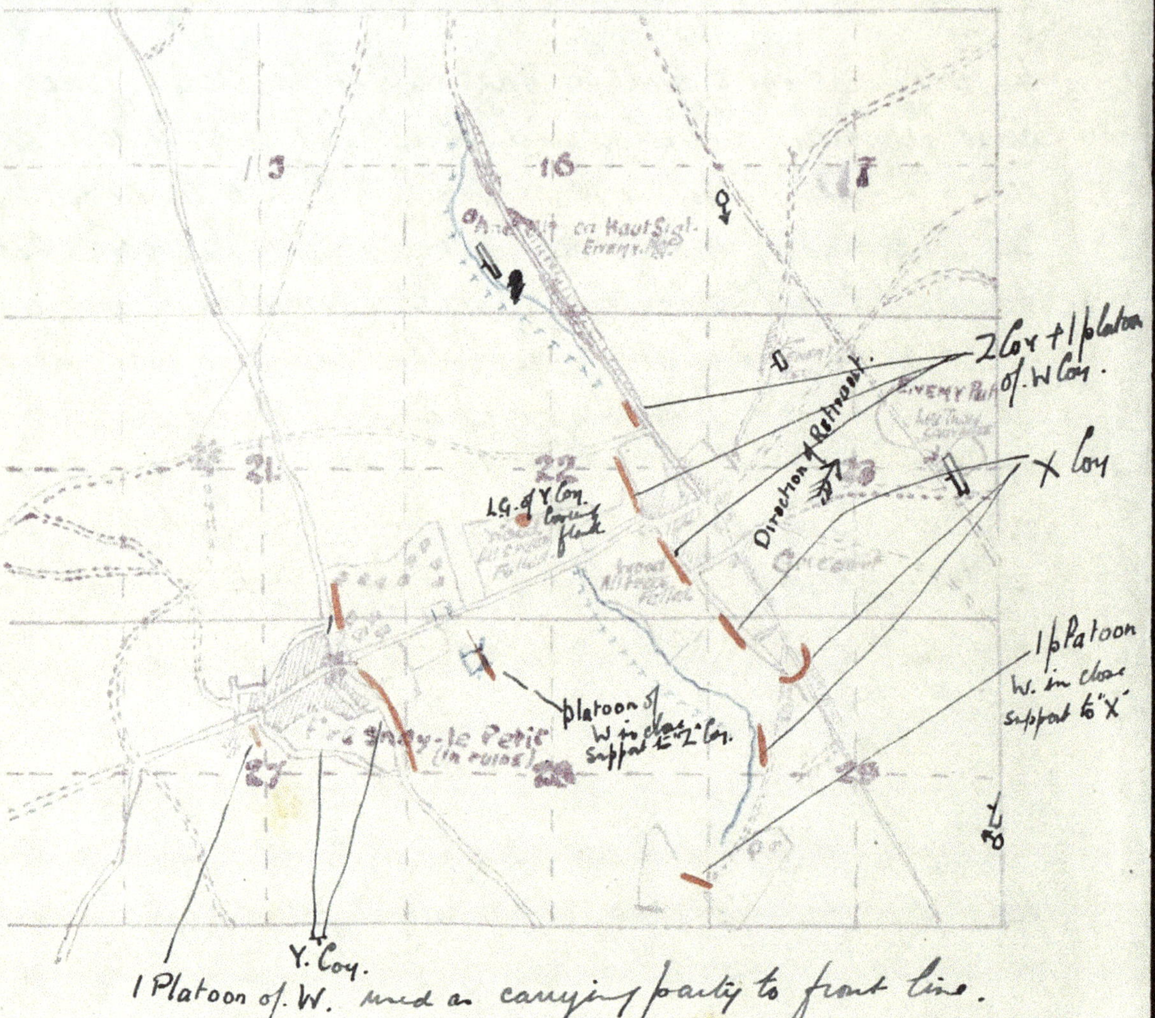


Enemy position

" M. G.

SCALE. $\frac{1}{20000}$.

TO. ATTACH TO WAR DIARY
17 LAN. FUS.

APRIL. 1917.

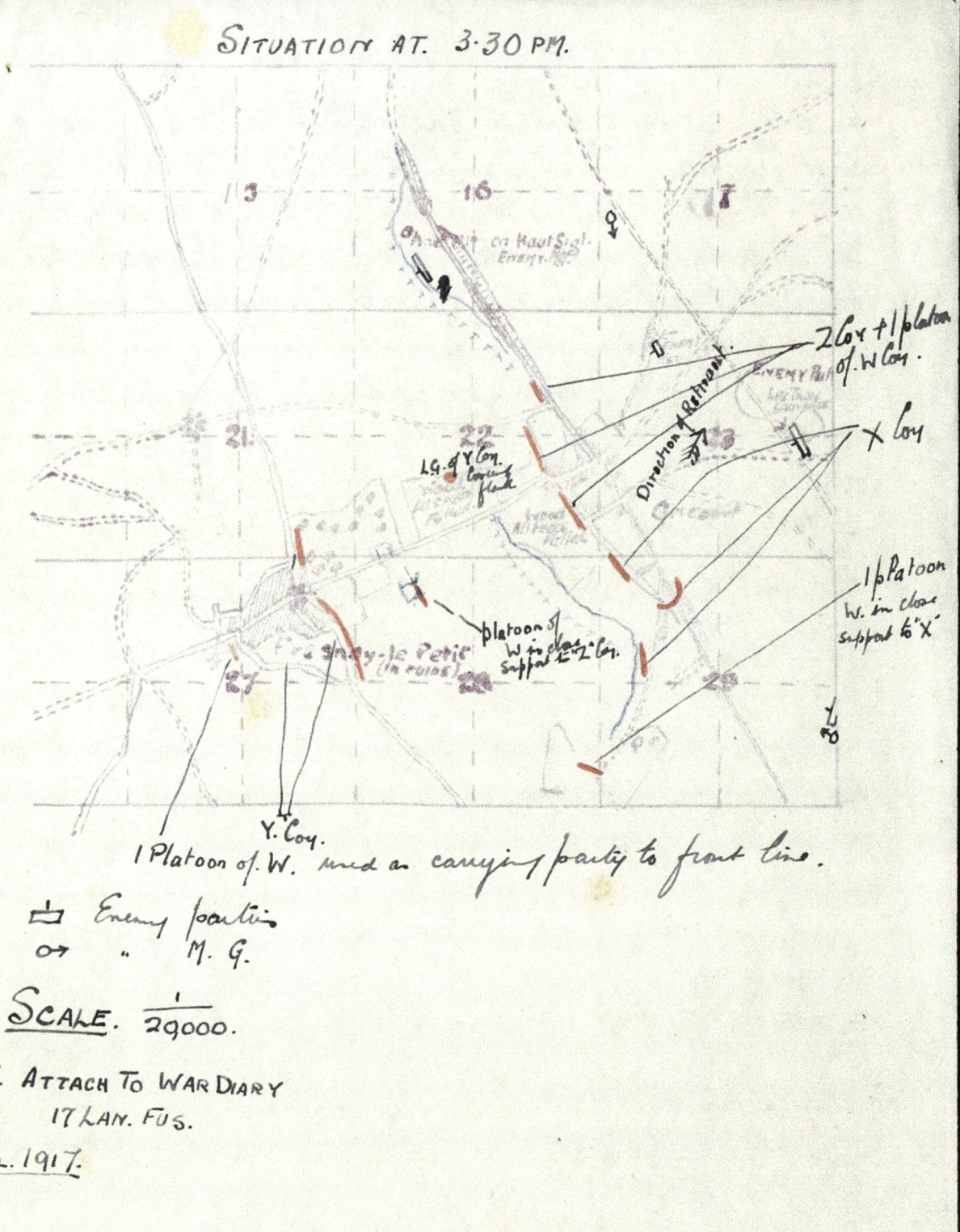

SKETCH MAP. Shewing positions at 7.45 PM 14/4/17 to 12.45 AM 15/4/17

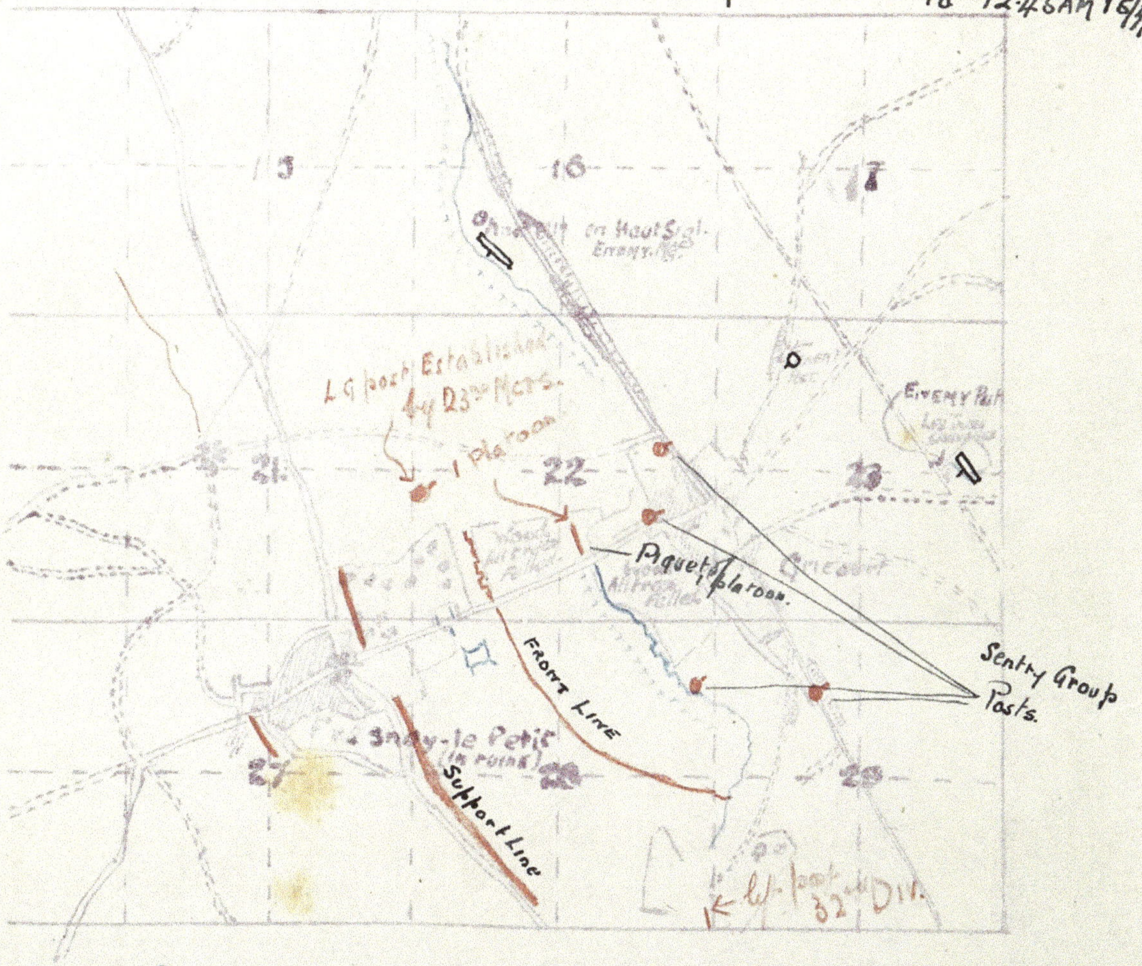


— German Trenches

— General Line (British) at 7.45 PM 14 4 1917

• Posts Established

▭ + o. Enemy Piquets & Posts.

Scale. 1/20,000.

To Attach To War Diary
17. Lan. Fus.

April. 1917.

Vol 16

Confidential

War Diary

— of —

17th Service (1st S.E.L.) Battalion, Lancashire Fusiliers.

From:- 1st May 1917. — To:- 31st May, 1917.

(Volume 16.)

16.V.
6 sheets

Instructions regarding War Diaries and Intelligence Summaries are contained in F. S. Regs., Part II. and the Staff Manual respectively. Title pages will be prepared in manuscript.

# WAR DIARY
*or*
# INTELLIGENCE SUMMARY.
*(Erase heading not required.)*

Army Form C. 2118.

| Place | Date | ~~Hour~~ | Summary of Events and Information — MAY. SHEET 1. | Remarks and references to Appendices |
|---|---|---|---|---|
| VILLECHOLLES | 1:5:17-2:6:17. | | Battalion in VILLECHOLLES. FIGHTING STRENGTH:- OFFS. 33. O.R. 744. | |
| LINE. | 3:5:17. | | Battalion moves to BIHECOURT & relieves 20TH LANCS. FUSRS in the Line in Left Subsector. | |
| LINE. | 4/5:5:17. | | Battalion in Line. 23RD MANCHESTER REGT. carry out a raid on SOMERVILLE WOOD (G.32 central) at 2.30 a.m. 4TH/5TH MAY. - Result, capture of Wood and four Prisoners. Our "Z" COY. provided 3 POSTS for the Wood during the consolidation thereof we captured 2 prisoners of 156th Regt. 1 to approach the wood. | |
| LINE. | 5/6:5:17. | | Battalion in Line. Germans attacked SOMERVILLE WOOD with 70 men at 9:30 P.M. & our Posts were driven out. A counter-attack at 12 midnight regained the wood for us & inflicted 9 killed and 1 prisoner upon the enemy we lost 1 killed & 6 wounded (See APPENDIX "A") | APPENDIX "A" |
| LINE. | 6:5:17. | | Battalion relieved by 20TH LANCS FUSRS and moves to VILLECHOLLES into Brigade Reserve. | |
| VILLECHOLLES | 7-8:5:17. | | Battalion in VILLECHOLLES. 4 Officers & 200 men found for digging ~~B~~ & wiring in front of BROWN LINE | |
| VILLECHOLLES | 8:5:17. | | Battalion moves to MAISSEMY and relieves 18TH LANCS FUSRS still in Brigade Reserve. Working Parties provided on new Brigade H.Q. at VADENCOURT - new line. | |
| MAISSEMY. | 10-13:5:17. | | Battalion at MAISSEMY. Working Parties of 4 Officers & 200 Other Ranks for work on Bde. H.Q., Shelters, and new front line. | |
| MAISSEMY. | 14:5:17. | | Battalion moves to POEUILLY & bivouacs in the Valley immediately S.W. of that place. | |
| POEUILLY. ~~MAISSEMY~~ | 15-20:5:17. | | Battalion at POEUILLY. Training carried out. On the 20th a Practice Attack was carried out by the 104th Bde. | |
| POEUILLY. | 21:5:17. | | Battalion marches to PERONNE and billeted there. | |
| PERONNE. | 22:5:17. | | Battalion in PERONNE. | |

1577 Wt. W10791/1773 500,000 1/15 D. D. & L. A.D.S.S./Forms/C. 2118.

Instructions regarding War Diaries and Intelligence Summaries are contained in F. S. Regs., Part II. and the Staff Manual respectively. Title pages will be prepared in manuscript.

# WAR DIARY

~~or~~

~~INTELLIGENCE SUMMARY.~~

(*Erase heading not required.*)

Army Form C. 2118.

| Place | Date | Hour | Summary of Events and Information — SHEET 2. | Remarks and references to Appendices |
|---|---|---|---|---|
| PERONNE. | 23·5·17. | | Battalion march to camp in the valley between HEUDICOURT - SORREL-LE-GRANDE. | |
| NR. HEUDICOURT. | 24·5·17. | | Battalion in camp. Training carried out. | |
| NR. HEUDICOURT. | 25·5·17. | | Battalion moved up the line & relieved the 13TH BATTN EAST SURREY REGT in the line running SOUTH of GONNELIEU. - Dispositions:- "W" COY: RIGHT FRONT. "Y" COY: LEFT FRONT. "X" " RIGHT SUPPORT. "Z" " LEFT SUPPORT. Relief reported complete at 11·40 P.M. | |
| LINE. | 26·5·17. | | Battalion in the Line. Our right front shelled with Gas Shells (about 300 sent over). We suffered 1 casualty ~~ies~~ wounded. | |
| LINE. | 27-28·5·17. | | Battalion in the Line. 2 men wounded. | |
| LINE. | 29·5·17. | | Battalion in Line. Dispositions altered to:- "X" COY: RIGHT FRONT. "Z" COY: LEFT FRONT. "W" " RIGHT SUPPORT. "Y" " LEFT SUPPORT. Relief complete without incident at 11·15 P.M. | |
| LINE. | 30-31·17. | | Battalion in the Line. 2/LT. W.M. HOLDEN, M.C. wounded 31·5·17. FIGHTING STRENGTH:- OFFS: 36 · O.R. 737. | |
| | | | Following recommended for immediate reward:- All of which have since been decorated.<br>L/CPL. WILLIAMSON, A. "Z" COY: ———— MILITARY MEDAL.<br>L/SGT. STRINGER, G. "Z" -"- ———— D°.<br>LIEUT. R.S. HEAPE. "Z" -"- ———— MILITARY CROSS.<br>For gallantry and devotion to duty in counter-attack on SOMERVILLE WOOD. | |
| | | | [signature] Major.<br>Commanding, 17TH (S) BN LANCASHIRE FUSILIERS. | |

A5834 Wt. W4973/M687 750,000 8/16 D. D. & L. Ltd. Forms/C.2118/13.

17th Service (1st S.E.L.) Battalion, Lancashire Fusiliers.

Appendix "A" to War Diary (Vol: 16)

-oOo- OPERATIONS ON NIGHT OF 5/6TH MAY 1917. -oOo-

At 9-30p.m. Enemy put up a fairly heavy Barrage on LONE TREE HILL and on Spur leading down to SOMERVILLE WOOD.

At 9-40p.m. He advanced against our Posts in SOMERVILLE WOOD in two parties both about 30 strong; one party against N.W. edge of Wood and the other from the direction of DOGS LEG. NUTTALL & WATSON POSTS fell back towards LONE TREE POSTS where they were reinforced by one Platoon. MORREY'S POST was however cut off and surrounded and severe hand-to-hand fighting took place. 3 out of 4 men got away - the Post having given an excellent account of itself, and it is believed accounted for four of the enemy.

At 11p.m. A report was received by O.C."Z"Coy. (Lt. Heape) to the effect that SOMERVILLE WOOD was in possession of the enemy. He immediately ordered and organised a counter-attack. Meantime, at 11-15 p.m. O.C. 17th L.F. instructed the Artillery to place an intense Bombardment on SOMERVILLE WOOD for 5 minutes, and ordered "X" Coy. to send a strong party to work round FISHER CRATER and threaten the enemy's left flank.

At 11-30p.m. "X"Coy. patrol moved forward and found enemy in occupation of FISHER CRATER. Patrol ~~moved round~~ worked round crater but garrison bolted Eastwards towards STE.HELENE LINE. They were fired on and chased for 300 yards but all enemy managed to escape.

At 12 midnight the Left Coy., "Z", were ready for the Counter-attack and moved forward and a barrage was put down East of SOMERVILLE WOOD. "Z"Coy. reached the outskirts of the Wood and charged and drove the enemy in full flight. The Company then consolidated position for our Posts to occupy.

At 1 a.m. Everything quiet.

RESULT OF OPERATIONS:- 1 Prisoner of 156th Regiment captured and 9 enemy dead counted.(Probably more accounted for by Shell and Rifle Fire.

Our Casualties:- 1 killed, 1 missing 6 wounded.

6/6/17.

[signature] Major,
Commdg. 17th (S) Bn. Lancs. Fusiliers.

# Sketch Maps Shewing Positions at 9.40 P.M. & 12 MD^NT Nights of 5/6 May 1917.

## Position at 9.40 P.M.

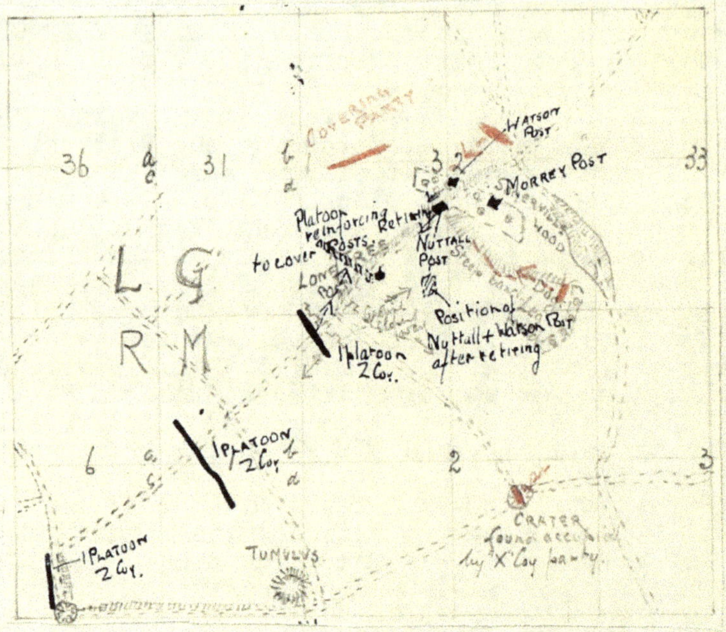


## Position at 12 Midnight

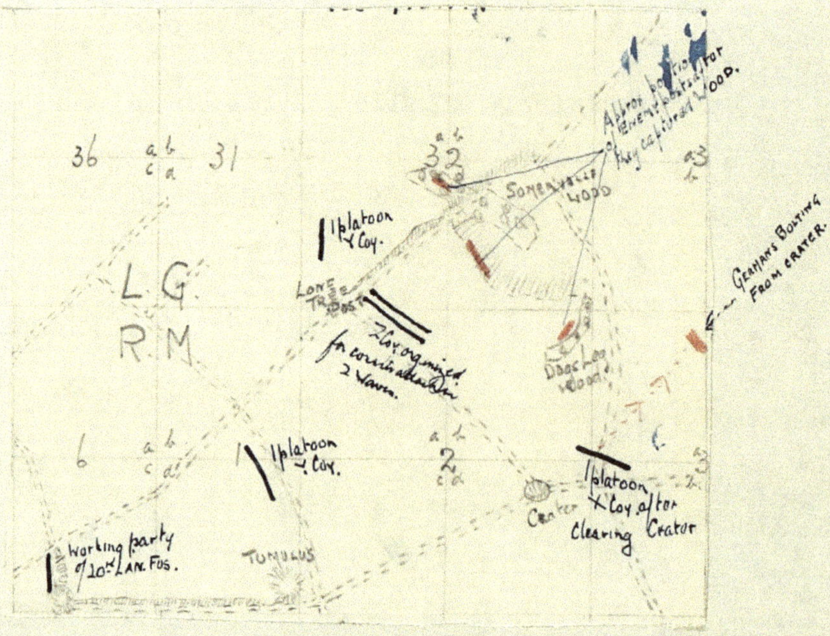


Scale 1/20,000

Ref. Map Hindenburg Line Sheet 4.

Key — = British Forces.

— = German Forces.

Vol 17

**Confidential**

# War Diary

of

17th Service (1st S.E.L) Battalion, Lancashire Fusiliers.

From:- 1st June 1917 —— To:- 30th June 1917.

(Volume 17)

17.V.
4 sheets

Instructions regarding War Diaries and Intelligence Summaries are contained in F. S. Regs., Part II. and the Staff Manual respectively. Title pages will be prepared in manuscript.

# WAR DIARY

~~or~~

~~INTELLIGENCE SUMMARY.~~

*(Erase heading not required.)*

Army Form C. 2118.

| Place | Date | Hour | Summary of Events and Information REF. MAP-SHEET 62c 1/40.000. | Remarks and references to Appendices |
|---|---|---|---|---|
| TRENCHES. | 1·6·17. | | Battalion in the Line GAUCHE WOOD Sector. STRENGTH:- OFFS: 37. O.R. 737. | |
| TRENCHES. | 2·6·17. | | Battalion relieved in the Line by 23rd Manchester Regt. and moves into Reserve to camp 1 mile E. of HEUDICOURT. named REVELON CAMP. | |
| NR. HEUDICOURT. | 3-9·6·17. | | Battalion in REVELON CAMP. Working Parties of 450 a day provided for night and day work on BROWN and GREEN lines and roads leading to BOX DUMP at Railton cross roads. | |
| NR. HEUDICOURT. | 10·6·17. | | Battalion is relieved by 19th D.L.I. and goes into Divisional Reserve in camp N. of AIZECOURT-LE-BAS. | |
| NR. AIZECOURT-LE-BAS. | 11-17·6·17. | | Battalion in camp; training carried out; - a special practice attack by Brigade, the co-operation with Contact Aeroplane being the principle feature of the practice. CASUALTY - 2/Lt. S. McVAY - DIAGNOSED WOUNDED (GASSED) 27·5·17. | |
| NR. AIZECOURT-LE-BAS. | 18·6·17. | | Battalion moves up to relieve 15th Cheshire Regt. in the Line - GUISLAIN SECTOR - "Y" Coy. Left Front, "X" Centre, "W" Right Front, and "Z" Coy. in Support. | |
| TRENCHES. | 19·6·17. | | Battalion in the Line - Nothing of importance occurs. | |
| TRENCHES. | 20·6·17. | | Battalion in the Line - "W" Coy. ~~relieved by 18th H.L.I. and~~ moves into Reserve. | |
| TRENCHES. | 21/22·6·17. | | Battalion in the Line - Nothing to report. CASUALTIES: 2 O.R. Wounded in Action. | |
| TRENCHES. | 23·6·17. | | Battalion in the Line. Inter Coy. reliefs "Z" Coy. take over left front, "W" right front, "Y" Coy. in Support "X" Coy. in Reserve. | |
| TRENCHES. | 24/25·6·17. | | Battalion in the Line - Nothing of importance occurs. CASUALTIES:- 2 O.R. Wounded in Action. | |
| TRENCHES. | 26·6·17. | | Battalion relieved by 23rd Manchester Regt., and moves into Support. CASUALTY:- 1 O.R. Wounded in Action. | |

T2134. Wt. W708—776. 500000. 4/15. Sir J. C. & S.

Instructions regarding War Diaries and Intelligence Summaries are contained in F. S. Regs., Part II. and the Staff Manual respectively. Title pages will be prepared in manuscript.

# WAR DIARY

-or-

~~INTELLIGENCE SUMMARY.~~

(Erase heading not required.)

Army Form C. 2118.

| Place | Date | Hour | Summary of Events and Information — SHEET II. | Remarks and references to Appendices |
|---|---|---|---|---|
| IN SUPPORT. | 27.6.17. | | Battalion in Support, a reconnoitring patrol investigating enemy defences with a view of a raid being made by the Battalion. Enemy found to be holding well advanced posts - the raid is not considered advisable. | |
| IN SUPPORT. | 28/30.6.17. | | Battalion in Support; working parties provided nightly for work on Front Line. STRENGTH:- OFFS. 38 : O.R. 715 | |
| | | | TOTAL CASUALTIES FOR MONTH:- OFFS:- 2/LT. S. McVAY - WOUNDED (GASSED) OTHER RANKS:- 5 WOUNDED IN ACTION. | |

1ST JULY 1917.

J. J. Cook [signature]
Major
Commanding 17th (S) Bn. Lancashire Fusiliers.

T2134. Wt. W708—776. 500000. 4/15. Sir J. C. & S.

Vol 18

Confidential

War Diary

— of —

17th Service (1st S.E.L.) Battalion, Lancashire Fusiliers

From 1st July 1917 — To:- 31st July 1917.

(Volume 18)

18. V.
4 sheets

Instructions regarding War Diaries and Intelligence Summaries are contained in F. S. Regs., Part II. and the Staff Manual respectively. Title pages will be prepared in manuscript.

# WAR DIARY
~~or~~
~~INTELLIGENCE SUMMARY.~~
*(Erase heading not required.)*

Army Form C. 2118.

| Place | Date | Hour | JULY. Summary of Events and Information | Remarks and references to Appendices |
|---|---|---|---|---|
| VILLERS-GUISLAIN. | 1·7·17. | | Battalion moves into camp near AIZECOURT-LE-BAS by Light Railway to LIERAMONT: STRENGTH – OFF. 38 O.R. 715 | |
| AIZECOURT-LE-BAS. | 2/13·7·17. | | Battalion in camp. General Training Programme carried out. "Y" Coy. detached to 180TH TUNNLG. COY. | |
| – Do. – | 14·7·17. | | Battalion moves to EPEHY to relieve the 14th GLOSTERS in Reserve. "X" Coy. detached to 180TH Tunnelling Coy. | |
| EPEHY. | 14/22·7·17. | | Battalion in Reserve. 350 men found nightly for work on Front Line Trenches. | |
| – Do. – | 23/7/17. | | Battalion moves up to relieve 23rd Manchester Regt. in the line. Cos. disposed in the line as follows:– ~~X~~ "W" COY. – RIGHT FRONT. "Y" COY. – LEFT FRONT. ~~W~~ "X" COY. – RIGHT SUPPORT. "Z" COY. – LEFT SUPPORT. | |
| TRENCHES. | 24·7·17. | | Nothing to report. | |
| – Do. – | 25·7·17. | | 2 Patrols, each of 1 Officer & 12 O.R. out at night – No contact with enemy. – Nothing to report. | |
| – Do. – | – " – | | Enemy Artillery & Trench Mortars active in registering our wire, ~~and~~ trenches on the Right of Battalion, ~~on~~ on our Left (13TH YORKS). News received from deserter that enemy intend to attack between 2·0 & 4·0 a.m. tomorrow morning. | |
| – Do. – | 26·7·17. | 6·0 a.m. | At 6·0 a.m. enemy heavily bombarded trenches on our Left and placed a flank barrage across our Left post & supports. | |
| | | 6·10 a.m. | Enemy raided 13 YORKS on our left under cover of smoke barrage. Enemy fired on by ~~our~~ Artillery & our Lewis Gun fire result not ~~known~~ certain. Casualties:– OFFS. WOUNDED:– LIEUT. R.S. HEAPE, M.C. 2/LT. G.M. THOMPSON. CAPT. S.H. BULL (R.A.M.C.) O.R.– KILLED. 4. WOUNDED. 39 | |

T2134. Wt. W708–776. 500000. 4/15. Sir J. C. & S.

Instructions regarding War Diaries and Intelligence Summaries are contained in F. S. Regs., Part II. and the Staff Manual respectively. Title pages will be prepared in manuscript.

# WAR DIARY

*or*

~~INTELLIGENCE SUMMARY.~~

*(Erase heading not required.)*

Army Form C. 2118.

| Place | Date | Hour | Summary of Events and Information SHEET 2. | Remarks and references to Appendices |
|---|---|---|---|---|
| TRENCHES. | 26·7·17 | (contd.) | Nothing to report during remainder of day. | |
| -Do- | 27·7·17. | | Front line Cos relieved from Supports. DISPOSITIONS:- "W" COY. LEFT FRONT - "Z" COY. RIGHT FRONT. "Y" COY. -"- SUPPORT - "X" COY. -"- SUPPORT. | |
| -Do- | 28·7·17. | | Nothing to report. | |
| -Do- | 29·7·17. | | 23rd Manchester Regt. raided enemy opposite our Right post capturing 2 M.Gs. Enemy retaliated on our Right Coy. No casualties. | |
| -Do- | 30·7·17. | | 20th Lancashire Fusiliers raided enemy on our left. We carried out a diversion by means of a strong patrol from "X" Coy, who threatened that portion of the enemy trenches raided by 23rd Manchesters the previous evening. The diversion was wholly satisfactory. Casualties:- 4 O.R's. WOUNDED. | |
| -Do- | 31·7·17. | | Battalion relieved in the line by 23rd Manchesters & move into Support. | |
| | | | STRENGTH:- OFF. 40 O.R. 656. | |
| | | | TOTAL CASUALTIES FOR MONTH:- OFF.-WOUNDED 3. (2 SINCE REJOINED). O.R.- KILLED 4, WOUNDED 43. | |
| | | | [signature] Lieut. Colonel. Commanding 17th (S) Battn. Lancashire Fusiliers | |

T2134. Wt. W708—776. 500000. 4/15. Sir J. C. & S.

Vol 19

Confidential

War Diary

— of —

17th Service (1st S.E.L.) Battalion, Lancashire Fusiliers.

From:- 1st August, 1917. To:- 31st August 1917.

(Volume 19.)

19. V.
9 sheets

Instructions regarding War Diaries and Intelligence Summaries are contained in F. S. Regs., Part II. and the Staff Manual respectively. Title pages will be prepared in manuscript.

# WAR DIARY
or
# INTELLIGENCE SUMMARY.
(Erase heading not required.)

Army Form C. 2118.

| Place | Date | Hour | Summary of Events and Information | Remarks and references to Appendices |
|---|---|---|---|---|
| | | | AUGUST, 1917. SHEET 1. | |
| | | | REF. MAP 66D. S.W. STRENGTH:- OFFS 40 - O.R. 656. | |
| SUPPORT LINE | 1-5:8:17. | | The Battalion in Support in the EPEHY SECTOR. Dispositions:- Battn. Hdqrs:- PARR'S BANK. "W" Coy:- LIMERICK & MEATH POSTS. "X" Coy:- COX'S BANK. "Y" Coy:- KILDARE POST. "Z" Coy:- HOLTS BANK. | SHW. |
| SUPPORTS. | 6/7:8:17. | | Battalion were relieved on night of 6/7:8:17 - "X" Coy. by ½ Coy. 29TH LANCERS. Remainder by 36TH JACOBS HORSE - and proceeded by motor busses to GURLU WOOD which was reached at 5 o'clock on morning of 7:8:17. | SHW |
| GURLU WOOD. | 8:8:17. | | Battalion was inspected & addressed by Brig. Gen. J.W. Sandilands, C.M.G., D.S.O., in the morning, on the Battle of Minden. All ranks wore red & white roses in their Steel Helmets, & under authority of G.O.C. the rest of the day was set aside for the usual Minden Day Celebrations. | SHW |
| GURLU WOOD. | 9-11:8:17. | | Company parades & training of specialists. | SHW |
| GURLU WOOD. | 12:8:17. | | Brigade Church Parade, attended by Maj. Gen. G. M. Franks, C.B. (Commdg. 35th Division) and Brig. Gen. J.W. Sandilands, C.M.G., D.S.O., followed by distribution of medals by Div. Commander. | SHW |
| GURLU WOOD. | 13-18:8:17. | | Training & practising for prospective raid. Companies fired for MILLS VASE, which was won by "Z" Coy. for second time in succession. In the afternoon & evening of the 18th there was a very interesting Regtl. Boxing Competition & Concert. | SHW |
| GURLU WOOD. | 19:8:17. | | Battalion moved up & relieved troops of the 4th Dismounted Cavalry Brigade in the Northern portion of | SHW |

T2134. Wt. W708—776. 500000. 4/15. Sir J. C. & S.

Instructions regarding War Diaries and Intelligence Summaries are contained in F. S. Regs., Part II. and the Staff Manual respectively. Title pages will be prepared in manuscript.

# WAR DIARY
~~or~~
# INTELLIGENCE SUMMARY.
*(Erase heading not required.)*

Army Form C. 2118.

SHEET 2.

| Place | Date | Hour | Summary of Events and Information | Remarks and references to Appendices |
|---|---|---|---|---|
| | 19:8:17. | (contd:) | the OSSUS Sub-sector. | |
| TRENCHES. | 20:8:17. | | All ranks took the maximum amount of rest in view of the raid to take place early next day. CASUALTIES: 4 KILLED. | Other ranks:- 10 WOUNDED. |
| | 21:8:17. | | In conjunction with 23RD MANCHESTER REGT. the Battalion raided the enemy trenches S. of CANAL WOOD. Result of raid was in every way most satisfactory, "W" COY. all reaching their final objective. 11 Prisoners were brought back & large numbers of dead & wounded Germans were left behind. Many more prisoners were actually taken, but had to be dispatched whilst our men were returning across "NO-MAN'S-LAND". Casualties:- OFFICERS:- 3 wounded. O.R.:- 2 killed. 40 wounded (chiefly slight). | (SEE APPENDIX FOR DETAILS) |
| | | | AWARD:- No. 20420 PTE. J. DIGGLE, "Y" COY: Awarded MILITARY MEDAL for bravery & devotion to duty on 21:8:17. | |
| | | | MENTIONED IN SPECIAL DIV. ORDER:- for gallant & soldierly conduct in connection with Operation on 21:8:17:- | |
| | | | OFFICERS:- LT. COL. F.J.F. CROOK, D.S.O.; LIEUT. G. MACKERETH, M.C. (WOUNDED); 2/LT. J.K.B. CRAWFORD.; CAPT. W.D. CHESHIRE.; 2/LT. P. FORMAN.; 2/LT. J. GOODIER. | |
| | | | OTHER RANKS:- 14182 CPL. W. SHEPHERD.; 26753 ~~25061~~ PTE. P. GOULDING.; 25061 PTE. J.A. HALL.; 28982 PTE. J.W. SADLICAR.; 14827 PTE. J.J. MOLYNEUX.; 20420 PTE. J. DIGGLE. | |
| -Do- | 22:8:17. | | Inter-Company reliefs:- "W" COY: to LIMERICK & MEATH POSTS. "X" COY: to COX'S BANK. "Y" COY: to Front Line, OSSUS 3 & 4. "Z" COY: to FOURTEEN WILLOWS. | |
| -Do- | 23-31:8:17. | | Nothing out of the ordinary Trench Warfare occurred, Company reliefs taking place every 4 days to ensure each Company getting 4 days rest at FOURTEEN WILLOWS. CASUALTIES, 25/8/17 - 3 O.R. WOUNDED. | |

TOTAL CASUALTIES:- OFFICERS:- LIEUT & ADJT. G. MACKERETH, M.C.
2/LT. W.B.K. GLASS } SLIGHTLY
2/LT. J.R. HAMILTON } WOUNDED.
OTHER RANKS:- 6 KILLED. 54 WOUNDED.

STRENGTH:- OFFS:- 36: O.R. 652.

Major
Commanding 17th (S) Battn., Lancashire Fusiliers

T2134. Wt. W708—776. 500000. 4/15. Sir J. C. & S.

APPENDIX.

17th Service (1st S.E.L.) Battalion, Lancashire Fusiliers.

OPERATION ORDER No.S/49.

---

1. The 104th Brigade will raid the CANAL WOOD - OSSUS trenches on the morning of August .....

2. Two parallel columns - 23rd Manchester Regt. on right,
   17th Lancashire Fusiliers on left.
   Approximate boundaries between Battalions is CHARING CROSS ROAD.

3. The 17th Lan Fus will move on a front of 160 yards with the centre of the 2 banks in X.24.a. as the centre of their furthest (2nd) objective. 1st Objective:- CANAL WOOD TRENCHES.

4. Formation:- "W"Coy. on right, "X"Coy. on Left, "Y"Coy.-Moppers up- and Flankers distributed as in separate diagram already issued.

5. The advance will conform to the lifts of the Artillery Barrage, which will be as follows:-
   1st Objective:- Zero to Zero plus 9.
   2nd Objective:- Zero plus 9 to Zero plus 12.
   All Infantry will be withdrawn from 2nd Objective by Zero plus 22. In addition there will be standing barrage in CANAL WOOD and OSSUS, which will begin to die down at Zero plus 45.

6. The raiders will assemble at the WESTERN end of CHARING CROSS ROAD (X.17.c.2.1.) at........ and will move off to the forming-up position astride CHARING CROSS ROAD X.23.b.3.6. at ...... a.m.
   Line of formation, N--- S---, move off on a bearing of 83° true.

7. O.C. "Z"Coy. will be responsible for patrolling X.23.b. from midnight until forming-up time. His patrol will act as covering party until Zero. Patrols must send in reports every half-hour; negative if necessary.

8. O.C. "Z"Coy. will also be responsible for observing and covering CANAL WOOD RAVINE during the raid. Any enemy movement observed on this flank must be immediately reported to the Artillery.

9. The whole raiding party will move at Zero, and the two first lines - ("W" & "X" Cos.) will move straight to the 2nd Objective conforming to the Artillery Barrage. - Moppers-up and H.Q. to 1st Objective. - Flankers echeloned to "W" & "X" Cos.

10. Prisoners and wounded must be sent back at once.

11. Signal to withdraw will be a RED Very Light fired by either O.C. "W" or "X" Coy. "Y"Coy. Moppers-up and Flankers will cover the withdrawal until "W" & "X" Cos. have passed through them.

12. DRESS:- Rifle & Bayonet, Belt and Pouches, only. Bombers to carry 6 Bombs each and spare bombs in buckets.
    Rifle Bombers ditto. Rifle Bombs.

13. Troops will return to the Stations occupiee by them previously to the Raid, and each Coy. must have an N.C.O. responsible for checking the number as they return.

14. Advanced Battn. H.Q. will be at LLoyds Bank X.22.d.6.7. Wires will be laid from here to OSSUS 3 on the day preceding the operation. Signallers going forward with H.Q. Raiding Party will connect up here when the party is forming up. All reports to H.Q. Raiding Party.

15. Collecting Station for Prisoners - WETSREN end CHARING CROSS ROAD., X.17.c.2.1.

16. Aid Posts, LLOYDS BANK (X.22.d.6.7.) and at Left Battn. H.Q.(X.22.C. central).

17. Zero will be notified separately.

18. Acknowledge.

(Signed) G.MACKERETH,Lieut.
A/Adjutant 17th (S) Bn. Lan. Fus.

Issued at ....... p.m., 16/8/17.

17th Service (1st S.E.L.) Battalion, Lancashire Fusiliers.

AMENDMENTS TO OPERATION ORDER No.S/49.

The following amendments are to be made:-

Para 5. All Infantry will be withdrawn fro 2nd Objective by Zero plus 25.

Para 11. Order to withdraw will be given by the Senior Officer in command of each Company independently. Light Signals will NOT beused.

Para 12. Cancel "Belt & Pouches", subsitute "Fatigue Dress" with bandolier and two clips in each side pocket of tunic.". Add:- Box Respirators in the "ALERT" position.

ADDITION:-

Para 11a. "Y"Coy. Mopper-up will each carry two flares, and these will be lit on command of an Officer when the withdrawal has begun and the leading lineshave passed back through the the Mopperseup and ane well clear of the 1st Objective.

Para 5a. RED Very Lights will be taken with the Raiding Parties and used if it is necessary to call upon the Artillery to lengthen barrage.

ACKNOWLEDGE.

Issued at ...... p.m; 18/8/17.

(Signed) G.MACKERETH,Lieut.
A/Adjutant 17th (S) Battn. Lancs. Fusiliers

17th Service (1st S.E.L.) Battalion, Lancashire Fusiliers.

ADDENDUM TO OPERATION ORDER No.S/49.

1. Raiding Paty from each Coy. to be at WESTERN end of CHARING CROSS ROAD at 3.50 a.m.

"W"Coy. move off first, followed by "X" Coy., followed by "Y"Coy. & H.Q.

3. LIEUT. MACKERETH M.C. and 2/LT.BASKETT will lay out a tape for forming up, not leter than 3.45 a.m.

4. Party to be formed up ready to move by 4.15 a.m.

5. The whole party will advance at ZERO whether it is formed up or NOT.

6. Gaps will be cut in the wire by special parties for the returning raiders. - These gps will be distributed along the front and will be marked by a "Gooseberry" on the flank of each gap.

7. ZERO 4.25 a.m.

8. All watches will be synchronised at 7 p.m. on the 20th and again at 3.50 a.m. on the 21st.

9. "Y"Coy. will detail an Officer to be at Battn. H.Q. (X.22.c.central) from 4 a.m. onwards. Any information received here to be passed direct to Brigade H.Q. at KILDARE Dug-Outs.

10. "Z"Coy. will detail an Officer to be at Prisoner Collecting Station, WESTERN end CHARING CROSS ROAD from 4.15 a.m. onwards.

Issued at 1.30 p.m., 20/3/17.

(Signed) G.MACKERETH, Lieut.
A/Adjt., 17th (S) Bn., Lacashire Fusiliers.

Reference Addendum to Operation Order N.S/49, issued to-day, please make the following ame,dment:-

Para 6. Gaps will be marked by cotton wool balls of White material and NOT be Gooseberries.

20/3/17.

(Signed) G.MACKERETH, Lieut.
A/Adjt., 17th (S) Bn., Lacashire Fusiliers.

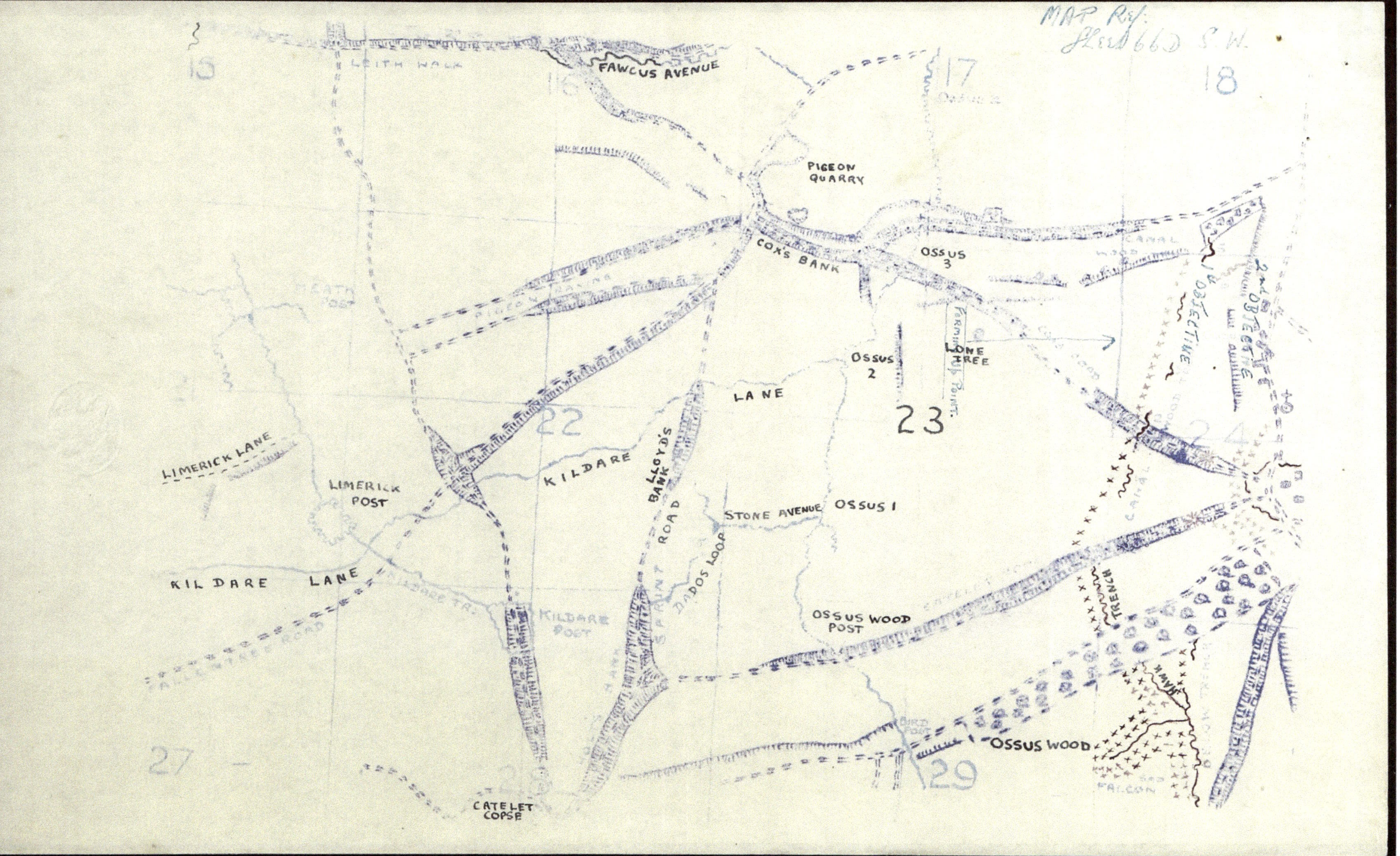
MAP Ref.
Sheet 66D S.W.
15
16
17
18
22
23
24
27
28
29
FAWCUS AVENUE
LEITH WALK
PIGEON QUARRY
COX'S BANK
OSSUS 3
OSSUS 2
OSSUS 1
LONE TREE
FORMING UP POINT.
1st OBJECTIVE
2nd OBJECTIVE
CANAL
LANE
LLOYD'S BANK
SPRINT ROAD
DADOS LOOP
STONE AVENUE
KILDARE
LIMERICK LANE
LIMERICK POST
KILDARE LANE
KILDARE POST
OSSUS WOOD POST
OSSUS WOOD
TRENCH
HAWK
FALCON
CATELET COPSE
BIRD

17th Service (1st S.E.L.) Battalion, Lancashire Fusiliers.

DAILY INTELLIGENCE SUMMARY
from 6 a.m. 20/8/17 to 6 a.m. 21/8/17.

OPERATIONS:-
All quiet up to midnight.

From midnight till 3.30 a.m. Patrolsin X.23.b. to keep "No-man's-land" clear. At 3.30 a.m. these Patrols formed up as a covering party to the raiding party which formed up at 4.10 a.m. on a NORTH & SOUTH line by the LONE TREE, X.23.b.3.5.

At 4.25 a.m.-Zero hour-, The raiding party advanced in three lines under cover of a heavy and accurate barrage. They reached the enemy wire 3 minutes before the time for the barrage to lift, and lay down in front of it.

At Zero plus 9 the advance was begun again but was immediately held up by 3 belts of wire, the first two of which were thick. A sharp fire and bomb fight took place whilst the party were getting through this wire and several casualties were sustained. In spite of this, the right party were able to force their way through, and after dealing with a few enemy in the first line, advanced on their second Objective - the bank at X.24.a.5.5. Here several prisoners were taken and four dug-outs bombed and blown in with Stokes Shells.

The time allotted for the Infantry at this bank had now expired and the signal was given to withdraw. Meanwhile the left party had also penetrated the wire, but the enemy were able to escape into CANAL WOOD. This party were unable to reach their 2nd Objective, owing to the time being up. They accordingly withdrew.

Flanking Parties covered both flanks, and the right flank party maintained touch with the 23RD MANCHESTER REGIMENT.

The raiders claim 11 prisoners, but this has not yet been checked.

Casualties estimated at:-
Officers:- 2 Wounded.
Other Ranks:- 2 Killed.
35 wounded.

HOSTILE ATTITUDE:-
Activity - Quiet up to the time of the raid.
The Germans in the front line put up a spirited resistance until the raiders had actually penetrated the wire.

Artillery - Some shelling - chiefly 77mm - in the morning about PIGEON QUARRY and Sprint Road.
At 8.30 p.m. the enemy put down a barrage on PIGEON QUARRY and about the LONE TREE in X.23.b. This ceased about 8-40 p.m.
Desultory shelling during the night.
During the raid the enemy's barrage was slow in coming down but very heavy during the return, especially about COX'S BANK and NORHT end of SPRINT ROAD.

Aviation:- 3 enemy aeroplanes over PIGEON QUARRY about 11 a.m. and four over whole front between 6 & 7 p.m.

HOSTILE DEFENCES:- The wire in front of CANAL WOOD TRENCHES consists of of three belts of wire - two strong apron wire about 15 feet deep, and one concertina wire.

21/8/17.

(Signed) F.J.F.Crook, Lt.Colonel.
Commanding 17th (S) Battn., Lancashire Fusiliers.

Vol 20

Confidential

# War Diary

of

17th Service (1st S.E.L.) Battalion, Lancashire Fusiliers

From:- 1st September 1917 —— To:- 30th September, 1917.

(Volume 20)

20 V
3 sheets

Instructions regarding War Diaries and Intelligence Summaries are contained in F. S. Regs., Part II. and the Staff Manual respectively. Title pages will be prepared in manuscript.

# WAR DIARY

~~or~~

~~INTELLIGENCE SUMMARY.~~

(Erase heading not required.)

Army Form C. 2118.

| Place | Date | Hour | Summary of Events and Information | Remarks and references to Appendices |
|---|---|---|---|---|
| | | | REF: MAPS:- SHEETS 57c S.E. & 62c. STRENGTH:- OFFS: 36 O.R. 632 | |
| TRENCHES | 1-5-9-17 | | The Battalion in the line in the Northern portion of the OSSUS Subsector. | |
| Do | 6-9-17 | | Battalion were relieved on night 6th/7th as follows:-<br>"W" Coy: by "Y" Coy: 17th Royal Scots. "Y" Coy: by "W" Coy: 17th West Yorks.<br>"X" Coy: " "Z" Coy: 17th West Yorks. "Z" Coy: " "X" Coy: 17th Royal Scots.<br>On relief Battalion mached to Camp at TEMPLEUX-LA-FOSSE. | |
| TEMPLEUX-LA-FOSSE | 8-10-9-17 | | Company in Parades & training of Specialists. | |
| Do | 11-9-17 | | The Battalion relieved the 16th Cheshires in the Right Subsector of the GILLEMONT Sector on the night of 11th/12th Dispositions:— "X" Coy:- CAT POST. "Y" & "W" Cos:- GILLEMONT FARM. "Z" Coy:- 1 Platoon - DOLEFUL POST. 3 Platoons - in Reserve in KEN LANE. | |
| TRENCHES. | 12-19-9-17 | | Nothing out of the ordinary trench warfare occurred. "Z" Coy relieved "W" Coy in the Front Line on the night of the 15th/16th. | |
| Do | 19-9-17 | | The Battalion were relieved by the 23rd Manchester Regt. on the night of the 19th/20th. Two Companies moved to LEMPIRE, where they were attached to the 180th Tunnelling Coy for work. Bn. Hd. Qrs. & the remaining two Companies moving to St EMILIE. | |
| St EMILIE. | 20/24-9-17 | | One of the Cos. at St EMILIE provided Working Parties, whilst the other practiced a proposed raid. | |
| GILLEMONT SECTR | 24-9-17 | | "Z" Coy raided ~~KNOLL~~ WILLOW TRENCH on the night of the 24th/25th. Strength of Raiding Party:- 1 Off & 46 O.R. The party reached their objective which had been evacuated by the enemy. A great coat belonging to the 184th Regt. was brought back. Casualties:- Lieut J.A. Wallis - Wounded. 1 O.R. Wounded (remained at Duty) | |

T2134. Wt. W708—776. 500000. 4/15. Sir J. C. & S.

Instructions regarding War Diaries and Intelligence Summaries are contained in F. S. Regs., Part II. and the Staff Manual respectively. Title pages will be prepared in manuscript.

# WAR DIARY

~~or~~

~~INTELLIGENCE SUMMARY.~~

*(Erase heading not required.)*

Army Form C. 2118.

SHEET II

| Place | Date | Hour | Summary of Events and Information | Remarks and references to Appendices |
|---|---|---|---|---|
| St. EMILIE. | 25:9:17 | | A small Working Party was provided for work on Cable trenches | |
| Do. | 26:9:17 | | The Battalion were relieved on the night of the 26th/27th & proceeded to camp at TEMPLEUX·LA·FOSSE | |
| TEMPLEUX·LA·FOSSE. | 27 & 28:9:17 | | Company Parades. "W" Coy. won the "Mills Vase" for rapid firing, 28:9:17. | |
| Do. | 29:9:17 | | The Battalion marched to PERONNE. Draft of 154 Other Ranks received. | |
| PERONNE. | 30:9:17 | | Further Draft of 110 Other Ranks received. | |
| | | | Total casualties for month:- 1 Officer - Wounded.<br>1 Other Rank - do: (at duty)<br>3 Other Ranks - Wounded<br>STRENGTH:- OFFS. 36. O.R. 961. | |

[illegible]

Lieut Colonel.

Commdg. 17th (S) Battn, Lancashire Fusiliers.

T2134. Wt. W708—776. 500000. 4/15. Sir J. C. & S.

4 104/35.

Vol 21

Confidential.

# War Diary

of

17th Service (1st S.E.L.) Battalion, Lancashire Fusiliers.

From:- 1st October, 1917. To:- 31st October, 1917.

(Volume 21.)

21. V.
9 sheets

Instructions regarding War Diaries and Intelligence Summaries are contained in F. S. Regs., Part II. and the Staff Manual respectively. Title pages will be prepared in manuscript.

# WAR DIARY
~~or~~
~~INTELLIGENCE SUMMARY.~~
*(Erase heading not required.)*

Army Form C. 2118.

17th Lancashire Fusiliers.
October 1917.

| Place | Date | Hour | Summary of Events and Information | Remarks and references to Appendices |
|---|---|---|---|---|
| | | | STRENGTH:- OFFS. 36. O.R. 961. | |
| PERONNE. | 1:10:17. | | Battalion resting at PERONNE. Advance parties sent to LATTRE ST. QUENTIN. Coy. parades for training. | |
| Do. | 2:10:17. | | Battalion entrained for AUBIGNY. | |
| AUBIGNY. | 3:10:17. | | Arrived AUBIGNY and marched to billets at LATTRE ST. QUENTIN | |
| LATTRE ST. QUENTIN: | 4:10:17. | | Training of Specialists, Bathing etc. | |
| Do. | 5:10:17. | | Company Training. | |
| Do. | 6:10:17. | | Y & Z Cos. fired on range at IZEL-LES-HAMEAU. Lecture by C.O. on "SHELL-HOLE WARFARE. | |
| Do. | 7:10:17. | | Church Parade. W & X Cos. on rifle range. | |
| Do. | 8:10:17. | | Companies practiced the attack. Sgts. Tomlinson & Johnston and Pte. Rowles, "Z" Coy. presented with M.M. ribands by ~~C.O.~~ ~~[illegible]~~ COL: F. AMBER late Commdg Officer 2nd Battn Lancs Fusiliers | |
| Do. | 9:10:17. | | Battalion practiced the attack | |
| Do. | 10:10:17. | | Battalion route march to IZEL-LES-HAMEAU. | |
| Do. | 11:10:17. | | Battalion practiced the attack. Conference of Officers - Subject:- Expected future operations. | |
| Do. | 12:10:17. | | Day spent in general cleaning up etc. Battalion marched to AUBIGNY STATION. | |
| Do. | 13:10:17. | | Battalion entrained at AUBIGNY for ESQUELBECQ. Marched to billets at ERINGHAM. | |
| ERINGHAM. | 14:10:17. | | Church Parade. | |

Instructions regarding War Diaries and Intelligence Summaries are contained in F. S. Regs., Part II. and the Staff Manual respectively. Title pages will be prepared in manuscript.

# WAR DIARY
~~or~~
~~INTELLIGENCE SUMMARY.~~
(*Erase heading not required.*)

Army Form C. 2118.

| Place | Date | Hour | Summary of Events and Information SHEET 2. | Remarks and references to Appendices |
|---|---|---|---|---|
| ERINGHAM. | 15:10:17. | | Battalion moved by train to PROVEN. Crossed Belgian Frontier at 1·45 pm. Camped near PROVEN for the night. | |
| PROVEN. | 16:10:17. | | Battalion moved by Light Railway to BOESINGHE and proceeded up the line and relieved the 2ND GRENADIER GUARDS in HOUTHULST FOREST SECTOR. | APPENDIX "A". |
| FRONT LINE. | 17:10:17. | | Held front line. Conditions extremely bad. | |
| Do. | 18:10:17. | | Battalion relieved in front line by 19TH D.L.I. CASUALTIES:- 2/LT. YOUNG J.D. WOUNDED (GAS SHELL). 2/LT. LEWIS H.N. KILLED. 8 O.R. WOUNDED | |
| CAMP. | 19:10:17. | | Battalion rested at "H" CAMP. | |
| CAMP. | 20:10:17. | | Battalion proceeded up the Line ready for an immediate attack. Details remained at DEWIPPE CAMP. | APPENDIX "B". |
| FRONT LINE. | 21:10:17. | | Battalion holding Line. W & X Cos. Front line. Y & Z Cos: behind in Shell-Holes. Battn. H.Q. moved at 5 pm from PASCALL FARM to EGYPT HOUSE. | |
| FRONT LINE. | 22:10:17. | | Battalion formed up for attack at 2 a.m. & went over the top at Zero hour - 5.35 am. see APPENDIX | |
| FRONT LINE. | 23:10:17. | | Battalion relieved at night by 17TH ROYAL SCOTS and proceeded to BABOON CAMP for the night. | |
| BABOON CAMP. | 24:10:17. | | Battalion entrained at 2 pm for DYKES CAMP. | |
| DYKES CAMP. | 25:10:17. | | Battalion rested & cleaned up. | |
| Do: | 26 & 27:10:17. | | Refitting etc. 2/LTS KEANE & WILLIAMS reported for duty. | |
| Do. | 28:10:17. | | Church Parade with 20TH LANCS FUSRS. Informal address by MAJ. GEN. G. McK. FRANKS, C.B., who congratulated Battn., Officers, N.C.O's & men & told COL. CROOK that he had a "damn fine Battalion". | |

T2134. Wt W708—776. 500000. 4/15. Sir J. C. & S.

Instructions regarding War Diaries and Intelligence Summaries are contained in F. S. Regs., Part II. and the Staff Manual respectively. Title pages will be prepared in manuscript.

# WAR DIARY

~~or~~

~~INTELLIGENCE SUMMARY.~~

*(Erase heading not required.)*

Army Form C. 2118.

| Place | Date | Hour | Summary of Events and Information — SHEET 3. | Remarks and references to Appendices |
|---|---|---|---|---|
| DYKES CAMP | 29:10:17. | | Training of Specialists. Companies constructing sandbag traverses round their huts as protection from Bombs. Companies had physical training under Bde. Instructor. CASUALTIES:- LIEUT. C.P. JOHNSTONE, 1 O.R. & 1 Horse wounded by Bomb dropped on Transport Lines. 2/LT. R.L. KEANE took over duties as Transport Officer. | |
| Do. | 30:10:17. | | Battalion moved forward to NEW BOESINGHE CAMP. | |
| NEW BOESINGHE CAMP. | 31:10:17. | | Working parties of 5 Offs. & 250 OR. supplied for work with R.E's. | |

TOTAL CASUALTIES:- STRENGTH:- OFFS: 24. OTHER RANKS:- 749.

| | OFFICERS. | OTHER RANKS. |
|---|---|---|
| KILLED:- | 4. | 32. |
| WOUNDED:- | 9 | 150. |
| MISSING:- | | 5. |

OFFICER CASUALTIES:

| KILLED. | WOUNDED. |
|---|---|
| 2/LT. LEWIS H.N. | CAPT. R.S. HEAPE M.C. |
| | " L. KITCHIN. |
| 2/LT. HAMILTON J.R. | LIEUT. H.G. LEAVER. |
| | " J. GOODIER. |
| 2/LT. CRANK H. | 2/LT. YOUNG J.D. (GAS SHELL). |
| | 2/LT. FORMAN P. |
| 2/LT. ALLIN H.A. | " ESSON A.C. (SINCE DIED). |
| | " SHEARSTON J.A. |
| | LIEUT. C.P. JOHNSTONE (H.L.I.) |

C. Lewely Major.
Commdg. 17th (S) Battn. Lancs. Fusiliers.

T2134. Wt. W708—776. 500000. 4/15. Sir J. C. & S.

APPENDIX "A"

17th Service (1st S.E.L.) Battalion, Lancashire Fusiliers.

## REPORT ON OPERATIONS 15th to 18th October, 1917.

On the 15th October 1917 the Battalion was moving up from ERINGHAM to the PROVEN Area and the Commanding Officer, together with other C.O's of the Brigade, went forward to reconnoitre the Sector of the Flanders front held by the Guards Division, with a view to the relief which took place on the night of the 16th/17th.

This Battalion relievd the 2nd Bn. GRENADIER GUARDS on the 5 Chemins sector.

The relief, an extraordinarily quickly and smoothly performed operation, was complete by 7.10 p.m. on the night of the 16th/17th.

The disposition of the Battalion was as follows:-
XXXX "X" Coy., "Z"Coy., & "W"Coy. from Right to Left on a 1000 frontage with their centre some 150 yds. N. of LES 5 CHEMINS Road junction; each Coy. with 1/2 Coy. in the Front Line, and 1/2 in Support. The "Front Line" consisted merely of a chain of shell-holes upon which a certain amount of work had been done, but which, even at their best, were half full of water. "Y"Coy. were disposed in Support about Egypt House. Battalion H.Q. were at VEE BEND, a partially detsroyed "Pill-Box" some 1200 yds. S.W. of EGYPT HOUSE.

Duckboard tracks led from BOESINGHE to VEE BEND. From that point to the Front Line was a sticky morass of muddy shell-holes with only tapes to show the routes to the forward lines.

This made the carrying up of rations, and the evacuation of wounded, an extraordinarily difficult operation. In spite, however, of the most inclement sonditions of wet and cold, accompanied at night by blank darkness, "Y"Coy. performed their allotted task with admirable pluck and endurance.

The morning of the 17th was notable, in as much as the Battalion was honoured by a visit from H.R.H. THE PRINCE OF WALES, acting as Staff Captain to the B.G.G.S., XIV Corps.

Throughout the next two days (17th & 18th Octr.) all positions were repeatedly and heavily shelled. Fortunately however, the casualties were light until the night of the relief, 18th/19th Oct., when the Battalion was relieved by the 19th D. L. I., Commanded by LT.COL. GREENWOOD. Relief was reported complete about 10 p.m., but the Companies experienced the greatest hardships in crossing the 1200 yds. to VEE BEND, which owing to a steady rain had now become a soggy mass of mud through which the men could move only with the greatest difficulty. A party of Stretcher Bearers carrying a wounded man down from "Y" Company took nearly 5½ hours to reach VEE BEND and arrived completely exhausted.

At about 11 p.m. the enemy commenced a violent gas-shell bombardment with "mustard gas"shell and all ranks were compelled to put on their Respirators. Even so, many cases of blisters and sores were reported - none of them, fortunately, serious.

The last of the Battalion arrived back in Camp near International Corner after daybreak on the morning of the 19th.

1:11:17.

Lieut. Colonel,
Commanding 17th (S) Battn., Lancs. Fusiliets.

War Diary

APPENDIX "B"

17th Service (1st S.E.L.) Battalion, Lancashire Fusiliers.

-----------

## REPORT ON OPERATIONS of OCTOBER 22nd 1917.

Battalion Commander:- LIEUT.COLONEL F.J.F.CROOK,D.S.O.

Company Commanders:- "W"Coy.- CAPT. R.S.HEAPE,M.C.
"X"Coy.- CAPT. L.KITCHIN.
"Y"Coy.- LIEUT. J.GOODIER.
"Z"Coy.- LIEUT. H.G.LEAVER.

-----------------------------

At 11.30 a.m. October 20th 1917 the Battalion moved out of Camp and marched to BOESINGHE here a halt was made for, dinners, issue of 2 days rations, stores, extra grenades, S.A.A., etc.

Operation Orders for the attack were issued during this halt, and at 4.0 p.m. the Battalion moved off via HUNTER STREET to the EGYPT HOUSE Sector of the Front Line.

There was considerable shelling on the way up and about 10 casualties were sustained before the Battalion got into position about LES 5 CHEMINS. Dispositions were as follows:-
"W" & "X" Companies from left to right on a frontage of 400 yards from the 5 CHEMINS - COLOMBO HOUSE Road in the Front Line and Support systems. "Y" Coy. in shell holes immediately N. of EGYPT HOUSE, and "Z" Coy. in shell holes S.W. of EGYPT HOUSE. Battn. H.Q. at PASCAL FARM.

Throughout daylight of the 21st October the Battalion lay quiet in its shell holes and avoided the attention of numerous enemy aeroplanes flying low over the Front Line.

During the night of 21/22 Oct. Battn. H.Q. moved up to EGYPT HOUSE and the Battalion formed up, ready for the assault, about 100 yards in front of the Front Line (i.e., 300 yards N. of LES 5 CHEMINS), and on a frontage of 400 yards with the Left resting on the 5 CHEMINS - COLOMBO HOUSE Road and in actual contact with the 15th CHESHIRE REGT. "X"Coy. on the Right were in contact with the 23rd MANCHESTER REGT., who were however, on a line rather South of that occupied by the Battalion. Capt. KITCHIN of "X" Coy. visited the Left Coy. Commander of the 18th LANCASHIRE FUSILIERS, who was to come up on his Right during the advance, and Capt. HEAPE ("W"Coy.) visited the CHESHIRES. Lieut. GOODIER of "Y"Coy. further detailed his No.1 Platoon as a contact platoon with the Brigade on our Left, and this Platoon acted accordingly during the advance.

The first Objective assigned to the 17th LANCASHIRE FUSILIERS was a line on the road running almost due EAST from MARECHAL FARM - always on a frontage of 400 yards.

The Battalion working with 2 Platoons per Company formed up in 4 waves:-
1st Wave:- 1 Platoon "W"Coy.,1 Platoon "X"Coy.- extended.
2nd Wave:- 1 Platoon "W"Coy.,1 Platoon "X"Coy.- in Sections.
3rd Wave:- "Y" Company in Sections.
4th Wave:- "Z" Company in Sections.

At Zero, 5.35 a.m. on the morning of the 22nd October 1917 the barrage opened and the Brigade advanced. At 6 a.m. the following message was received from Capt. HEAPE,M.C., Commanding "W"Coy:-

"Have captured COLOMBO HOUSE. - Best sport going - Right in our own Barrage."

and at 6.45 a.m. messages were received from Capt.HEAPE, Capt. KITCHIN (Comndg. "X"Coy.), and LIEUT. GOODIER (Comndg. "Y"Coy.), almost simultaneously stating that the final objectives had been reached and consolidation was in progress, "W" Coy. reporting in addition the capture of a Machine gun, which was brought down later by a runner. About 20 Prisoners were also brought in.

As "W"Coy. succeeded in keeping closer under the barrage than did the CHESHIRES on the Left, Capt. HEAPE was obliged to take COLOMBO HOUSE and MARECHAL FARM in his advance, as he dared not leave his flank exposed to these strong points. The CHESHIRES reached both these points as "W"Coy. men were leaving them and firm contact was established.

So far all was going well, but no messages at all had been received from the other Battalions of the Brigade, and then without warning Battn. H.Q. at EGYPT HOUSE became aware of a straggling crowd of men falling back on them from the direction of the YPRES-STADEN Railway. The Officers at H.Q. immediately turned out and stopping the rot, put the men - a mixture of Manchesters, and 16th Royal Scots from the Division on our Right - into a shell-hole line immediately covering EGYPT HOUSE. From what could be learnt from these men, it appeared that the left of the Right Division had for some reason or other failed to come up, and had consequently left uncovered the Right of the MANCHESTERS, who in their turn went wide and lost touch with the 18th LANCASHIRE FUSILIERS.

The position now began to look critical and Capt. F.L. WAINWRIGHT, M.C., attached to the 104th Brigade as Liaison Officer, went to Brigade to report what was known of the situation, and warnings were sent forward to the Front Line. At 8-30 a.m. reports began to come in from the advanced Companies of the 17th LANCASHIRE FUSILIERS indicating a certain uneasiness and that the situation on their immediate Right was unclear. "X"Coy. in front, and "Y"Coy. in Support both reported their Right flanks to be in the air. At the same time "X"Coy. reported that some of the 18th LANCASHIRE FUSILIERS had come up on their Left flank. Orders were at once sent forward to establish strong points on the Right flank of each line, and the fourth line, "Z"Coy., which had reached its objective and began work on the construction of a strong point at U.6.d.central as ordered, was now swung round half right to cover the exposed right rear flank.

Meanwhile the Brigade had ordered up two Companies from the reserve Battalion (20th LANCASHIRE FUSILIERS) to fill up the gap from ANGLE POINT to ADEN HOUSE, and to try and get touch with the Right Division on the Railway.

The two Companies moved up and were in position about midday. The remaining two Companies moved up later in the day.

All Companies of the 17th LANCASHIRE FUSILIERS were now well in on their new positions and in touch with the 15th CHESHIRES on their left, but with their right flank more or less in the air - although a certain number of the 18th LANCASHIRE FUSILIERS were now reforming on the right of the FRONT LINE. These were later swung back to form a defensive flank extending from the Front Line to Supports.

All this work was done under continual sniping and Machine Gun fire, and towards afternoon as the situation became clearer, the German Artillery began shelling the new positions.

At 4.15 p.m. a message was received from "Y" Coy. that the enemy were massing in the Wood on the right flank. Shortly afterwards confirmation was received from the other Companies. The Artillery was warned by 'phone, runner and Pigeon messages, and at once opened a counter preparation fire on the Wood.

At 4.31 p.m. the "S.O.S." was sent up from the Front Line and repeated at Battn. H.Q.

This "S.O.S." was fired owing to a counter-attack developing upon the CHESHIRES on the left flank. The CHESHIRES appear to have lost most of their Officers and about 4-45 p.m. began falling back onto COLOMBO HOUSE line. This rot was stopped by Capt. MEAPE and the "Y"Coy. Officers, of whom 2/Lt. CLARK was killed whilst running across to stop the retirement. About a score of the CHESHIRES were picked up and incorporated in "Y" Cos line, afterwards rejoining their Battalion when touch had been re-established at COLOMBO HOUSE. The leading Companies brought heavy Rifle and Lewis Gun fire to bear on the enemy, and the counter-attackers were also caught by the Artillery barrage which had now shut down in answer to the "S.O.S.". The enemy broke up under this combined fire and retired once more to the shelter of the forest.

Nevertheless the position was now extremely critical. "W" and "X" Cos. were holding a salient some 1000 yards deep and 300 yards wide with both their flanks in the air. Accordingly about 6 p.m. Capt. KITCHIN gave orders to fall back to the Support Line held by "Y" Coy.; "Y"Coy. to swing their left flank back and maintain touch with the CHESHIRES at COLOMBO HOUSE, and the Company of the 18th LANCASHIRE FUSILIERS to swing back and get touch with the 20th LANCASHIRE FUSILIERS who were now in the neighbourhood of the HUTS on the right flank. "Z"Coy. formed a strong point covering the right rear flank.

Consolidation was carried out on this line during the hours of darkness and rations, water and fresh S.A.A. were brought up over most difficult country and under exceptional difficulties by a special party of Headquarters men under the Transport Officer. The men also each received a ration of rum, the value of which can be understood when it is realised that they had lain all day in shell holes up to their waistes in water. There were still large numbers of wounded lying out as the supply of stretcher bearers was lamentably inadequate and continual sniping during daylight made the collection of the wounded exceedingly difficult. Advantage was taken of the darkness to bring in a number of these men.

Desultory shelling continued throughout the night, increasing at dawn to a heavy barrage fire. No counter-attack developed however, andthe second day dragged through without change in the dispositions.

At 4.30 p.m. however, the enemy put down a barrage on the Support Line and launched another counter-attack on the Left Brigade.

By the time this had been beaten off and the consequent shelling died down it was dark enough for the 17th ROYAL SCOTS, who had now come up, to proceed with the relief of the 17th and 18th LANCASHIRE FUSILIERS in the Front Line. The relief was completed without further incident by about Midnight.

Some of the men were so exhausted however by the frightful conditions of wet and cold, that they could scarcely be got out of the line, and it was not until 5 a.m. on the morning of the 24th that the whole of the Battalion was back in BARDON CAMP on the bank of the YSER CANAL.

The casualties during this operation were rather heavy, although not so heavy as the other Battalions of the Brigade who had failed to maintain their gains.

The 17th LANCASHIRE FUSILIERS lost 4 Officers Killed - (2/Lts. H.A.ALLIN, J.R.HAMILTON; H.CRANK, and H.H.LEWIS), and 8 Wounded. - 32 Other Ranks Killed, 142 wounded and 5 Missing.

Lieut. Colonel,

Commanding, 17th Ser. (1st S.E.L.) Bn., Lancashire Fusiliers.

31:10:17.

# SKETCH MAPS OF OPERATIONS
## HOUTHULST WOOD OCT 22/23rd 17.

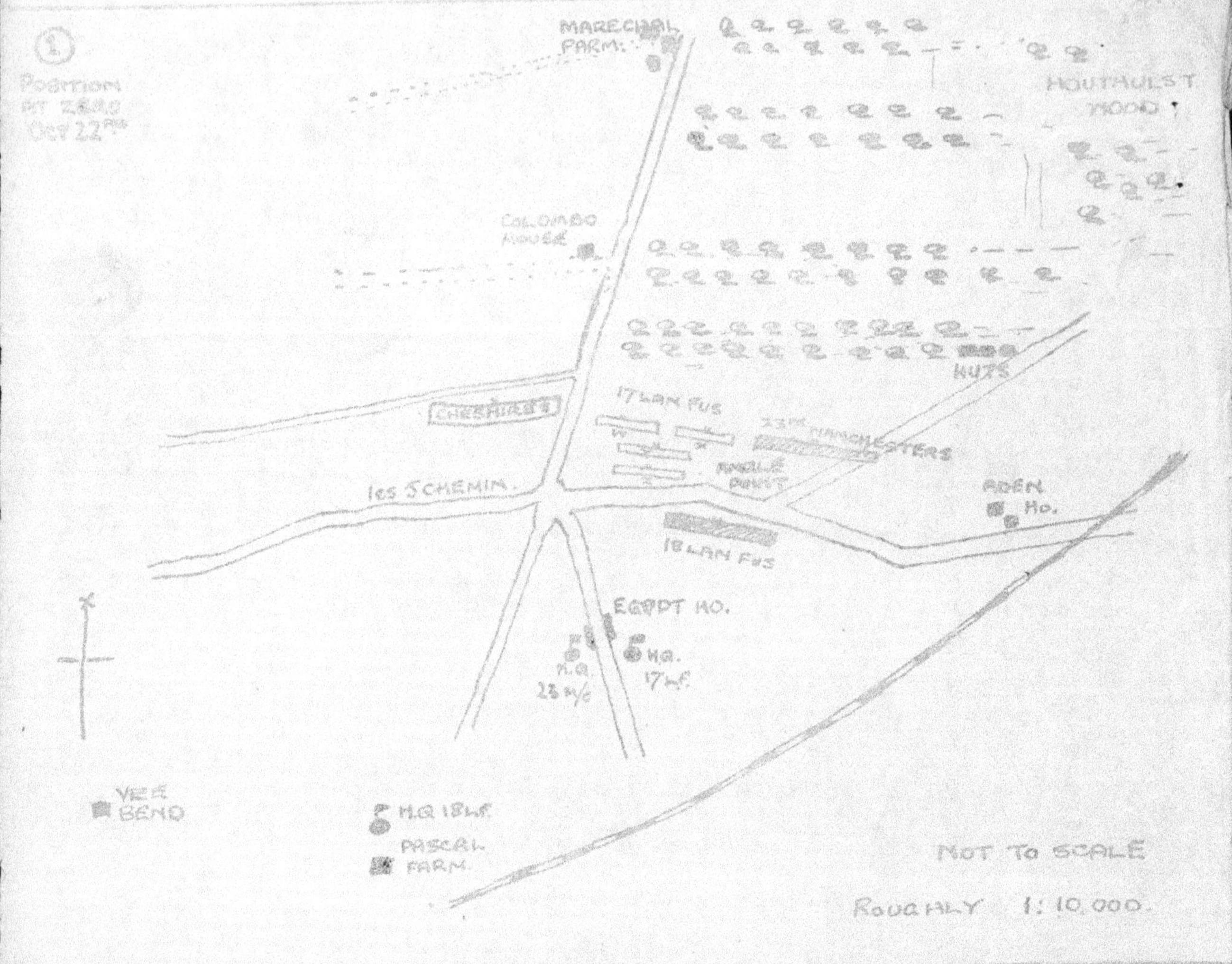


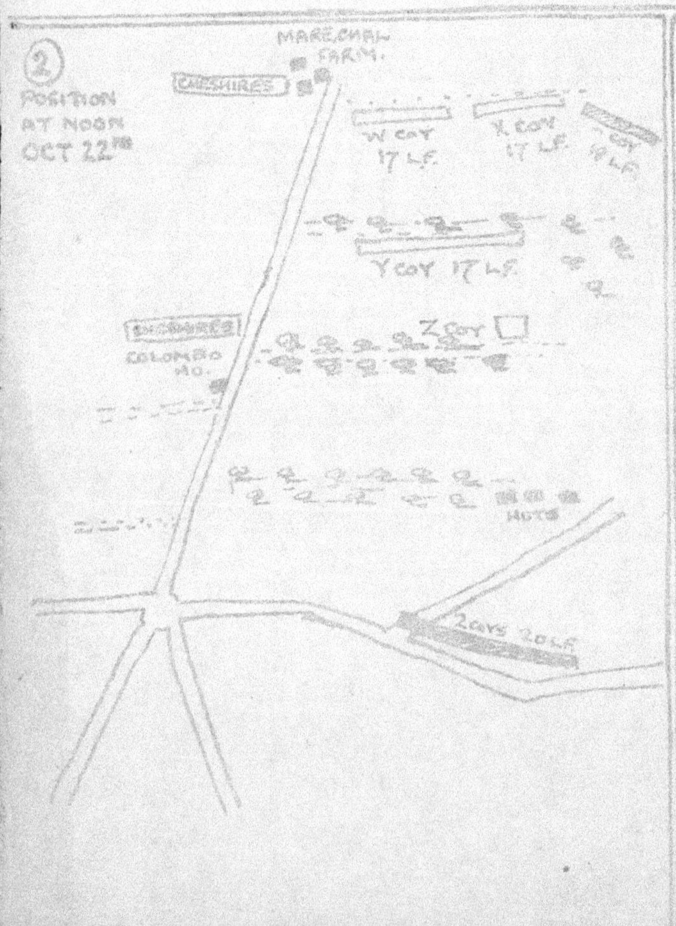


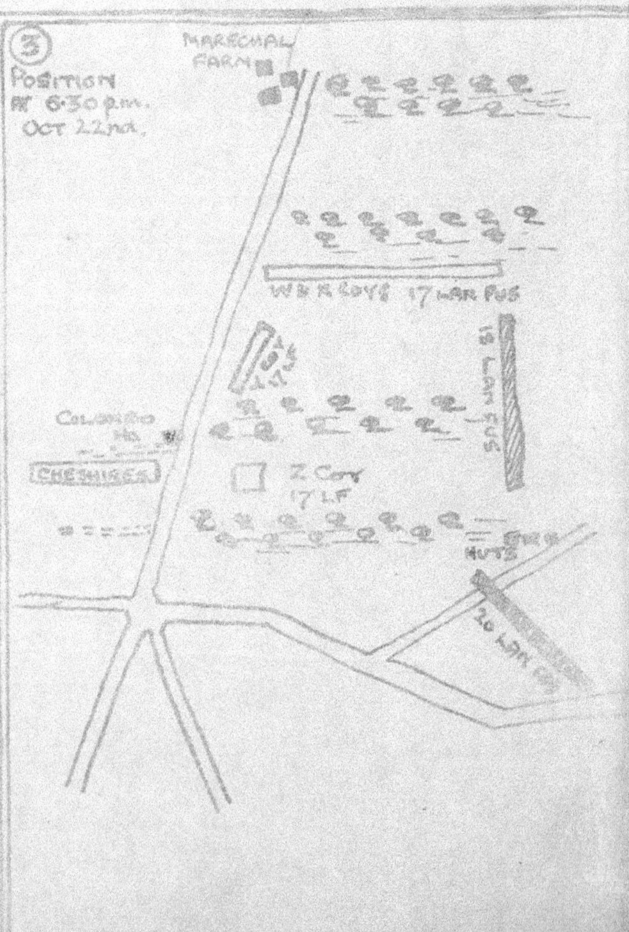

9

35

Vol 22

Confidential

# War Diary

of

17th Service (1st S.E.L.) Battalion, Lancashire Fusiliers

From:- 1st November, 1917. To:- 30th November, 1917.

(Volume 22)

22. V
3 sheets

Instructions regarding War Diaries and Intelligence Summaries are contained in F. S. Regs., Part II. and the Staff Manual respectively. Title pages will be prepared in manuscript.

# WAR DIARY

~~or~~

~~INTELLIGENCE SUMMARY.~~

(*Erase heading not required.*)

Army Form C. 2118.

| Place | Date | Hour | Summary of Events and Information | Remarks and references to Appendices |
|---|---|---|---|---|
| | | | SHEET 1. | |
| | | | STRENGTH:- OFF: 24. O.R. 749. | |
| CAMP. | 1-3.11.17 | | Battalion at NEW BOESINGHE CAMP. W. of the YSER CANAL 4 Offs & 250 O.R. working for R.E.'s daily | |
| Do. | 4.11.17 | | Battalion moved by train to PROVEN & encamped at PURBROOK; transport by road. | |
| PURBROOK. | 5.11.17 | | Cleaning up; improving Camp | |
| Do. | 6.11.17 | | Battalion moved by march route into billets at HERZEELE. | |
| HERZEELE. | 7-8.11.17 | | Company & Specialist training. | |
| Do. | 9.11.17. | | Battalion drill & ceremonial parade. 172 O.R.'s rejoined from Depot Battalion. | |
| Do. | 10.11.17 | | Company parades Inspection of transport by G.O.C. - very satisfactory! | |
| Do. | 11.11.17 | | Church Parade. | |
| Do. | 12.11.17 | | Company training of Specialists. | |
| Do. | 13.11.17 | | 8 Officers & Band entertained by French Army at BAMBECQUE. | |
| Do. | 14.11.17 | | Brigade Parade; medal ribands distributed by MAJ. GEN. G.M. FRANKS, C.B. | |
| | | | MILITARY MEDAL:- 14956 L/S. F. TETLOW, "Z" COY: 15518 PTE. WOODS T., "X" COY: 14718 PTE. L. BRIERS, "W" COY: 22160 PTE. O. WILLIAMS H.Q. RUNNER | |
| Do. | 15.11.17 | | Company Training. | |
| Do. | 16.11.17 | | Entertained Officers & Band of 233rd Regt. French Army at HERZEELE. | |
| Do. | 17.11.17 | | Battalion moved by train to ELVERDINGHE; Transport by road. H.Q., W & X Cos. to No. 4 SIEGE CAMP. Y & Z " No. 5 " " | |

T2134. Wt. W708—776. 500000. 4/15. Sir J. C. & S.

Instructions regarding War Diaries and Intelligence Summaries are contained in F. S. Regs., Part II. and the Staff Manual respectively. Title pages will be prepared in manuscript.

# WAR DIARY

or

~~INTELLIGENCE SUMMARY.~~

(Erase heading not required.)

Army Form C. 2118.

| Place | Date | Hour | Summary of Events and Information — SHEET 2. | Remarks and references to Appendices |
|---|---|---|---|---|
| SIEGE CAMP. | 18.11.17. | | Church Parade at Siege Camp. | |
| Do. | 19.11.17. | | Training of Specialists under Company arrangements. | |
| Do. | 20.11.17. | | Battalion moved into Bde. Reserve at CANAL BANK. Details remain at No. 1 Siege Camp. | |
| CANAL BANK. | 22.11.17. | | Battalion moved into the Line, right of POELCAPELLE – PADDEBEEK Sector & relieved 23rd Manchester Regt. Y & Z Cos. Front Line: X Coy. Support: W Coy. Reserve: Bn. HQ. Burns House. | |
| FRONT LINE. | 24.11.17. | | Battalion relieved in the Line by 15th CHESHIRES, & moved back by train to DIRTY BUCKET CAMP. | (A.30.a. – SHEET 28 N.W.) |
| CAMP. | 25.11.17. | | Church Parade. | |
| Do. | 26-30.11.17. | | Company Training, firing etc. – refitting. | |
| TOTAL CASUALTIES FOR MONTH:– | | | Other Ranks – Killed 3. (21.11.17.) Wounded 5 (22.11.17) — STRENGTH:– OFFS. 40 : O.R. 725. | |

[signature]
Lieut. Colonel
Commdg. 17th (S) Battn. Lancashire Fusiliers

Instructions regarding War Diaries and Intelligence Summaries are contained in F. S. Regs., Part II. and the Staff Manual respectively. Title pages will be prepared in manuscript.

# WAR DIARY
or
# INTELLIGENCE SUMMARY.
(*Erase heading not required.*)

17th (S) Bn.
LANCASHIRE FUSILIERS.
DECEMBER 1st – 31st 1917

Army Form C. 2118.

VII 23 SHEET 1.

| Place | Date | Hour | Summary of Events and Information | Remarks and references to Appendices |
|---|---|---|---|---|
| | | | STRENGTH – OFF. 39 O.R. – 725 | |
| CAMP | 1·12·17 | | Battalion at DIRTY BUCKET. Practice attack through wood. | |
| FRONT LINE | 2·3·12·17 | | Battalion proceeded by train to relieve 18th H.L.I. in the front line. (POELCAPELLE – PADDEBEEK SECTOR)<br>W & X coys FRONT LINE<br>Y COY. SUPPORT<br>Z " RESERVE<br>BATT. HQRS ALBERTA | |
| CANAL BANK | 4·5·12·17 | | Battalion relieved in the line by 23rd Manchester Regt. and moved into Reserve – CANAL BANK. | |
| CAMP. | 6·12·17 | | Battalion relieved in reserve and moved back to DIRTY BUCKET CAMP. | |
| DO. | 7·12·17 | | Company training | |
| CANAL. | 8·12·17 | | Battalion moved up to CANAL (MURAT CAMP) and were employed for 1 week on Corps Roads and supplying working parties for R.E's. | |
| WATOU | 15·12·17 | | Battalion relieved by 15th Cheshires and entrained for WATOU. Billeted in Farms, in HOUTKERQUE area. | |
| HOUTKERQUE AREA. | 16·12·17 | | Cleaning up and resting. | |
| DO. | 17-22·12·17 | | Company training, etc. | |
| DO. | 23·12·17 | | Church Parade. | |
| DO. | 24·12·17 | | Competition :- Firing for MILLS VASE. Won by W Coy. for 2nd time. | |
| DO. | 25·12·17 | | Christmas Day. Observed as holiday. | |

23. V
2 sheets

T2134. Wt. W708—776. 500000. 4/15. Sir J. C. & S.

Instructions regarding War Diaries and Intelligence Summaries are contained in F. S. Regs., Part II. and the Staff Manual respectively. Title pages will be prepared in manuscript.

# WAR DIARY
*or*
# INTELLIGENCE SUMMARY.
*(Erase heading not required.)*

Army Form C. 2118.

SHEET 2.

| Place | Date | Hour | Summary of Events and Information | Remarks and references to Appendices |
|---|---|---|---|---|
| HOUTKERQUE AREA. | 26.12.17. | | Company training. | |
| Do. | 27.12.17. | | Battalion Sports. | |
| Do. | 28.12.17. | | Company training. | |
| Do. | 29.12.17 | | Brigade Sports. Cross-Country race won by this Battalion. | |
| Do. | 30.12.17. | | Church Parade. | |
| Do. | 31.12.17. | | Company training. | |
| | | | TOTAL CASUALTIES FOR MONTH. Other Ranks. - Wounded 2. (3.12.17.) do. 1. (12.12.17.) STRENGTH- OFFS. - 40 O.RS. - 712. | |

17th (SERVICE) BATTN. 31 DEC 1917 LANC. FUS. & E. L.

[signature] Major.
Commdg. 17th (S) Bn. Lancashire Fusiliers.

T2134. Wt. W708—776. 500000. 4/15. Sir J. C. & S.

35

Army Form C. 2118.

17 Lanc Fus

Vol 24

Instructions regarding War Diaries and Intelligence Summaries are contained in F. S. Regs., Part II. and the Staff Manual respectively. Title pages will be prepared in manuscript.

# WAR DIARY
*or*
~~INTELLIGENCE SUMMARY~~.

*(Erase heading not required.)*

| Place | Date | Hour | Summary of Events and Information | Remarks and references to Appendices |
|---|---|---|---|---|
| HOUTKERQUE. | 1-2:1:18. | | Battn. at rest in HOUTKERQUE AREA. Company training. STRENGTH:- OFFS. 40. O.R. 712. | |
| Do. | 3-4:1:18. | | Divisional Sports. MILITARY CROSS – HON. LT. & QR. MR. T. KEAY, ~~M.C.~~ awarded the M.C. | |
| Do. | 5:1:18. | | Inspection of Transport by G.O.C. Division. Company & Specialists Training. | |
| Do. | 6:1:18. | | Voluntary Church Parades. | |
| Do. | 7:1:18. | | Battn. marched to & entrained at PROVEN, for ELVERDINGHE, & stayed the night at CANAL BANK. | |
| CANAL BANK. | 8:1:18. | | Relieved 7/4th LONDON REGT. in the LEFT POELCAPELLE SUB-SECTOR. Dispositions:- Z. W. Y. Cos:- FRONT LINE. X. Coy:- SUPPORT. BN. HDQRS:- SOUVENIR HOUSE. | |
| TRENCHES. | 10:1:18. | | Relieved in the Front Line by 23RD MANCHESTER REGT. & moved into SUPPORTS as follows:- X & W Cos:- EAGLE TRENCH. W & Z Cos:- CANDLE TRENCH. BN. H.Q. - PIG & WHISTLE. | |
| SUPPORTS. | 12:1:18. | | Battn. relieved 23RD MANCHESTERS in Front Line. DISPOSITIONS:- W. X. Y. Cos. - FRONT LINE. Z. Coy. - SUPPORT. BN. H.Q. - SOUVENIR HOUSE. | |
| TRENCHES. | 14:1:18 | | Relieved by 23RD MANCHESTERS & moved back to Supports:- W & Z - EAGLE TRENCH. X & Y - CANDLE TRENCH. BN. H.Q. PIG & WHISTLE. | |
| SUPPORTS. | 16:1:18. | | Battn. relieved in Supports by 15th. NOTTS. & DERBY REGT. & moved into Divnl. Support at TURCO CAMP. | |
| TURCO CAMP. | 17:1:18-23:1:18. | | Cleaning up etc. & improving camp. Day & night working parties found for 203RD & 205TH Field Coy. R.E. and 19TH NORTHUMBERLAND FUSRS. (Pioneer Battn.) Casualties:- O.R. - 1 killed 9 wounded 19:1:18. | |
| Do. | 24:1:18 | | Battn. relieved 15TH NOTTS. & DERBY in the Left POELCAPELLE Sub-sector. | |
| TRENCHES. | 26:1:18. | | Relieved by 23RD MANCHESTERS in the Front Line & moved into Supports:- Y & Z Cos:- EAGLE TRENCH. W & X " CANDLE TRENCH. BN. H.Q. PIG & WHISTLE. | |

A7092 Wt. W128.9/M1293 750,000. 1/17. D. D & L. Ltd. Forms/C2118/14.

24 V
2 sheets

Instructions regarding War Diaries and Intelligence Summaries are contained in F. S. Regs., Part II. and the Staff Manual respectively. Title pages will be prepared in manuscript.

# WAR DIARY

~~or~~

~~INTELLIGENCE SUMMARY.~~

(Erase heading not required.)

Army Form C. 2118.

| Place | Date | Hour | Summary of Events and Information SHEET 2. | Remarks and references to Appendices |
|---|---|---|---|---|
| SUPPORTS. | 28:1:18 | | Relieved 23RD MANCHESTER REGT. in the Front Line. | |
| TRENCHES. | 30:1:18. | | Battn. relieved by 23 Manchesters in Line & moved back into Supports as follows:- Y & Z Cos.- CANDLE TRENCH. W & X Cos.- EAGLE TRENCH. BN.H.Q.- PIG & WHISTLE. | |
| SUPPORTS. | 31:1:18. | | Battalion remained in Supports. STRENGTH:- OFFS. 41. O.R. 680. | |
| | | | Total Casualties for month of January:- Officers:- NIL. Other Ranks:- 11. | |

[signature] Lieut: Colonel.
Commanding 17th (S) Bn., Lancashire Fusiliers.

35

Vol 25

Confidential

War Diary

— of —

17th Service (1st. S. E. L.) Battalion, Lancashire Fusiliers

From: 1st February 1918 To:- 28th February 1918.

(Volume 25.)

25-V.

Instructions regarding War Diaries and Intelligence Summaries are contained in F. S. Regs., Part II. and the Staff Manual respectively. Title pages will be prepared in manuscript.

# WAR DIARY

*or*

~~INTELLIGENCE SUMMARY~~.

*(Erase heading not required.)*

Army Form C. 2118.

| Place | Date | Hour | Summary of Events and Information | Remarks and references to Appendices |
|---|---|---|---|---|
| TURCO CAMP | 1·2·18 | | Bn. relieved in supports and moved into Div. support at TURCO CAMP. STRENGTH:- OFFS 41 OR 680 | |
| do. | 2·2·18 | | Cleaning up etc. | |
| do. | 3·2·18 | | Church Parade | |
| do. | 4/8·2·18 | | Working Parties to R.E.s' and Tunnellers. | |
| IRISH FARM | 5·2·18 | | Z Coy moved to IRISH FARM to amalgamate with half-coy. Y Coy 20 L.F. | |
| TURCO CAMP | 6·2·18 | | W Coy and half Y Coy. 20 L.F. joined the Bn. at TURCO CAMP and were amalgamated. | |
| TRENCHES | 9·2·18 | | Bn. moved into Front line and relieved 15th Sherwood Foresters. 1 man killed and 7 men wounded on the way up. | |
| SUPPORT | 14·2·18 | | Bn. relieved by 1/9 D.L.I. and moved into support. | |
| CAMBRIDGE CAMP | 16·2·18 | | Relieved in support by 19th H.L.I. and moved into Div. support at CAMBRIDGE CAMP. | |
| do. | 17·2·18 | | Church Parade at BOESINGHE. | |
| do | 18/20·2·18 | | Working Parties 350 o.ranks. in Army line. | |
| do | 21·2·18 | | Bn. deloused at POPERINGHE Working Party 100 o.ranks with R.E.s'. | |

A7092 Wt. W128.9/M1293 750,000. 1/17. D. D & L. Ltd. Forms/C2118/14.

Army Form C. 2118.

# WAR DIARY
*or*
# INTELLIGENCE SUMMARY.
(*Erase heading not required.*)

Instructions regarding War Diaries and Intelligence Summaries are contained in F. S. Regs., Part II. and the Staff Manual respectively. Title pages will be prepared in manuscript.

| Place | Date | Hour | Summary of Events and Information | Remarks and references to Appendices |
|---|---|---|---|---|
| LARRY CAMP | 22.2.18 | | Working Party 350 ORanks. Bn. moved into LARRY CAMP in Div. Reserve. | |
| do. | 23.2.18 | | Working Party 60 ORanks with R.E.'s | |
| do. | 24.2.18 | | Church Parade. Working Party 54 ORanks at Transport Lines. | |
| do | 25.2.18 | | Working Party of 180 ORanks for various jobs. | |
| do. | 26.2.18 | | Working party of 170 ORanks for various jobs. | |
| do | 27.2.18 | | Working party 170 ORs. Lecture to officers by G.O.C. 104th Bde. | |
| ~~TRENCHES~~ do | 28.2.18 | | ~~Bn. moved into Front line and relieved 15 Cheshire Regt.~~ Working Party 170 ORS. Miscellaneous work. | |
| | | | Total casualties for month of February. 1 OR. KILLED. 1 OR. W + MISSING. 9 ORS. WOUNDED. STRENGTH OFFS 34 ORS. 642. | |

[illegible] Lieut
for Major. Commdg.
17th (S) Bn Lancs. Fusiliers

A7092 Wt. W128.9/M1293. 750,000. 1/17. D. D & L. Ltd. Forms/C2118/14.

104th Inf.Bde.
35th Div.

WAR DIARY

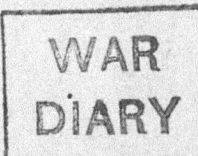

17th BATTN. THE LANCASHIRE FUSILIERS.

M A R C H

1 9 1 8

17th Lancs. Fusiliers

17 L F 1st–31st March 1918 Vol 26

104/35 Army Form C. 2118.

Instructions regarding War Diaries and Intelligence Summaries are contained in F. S. Regs., Part II. and the Staff Manual respectively. Title pages will be prepared in manuscript.

# WAR DIARY
or
~~INTELLIGENCE SUMMARY.~~
(Erase heading not required.)

MARCH 1918.

| Place | Date | Hour | Summary of Events and Information | Remarks and references to Appendices |
|---|---|---|---|---|
| LARRY CAMP | 1. | | Battalion moved by train to Forward Area and relieved 15th Cheshire Regt in the front line R. sub. sector. | |
| | | | Dispositions :– X Coy – Y Coy – Front Line; W Coy – Support; Z Coy – Reserve (counter attack); Battn Hqrs – SOUVENIR HO. | |
| | 3. | | Battalion relieved by 18th Lan. Fus. and moved into Brigade Support. X and Y Coys – LANGEMARCK; W " Z " – BEAR TRENCH & KOEKUIT; Battn Hqrs – PIG & WHISTLE | |
| | 5. | | Battalion relieved the 19th D.L.I. in the front line L sub sector. Dispositions Z Coy – W Coy – Front Line; Y Coy – Close Support; X Coy – Reserve; Batt. Hqrs. – PASCAL FARM. | |
| | 7. | 4.15 A.M. | 3 Officers & 50 other ranks of X Coy raided COLLIBRE HOUSE from the R. sub sector. No identification was established, as enemy got away, owing probably to our artillery barrage opening 4½ minutes too soon. Casualties – 3 other ranks slightly wounded. | |
| | 7/8 | | Battalion relieved by 17th Royal Scots, and moved back by road route to LARRY CAMP. Near IRON CROSS Battalion caught in enemy gas shell barrage (mustard and phosgene gas), and moved along in Box Respirators. 1 casualty (slight) | |
| LARRY CAMP. | 8 | | Day devoted to cleaning up of arms equipment etc. and resting. | |
| | 9 | | Training under company arrangements – local working parties – S. Box Respirators inspected by Brigade Gas N.C.O. | 26 V. 3 sheets |

A7092 Wt. W128 9/M1293 750,000. 1/17. D. D & L. Ltd. Forms/C2118/14.

Instructions regarding War Diaries and Intelligence Summaries are contained in F. S. Regs., Part II. and the Staff Manual respectively. Title pages will be prepared in manuscript.

# WAR DIARY
*or*
# INTELLIGENCE SUMMARY.
*(Erase heading not required.)*

Army Form C. 2118.

MARCH 1918 (Cont)

| Place | Date | Hour | Summary of Events and Information | Remarks and references to Appendices |
|---|---|---|---|---|
| LARRY CAMP | 10 | | 7 Officers and 350 O.R. on work in the Army Battle Zone | |
| | | 10 AM. | Major General G.M. FRANKS, C.B. distributed medal ribands, as under at WHITEMILL CAMP. 4 Officers and 70 O.R. on Parade.<br>Sergt Battle – CROIX-DE-GUERRE (French) Sergt Birmingham, CROIX DE GUERRE (Belgian)<br>Private Birtwell – D.C.M. Sergt Moat – "<br>Pte Taylor – M.M. | |
| | | 11 AM | Church of England Service at WHITEMILL CAMP | |
| | 11–15 | | Working parties of 7 Officers and 350 O.R. on work in the Army Battle Zone | |
| | 16. | | Company training | |
| | 17 | | Bathing | |
| | 18 | | Company training | |
| | 19 | | Nucleus of Battn visited Army Battle Zone of VIII Corps | |
| | 20 | | Brigade Stretcher Bearer Competition won by Battn team | |
| | ~~21~~ | | Transport Inspection & Competition | |
| | 21 | | Company Training | |
| | 22. | | Packing up and making preparations for move. | |
| | 23 | | Battalion, with Transport, proceed by road route to PESELHOEK and entrain at 7 am. W Coy entrained 3 hours earlier. Detrain at CORBIE and march to billets at VAUX. | |
| MARICOURT | 24 | | Battalion proceeded by motor lorries to near BRAY-sur-SOMME and thence by march route to MARICOURT, taking up front line battle positions | |
| | 25 | | Battalion took part in the ~~Battle of~~ ACTION at MARICOURT, and retired during the night to BRAY, via SUZANNE. | |
| BRAY | 26 | | Battalion took part in the ~~Battle of~~ action at BRAY, and after fighting for six hours retired to MORLANCOURT, later taking up battle position on the River ANCRE near BUIRE | |

A7092 Wt. W123 9/M1293 750,000. 1/17. D. D & L. Ltd. Forms/C2118/14.

Instructions regarding War Diaries and Intelligence Summaries are contained in F. S. Regs., Part II. and the Staff Manual respectively. Title pages will be prepared in manuscript.

# WAR DIARY
*or*
# INTELLIGENCE SUMMARY.
(*Erase heading not required.*)

Army Form C. 2118.

MARCH 1918 (Contd)

| Place | Date | Hour | Summary of Events and Information | Remarks and references to Appendices |
|---|---|---|---|---|
| BUIRE sur l'Ancre. | 27 | | Battalion entrench themselves & hold on to position. | |
| | 28 | | Battalion relieved by 15th Cheshire Regt and moved for one day into Support | |
| | 29. | | Battalion relieved the 18th HLI on the Railway Embankment at DERNENCOURT. Batt H.Q. in the front line in a Tank. | |
| | 30 | | Battalion relieved by the 12th and 13th Australian Brigades, and moved back into rest billets at LA HOUSSLYE. | |
| LAHOUSSLYE | 31. | | Day devoted to resting and general cleaning up. | |
| | | | CASUALTIES for month. – OFFICERS: Killed — ; Wounded 8 ; Missing 1 ; Died of Wounds 1 ; [Total] 10 | |
| | | | OTHER RANKS: Killed 6 ; Wounded 82 ; Missing 37 ; [Total] 125 | |

Major C.E. Jewels M.C. commanded the Batt. up to 28/3/18 inclusive.
Lt Col F.J.J. Cook D.S.O. from 29/31/3/18

[signature] Lt Col
Cdg 1/7 LAN. FUS.

A7092 Wt. W128.9/M1293 750,000. 1/17. D. D & L. Ltd. Forms/C2118/14.

Marching Out state
W. Company.

| | Off. | O.R. | Total |
|---|---|---|---|
| | 6 | 120 | 126 |
| Attached | 1. | 3. | 4. |
| | 7. | 123. | 130 |

22. 3. 18 Sharples RSM.

Marching Out state

| | Off. | O.R. | Total. |
|---|---|---|---|
| H.d Q.rs | 8. | 126 | 134. |
| X. | 7 | 127 | 134. |
| Y. | 6 | 135 | 141. |
| Z. | 6 | 136 | 142. |
| Total's | 27. | 524. | 551. |

22. 3. 18.

T Sharples R.S.M.

C.O. Japan

The reconnoitring patrol I sent out reports the following information.

'The quarry was held by the 19th D.L.I to the strength of about two dozen men. On their right on the crest are some posts of the 18th L.F. a distance of about 100 yards between their left post and the D.L.I.

The platoon of the D.L.I. have now retired to this side of the railway leaving the quarry now unoccupied.'

Please

J.H. Lakes Capt
O.C. W Coy

28/3/18.

W Coys  
X —  
Y —

The D.L.I. are withdrawing from the QUARRY – and it appears that the enemy are preparing to attack in accordance with previous information.

28/3/16

8 am.

Ainsworth Capt Adjt  
JAPAN

W Coy 17th Lancs Fus

Casualty Return from Noon 29.3.18 to Noon 30-3-18

| Regt No | Rank | Name | | Casualty | Date |
|---|---|---|---|---|---|
| 15311 | Pte | Doran | H | Wounded | 29 3 18 |
| 24456. | " | Kisbey | W | " | 29 3 18 |
| 11162 | " | Rigby | J | " | 29 3 18 |
| 32647 | Cpl | Braithwaite | A (X Coy) | " | 30 3 18 |
| 44315 | Pte | Leishman | D (X) Coy | " | 30. 3 18 |

[illegible] Capt
Commdg W Coy

30-3-18

17TH (SERVICE) BATT.N.
S.1.290.
1 MAY 1918
LANC. FUS.

Vol 27

104/35

(Confidential)

War Diary

of

17th Service (1st S.E.L.) Bn., Lancashire Fusiliers

From:- 1st April 1918. — To:- 30th April, 1918.

Volume 27

27.V.
3 sheets

Army Form C. 2118.

Instructions regarding War Diaries and Intelligence Summaries are contained in F. S. Regs., Part II. and the Staff Manual respectively. Title pages will be prepared in manuscript.

# WAR DIARY
or
# ~~INTELLIGENCE SUMMARY.~~

(Erase heading not required.)

| Place | Date | Hour | (SHEET 1) Summary of Events and Information | Remarks and references to Appendices |
|---|---|---|---|---|
| LA HOUSSOYE | 3/4/18 | | Battalion at LA HOUSSOYE in Billets, cleaning up, resting & re-fitting. STRENGTH - OFFS. 42 O.R. 783 | |
| Do | 4/4/18 | | Battalion moved by march route to BONNAY & halted for tea. When entering new billets orders were received to take up a position to defend VAUX-sur-SOMME on the Right flank of the Australian Corps. Dispositions - "Z" & "Y" Cos. - S. of River ANCRE; "X" Coy & Battn. Hdqrs. in VAUX; "W" Coy S. of River ANCRE, under orders of O.C. 18th Bn. Lan. Fus. | |
| | 5.6.7 & 8 | | CASUALTIES Officers - 1 Wounded. 1 Wounded (at duty). O. Ranks - 1 Killed. 4 Wounded | |
| TRENCHES | 8/4/18 | | Battalion relieved by 51st Australian Battn. & moved into billets at BONNAY. | |
| BONNAY. | 9/4/18 | | Battalion moved by march route & lorries to HEDAUVILLE, & went into billets. When marching through LA HOUSSOYE village was shelled. CASUALTIES - Officers - 1 Wounded; O. Ranks - 1 " 1 Wounded (at duty) | |
| HEDAUVILLE | 10/4/18 | | Battalion resting & cleaning up. | |
| Do | 11/4/18 | | Battalion "stood-to" at 3.30 am. & in the evening moved up into the line at AVELUY WOOD relieving 12th H.L.I. in the Left Divl. Sub Sector. Dispositions - "Z" "W" "X" Cos. - Front Line; "Y" Coy. - Close Support. Details left out of Line moved to Camp in valley between CONTAY & VARENNES. | |
| TRENCHES | 12/4/18 | | 2/Lt. E. C. Webster & 1 O.Rank Missing from Patrol on night 12th/13th. | |
| | 13/4/18 | | Draft of 145 O.Ranks joined details. "Z" Coy withdrawn from front line: W & X front line - Y & Z in Support. | |
| | 14/4/18 | | 100 O.Ranks (from Draft) to 205th Field Coy. R.E. as working party. | |
| | 15/4/18 | | "Z" Coy relieved "W" Coy in front line. | |
| | 17/4/18 | | Battn. relieved in front line by 15th SHERWOOD FORRESTERS. Casualties during tour - 1 Officer & 1 O.Rank - Missing. O.Ranks - 2 Killed 3 Wounded | |
| HEDAUVILLE | 18/4/18 | | Hdqrs., Y & Z Cos. in billets at HEDAUVILLE; W & X Cos. bivouaced in Valley E. of HEDAUVILLE. Afternoon - Cleaning up. | |
| Do | 19/4/18 | | W & X Cos. shelled & moved to Valley further N. towards HEDAUVILLE. HEDAUVILLE shelled by 105 mm Gun, at 6pm. Billets temporarily vacated. Casualties - 6 O.Ranks Wounded. Village again shelled at 10 pm. | |

A7092 Wt. W128 9/M1293 750,000. 1/17. D.D. & L. Ltd. Forms/C2118/14.

Instructions regarding War Diaries and Intelligence Summaries are contained in F. S. Regs., Part II. and the Staff Manual respectively. Title pages will be prepared in manuscript.

# WAR DIARY
~~or~~
# ~~INTELLIGENCE SUMMARY.~~

(Erase heading not required.)

Army Form C. 2118.

| Place | Date | Hour | (SHEET 2) Summary of Events and Information | Remarks and references to Appendices |
|---|---|---|---|---|
| HEDAUVILLE | 20/4/18 | | Village shelled at 3am & 7am. Casualties. 3 ORanks Wounded | |
| D° | 20/4/18 | | In evening Battn relieved 12th H.L.I. in front line - Right Battn of Divl Sub Sector. Dispositions - W & X Cos - Front Line; Z Coy - Close Support; Y Coy - Main Support. Bn H.Q. & Aid Post in BOUZINCOURT. | |
| TRENCHES. | 21/4/18 | | Battalion withdrawn from Front Line during attack by 38th, 35th & 17th Divisions at 7.30pm 22/4/18. W. & X Cos of this Battn moved forward at Zero & occupied Support & Reserve Lines. | |
| | 23/4/18 | | Battalion re-occupied Front Line - Y & Z Cos - Front line, W & X Cos in Support. Casualties during tour: ORanks:- 4 Killed. 8 Wounded | |
| | 26/4/18 | | Battalion relieved in Line by 4th N. STAFFS & moved to bivouacs in Bank at 1.5.a. (Sheet 57d.) near HEDAUVILLE | |
| BIVOUACS | 27 to 29/4/18. | | Resting & cleaning up | |
| D° | 30/4/18 | | Battalion relieved 12th H.L.I. in front line at AVELUY WOOD - L. Div. L. Sub Sector. Dispositions - W. & X Cos Front Line Y & Z Cos Support. CASUALTIES - 3 O.R. Wounded. STRENGTH - Offs 41, O.R. 893 | |
| | | | Total casualties for month of April. Officers - 2/LT. E.C. WEBSTER - MISSING. 2/LT H.E. TUPLING - WOUNDED. LIEUT. T.G. GRIBBLE - WOUNDED. 2/LT W.W. COTTON - WOUNDED (at duty). ORanks - Killed - 7. Wounded 28. Missing 1. Wounded (at duty) 1. | |
| | | | [signature] Major for Lieut Colonel Commdg 17th (S) Battn Lancashire Fusiliers. | |

A7092 Wt. W128.9/M1293 750,000. 1/17. D. D & L. Ltd. Forms/C2118/14.

cf. 45 35 Vol 28

(Confidential)

War Diary

of

17th Service (1st S.E.L.) Bn Lancashire Fusiliers

From:- 1st May 1918. —— To:- 30th May 1918

Volume 28

28. V

Army Form C. 2118.

Instructions regarding War Diaries and Intelligence Summaries are contained in F. S. Regs., Part II. and the Staff Manual respectively. Title pages will be prepared in manuscript.

# WAR DIARY
*or*
# INTELLIGENCE SUMMARY.
*(Erase heading not required.)*

| Place | Date | Hour | (SHEET 1) Summary of Events and Information | Remarks and references to Appendices |
|---|---|---|---|---|
| TRENCHES | 1/5/18 | | Battalion in the front line in AVELUY WOOD Left Division. Left sub. sector – usual trench warfare. Casualties 3 Other Ranks W/a. Strength OFFS 41 ORS. 893. | |
| do. | 2/5/18 | | Bn. relieved in the line by 38th Division and moved back into reserve in banks and trenches WEST of HEDAUVILLE. | |
| RESERVE | 3/5/18 | | Bn. moved back into Corps Reserve and occupied tents in TOUTENCOURT WOOD. | |
| TOUTENCOURT | 4/5/18 | | Cleaning up & resting. | |
| do. | 5/5/18 | | Training by Companies – shooting, platoons in attack etc. | |
| do | 6/5/18 | | Training by Companies. Afternoon – inspection by Corps Commander. 15 medal ribbands distributed to recipients of this Battalion. | |
| do | 7/5/18 | | Weather very bad – no training practicable. Lecture to officers & NCOs by GOC. 104 Bde | |
| do | 8/5/18 | | Company training | |
| do | 9/5/18 | | Mills Vase Competition, won by 'W' Coy. | |
| do | 10/5/18 | | Company Training | |
| do | 11/5/18 | | Brigade Church Parade | |
| do | 12/16/5/18 | | Company Training. | |
| do | 17/5/18 | | Divisional Rifle Meeting. Z Coy runners up in Chatti Competition. | |

A7092' Wt. W128/9/M1293 750,000. 1/17. D. D & L. Ltd. Forms/C2118/14.

Instructions regarding War Diaries and Intelligence Summaries are contained in F. S. Regs., Part II. and the Staff Manual respectively. Title pages will be prepared in manuscript.

# WAR DIARY
*or*
# INTELLIGENCE SUMMARY.
*(Erase heading not required.)*

Army Form C. 2118.

| Place | Date | Hour | (SHEET 2) Summary of Events and Information | Remarks and references to Appendices |
|---|---|---|---|---|
| TOUTENCOURT | 18.5.18 | | Company Training | |
| do | 19.5.18 | | Church Parade | |
| do | 20.5.18 | | Bn. moved by road to HEDAUVILLE and bivouaced until evening – then moved up to front line AVELUY WOOD Left subsector and relieved 15th Welsh Regt, 38th Division | |
| TRENCHES | 21.5.18 | | W Coy raided by the enemy – 1 man taken prisoner and 1 Lewis Gun lost. Casualties O.R. 2 W/A. " 2 M/A. | |
| do. | 22.5.18 | | W Coy raided 5 times by the enemy who were successfully driven off each time. Casualties 2 O.R. KILLED-IN-A. | |
| do | 23/25.5.18 | | Usual trench warfare Casualties OFFS 1 W/A O.Rs. 1 K/A. 4 W/A. | |
| do | 25.5.18 | | Bn. relieved by 12th H.L.I. and moved back to HEDAUVILLE (valley in V 5 a). Heavily gas[illegible] shelled during night. Casualties OFFS. 1 W/A O.R 13 W/A. | |
| RESERVES | 26.5.18 | | Heavily shelled with gas and H E shells. Casualties OFF. 3 W/A O.R K/A 5. W/A 5. W (gassed) 7. | |
| do. | 27.5.18 | | Moved to W of HEDAUVILLE (P33 c) Casualties OFF. 1 W/A. O.R 1 W/A. | |
| do | 28.5.18 | | Practiced attack. | |
| do. | 29.5.18 | | Bn. moved up to L. subsector AVELUY WOOD and relieved 12th H.L.I. Casualties O.R. 2 W/A. | |

Army Form C. 2118.

Instructions regarding War Diaries and Intelligence Summaries are contained in F. S. Regs., Part II. and the Staff Manual respectively. Title pages will be prepared in manuscript.

# WAR DIARY
*or*
# ~~INTELLIGENCE~~ SUMMARY.
*(Erase heading not required.)*

| Place | Date | Hour | Summary of Events and Information (SHEET 3.) | Remarks and references to Appendices |
|---|---|---|---|---|
| TRENCHES | 30.5.18 | | Prisoner of 179 Saxon Regt captured by "E" Company | |
| do. | 31.5.18 | | Usual trench warfare. | |
| | | | Strength OFFS. 38, O.RS. 857<br>Total casualties for month:-<br>Officers:- Capt J. L. Wainwright MC, Lt. H.G. Leaver MC, 2/Lt. J.C. Lucey, 2/Lt. G.H. Dransfield, 2/Lt. H.E. Benson, 2/Lt. H.R. Patrick } Wounded-in-Action.<br>2/Lt. J. Edwards, 2/Lt. W. Brookes } Wounded (at duty) 28.5.18.<br>Other Ranks:- Killed-in-Action - 5. Missing-in-Action - 2. Wounded-in-Action - 37 | |

[signature]
Lieut Colonel
Commdg 17th (S) Bn. Lancashire Fusiliers

A7092 Wt. W128 9/M1293 750,000. 1/17. D. D & L. Ltd. Forms/C2118/14.

35



Vol 29

(Confidential)

War Diary

of

17th Service (1st S.E.L.) Battalion, Lancashire Fusiliers.

From 1st June 1918 to 30th June 1918.

Volume 29

29. V.

Instructions regarding War Diaries and Intelligence Summaries are contained in F. S. Regs., Part II. and the Staff Manual respectively. Title pages will be prepared in manuscript.

# WAR DIARY
*or*
# INTELLIGENCE SUMMARY.
*(Erase heading not required.)*

Army Form C. 2118.

REF MAPS 57d SE & SW 1/20,000.

| Place | Date | Hour | Summary of Events and Information | Remarks and references to Appendices |
|---|---|---|---|---|
| | | | (SHEET 1.) STRENGTH:- OFFS:- 39 O.R:- 857 | |
| AVELUY WOOD | 1/6/18 | 3.25am | Y & Z Coys, in conjunction with 3 Coys of the 18th Lan Fus on the right, attacked the Western edge of AVELUY WOOD under cover of a barrage put down by Heavy & Field Artillery, & supported by Machine & Lewis Gun fire. | |
| | | 3.55am | Objective reported gained, but subsequently forced back to our original front line by heavy counter attacks. | |
| | | 5.5am | Both coys reported back. Heavy casualties inflicted on the enemy, many prisoners & several machine guns taken. Regiments identified - 139, 79, & 133 I.R. (24th (Saxon) Division). Casualties OFFRS: 5 W/A. 1 W/O. O.RKS 5 K/A. 64 W/A. 13 M/A. | |
| | | 9.0pm. | Batt relieved by 12th H.L.I. under Battle conditions and move back to Brigade reserve in P.33.d (W. of HEDAUVILLE.) | |
| HEDAUVILLE. | 2/6/18 | | Day devoted to cleaning up & resting. | |
| | 3/6/18 | | W, Y & Z Coys bathe at Hedauville Baths. | |
| | 4/6/18 | | Recommendations for awards forwarded to Bde. | |
| | | 8:0pm. | Operation Order No S.1. issued. | |
| | 5/6/18 | | HQ & X Coys bathe<br>Battn relieves the 15th Cheshires in the left BOUZINCOURT Sub Sector.<br>Coys. disposed:- X Coy. on the Left, W " Right, Y " in Support, Z " Reserve. Bn HQ - W.7.b.2.7. R.A.P. - W.7.c.9.4. | |
| | | 11.35pm | Relief reported complete. | |

A7092 Wt. W.128.9/M1293 750,000. 1/17. D. D & L. Ltd. Forms/C2118/14.

Instructions regarding War Diaries and Intelligence Summaries are contained in F. S. Regs., Part II. and the Staff Manual respectively. Title pages will be prepared in manuscript. (SHEET 2.)

# WAR DIARY
*or*
# INTELLIGENCE SUMMARY.
*(Erase heading not required.)*

Army Form C. 2118.

| Place | Date | Hour | Summary of Events and Information | Remarks and references to Appendices |
|---|---|---|---|---|
| TRENCHES. | 5/6/18 | | Casualties - 1 OR W/A. 1 OR W/D. | |
| | 6/6/18 | | Further recommendations for awards submitted | |
| | 8/6/18 | | 19 OR reinforcements received & posted to Coys. Casualties OFFS. 2 W/A. OR 1 K/A. 2 W/A. 1 W/D. | |
| | 9/6/18 | | Casualties - 1 OFF W/D. 2 OR W/A. | |
| | 9/10/6/18 | | Batt. relieved by 18 Lan. Fus & move to PURPLE SYSTEM. Bn HQ at V. 6. d. 9. 8. | |
| | | 11.45pm | Relief reported complete. | |
| | 10/6/18 | | 6 Offrs report for duty. 4 OR W/A. | |
| | 11/6/18 | | Claim for 3 German MGs, captured during the operations of the 1st inst, to be set aside for allotment as Trophies after the War, forwarded to Bde. | |
| | | | Draft of 61 OR reinforcements received & posted to Coys. | |
| | 12/13/6/18 | | Battn relieve 15th Cheshires in reserve<br>3½ Coys occupy BOUZINCOURT TRENCH. ½ Coy in SAUCHIEHALL RESERVE.<br>Bn HQ. - W. 7. c. 6. 2. | |
| | | 11.50pm | Relief reported complete. | |
| | 13/6/18 | | Draft of 118 OR received & posted to Coys. Casualties 1 OR W/A. 1 OR Died of natural causes | |
| | 13/14/6/18 | | Batt. relieve 18th Lan Fus in Left BOUZINCOURT Sub Sector. | |
| | | 11.55pm | Relief reported complete. | |
| | 14/6/18 | | 3 OR W/A. | |
| | 15/6/18 | | Capt & Adjt G. Mackereth M.C. & 2Lt A R Burr join for duty.<br>1 OR. D/W. 1 OR K/A. 9 OR W/A. | |
| | 16/6/18 | | Instructions for move to BEAUQUESNE received. 2 OR W/A. | |

A7092 Wt. W125.9/M1293 750,000. 1/17. D. D & L. Ltd. Forms/C2118/14.

Instructions regarding War Diaries and Intelligence Summaries are contained in F. S. Regs., Part II. and the Staff Manual respectively. Title pages will be prepared in manuscript. (SHEET 3)

# WAR DIARY

~~or~~

~~INTELLIGENCE SUMMARY.~~

(*Erase heading not required.*)

Army Form C. 2118.

| Place | Date JUNE. | Hour | Summary of Events and Information | Remarks and references to Appendices |
|---|---|---|---|---|
| | 17. | 1pm. | Billeting party of 2/Lieut J Galbraith & 5 OR proceed to BEAUQUESNE | |
| | | 3pm. | " " " 2/Lieut Lt. J. Baskett & 10 OR proceed to WARLOY | |
| | | 5pm. | Details and Transport move to BEAUQUESNE | |
| | 17/18 | | Batt. relieved in the line by 5th Bn Royal Berkshire Regt. (12th Division) & move to Billets at WARLOY. | |
| WARLOY | 18. | 4.30pm. | Battn. leave WARLOY and move by march route to BEAUQUESNE arriving in billets about 8.30 pm. Battn HQ - No 13 LA PLACE. | |
| BEAUQUESNE | 19 | | Day devoted to cleaning up & re-organization of platoons & sections. | |
| | | 3.30pm. | Lecture to Offrs by G.O.C. 104 Inf Bde | |
| | | 4pm. | Orders in case of Alarm whilst in G.H.Q. & Left Division Reserve, issued | |
| | 20 | | Major C.E. JEWELS, DSO, MC, leaves to assume command of the 18th Lan Fus. | |
| | | 8.10am. | Batt. parade & march to Range (H.26.c.). Address and inspection by Commanding Officer. Training in accordance with programme issued. | |
| | | | X Coy baths. | |
| | 21. | | Training. X Coy together with other detachments of the Bde under Major G.C. BELL, 19 DLI move to billets at ACHEUX for work under CRE. V Corps Troops | |
| | | | Lewis Guns brought up to the scale of 32 for the Battn. | |
| | | 5.30pm | Lecture by Major JAMES, RAF to Offrs & Senior N.C.Os on liaison between Infantry and RAF. | |
| | 22 | | Training. Coy baths &. Steam delousing of men's khaki clothing | |
| | | 3pm. | Demonstration of Gas drum projectors. | |
| | 23 | 10am | Church parade. Service on ground in N.15.b. | |
| | | | Mass for R.Cs in BEAUQUESNE CHURCH. | |

A7092 Wt. W128.9/M1293. 750,000. 1/17. D. D & L. Ltd. Forms/C2118/14.

Army Form C. 2118.

Instructions regarding War Diaries and Intelligence Summaries are contained in F. S. Regs., Part II. and the Staff Manual respectively. Title pages will be prepared in manuscript.

(SHEET 4)

# WAR DIARY
*or*
# INTELLIGENCE SUMMARY.
*(Erase heading not required.)*

| Place | Date JUNE | Hour | Summary of Events and Information | Remarks and references to Appendices |
|---|---|---|---|---|
| BEAUQUESNE. | 23. | | Staff Paymaster and Cox & Co notified of Capt Mackereth taking over duties of Imprest Holder A.R.1. | |
| | | 1.0pm | 15 OR i/c of CSM Forester leave for Third Army Rest Camp. | |
| | | 9.0pm | Operation Order No S2. (Practice) issued. – Counter Attack. | |
| | 24 | | Training | |
| | | 3.30pm | G.O.C. 104 Inf Bde presents Medal Ribands to the following:- | |
| | | | D.C.M: Pte Wm Sholicar. M.M: Cpl J. Lord. Pte B. Heyworth | |
| | | | Cpl F. Jones Pte A. Burges. | |
| | | | BAR to M.M: Pte B. Rees Cpl A. Carr. | |
| | | | Pte J. Diggle | |
| | 25. | | Training. | |
| | | | Band play at 104 Inf Bde HQ. Mess. | |
| | 26. | | Training | |
| | 27. | | Training. W Coy work on T head & D trench shelters, pattern laid down by 35th Div | |
| | | | Army Commander sees the Batt training on range H.26.c. | |
| | | | Demonstration of 'POPHAM' Signalling panel. 2/Lts W.H. Breasley & J. Halstead join. | |
| | 28 | | Training. | |
| | | | At the request of the Major General, Commanding 35th Div, Band play at 35th Div HQ Mess during the evening. | |
| | 29. | | BEAUQUESNE bombed by E.A. Fires break out & are dealt with by W Coy. 2/Lieut. R. Irvine M.C. & a party of 19 D.L.I. bring the French fire engine. After an 6 hours work the fires were got under. No assistance was given by the French civilians, who even hampered the work of our troops. | |
| | | | Casualties :- 2 OR Wounded. 1 OR W/D. | |

A7092 Wt. W128.9/M1293 750,000. 1/17. D. D & L. Ltd. Forms/C2118/14.

Army Form C. 2118.

# WAR DIARY
*or*
# INTELLIGENCE SUMMARY.
(*Erase heading not required.*)

Instructions regarding War Diaries and Intelligence Summaries are contained in F. S. Regs., Part II. and the Staff Manual respectively. Title pages will be prepared in manuscript. (SHEET 5)

| Place | Date JUNE | Hour | Summary of Events and Information | Remarks and references to Appendices |
|---|---|---|---|---|
| BEAUQUESNE | 29 | 11.15AM | Report on bombing forwarded to Bde. | |
| | | 12.30pm | Warning Order No J.581. issued - Preparations to be made for an early move. | |
| | | 6.0pm | Battle Surplus under Capt W.B.K.[illegible] M.C. move by march route to Divl Reception Camp TALMAS | |
| | | 7.45pm | Operation Order No 54. issued | |
| | | | 35th Divl Rifle Meeting held near ARQUEVES. - This Battalion's entries cancelled owing to forthcoming move. | |
| | 30 | 12.30pm | Final instructions for move issued. Office No J.611. | |
| | | 3.0pm | Y Coy, detailed as unloading party, leave billets & travel by the first train to the new area. Advance party of 2/Lt J. Gallbreath & 4 N.C.O.s move with Y Coy. | |
| | | | Canvas, targets, ablution bowls, etc handed over to Town Major. Certificate that billets had been left clean obtained. | |
| | | 4.30pm | First line Transport move to entraining station | |
| | | 6.15pm | Batt. leaves BEAUQUESNE & march to DOULLENS. On entering DOULLENS the Battn receives a hearty reception from the American troops. | |
| | | 10.22pm | Battn with Transport leave DOULLENS (North) Station for ST OMER. | |

Army Form C. 2118.

# WAR DIARY
*or*
# INTELLIGENCE SUMMARY.
*(Erase heading not required.)*

Instructions regarding War Diaries and Intelligence Summaries are contained in F. S. Regs., Part II. and the Staff Manual respectively. Title pages will be prepared in manuscript.

(SHEET 6)

| Place | Date | Hour | Summary of Events and Information | Remarks and references to Appendices |
|---|---|---|---|---|

CASUALTIES FOR MONTH.

OFFICERS:-

DIED OF WOUNDS:
2 Lieut J H Cartwright
2 Lieut J McGinerly

WOUNDED IN ACTION
Capt R S Hope, M.C.
Lieut J A Shearston
Lieut A G Coop.
2 Lieut H Langcaster
" E McGhey

WOUNDED AT DUTY.
Lieut A Powell
2/Lt R J Keane.

OTHER RANKS:-

KILLED IN ACTION. - 7.
DIED OF WOUNDS - 1.
DIED (NATURAL CAUSES) - 1.
MISSING. - 13.
WOUNDED - 90.
WOUNDED (AT DUTY) - 3.

STRENGTH - 30/5/18
OFFRS:- 40
O.RKS:- 956

G. Mackreth Captain
for Lieut Colonel
Comdg 17th (S) Bn Lancs Fusrs.

A7092 Wt. W128.9/M1293 750,000. 1/17. D. D & L. Ltd. Forms/C2118/14.

17th Service (1st S.E.L.) Battalion, Lancashire Fusiliers.

APPENDIX TO WAR DIARY FOR JUNE, 1918.

Extract from Battalion Orders dated 28th June, 1918.

490. AWARDS:

Under authority granted by His Majesty the King the Field Marshal Commanding-in-Chief has awarded decorations to the under-mentioned Officers and N.C.O. in recognition of their Gallantry and Devotion to duty during recent operations:-

The DISTINGUISHED SERVICE ORDER.

late 2/Lieut. P. McGIVENEY.

The MILITARY CROSS.

Lieut. (A/Capt.) C. S. ATKINSON.

The DISTINGUISHED CONDUCT MEDAL.

No. 3956 L/C. J. MULDOWNEY, M.M.

The Army, Corps, Divisional and Brigade Commanders and the Commanding Officer congratulate the recipients.

3333333333333333333333333333333333

Confidential

(C.L. 106.)

Vol 30

War Diary

– of the –

17th Service (1st S. E. L.) Batt. Lancashire Fusiliers

From 1st July 1918 – To 31st July 1918

Volume No. 30.

30. V.
5 sheets

30

Army Form C. 2118.

Instructions regarding War Diaries and Intelligence Summaries are contained in F. S. Regs., Part II. and the Staff Manual respectively. Title pages will be prepared in manuscript.

# WAR DIARY
*or*
# INTELLIGENCE SUMMARY.
*(Erase heading not required.)*

REF. MAPS:- HAZEBROUCK 5A 1/100,000
Sheet 27 & 28 1/40,000

| Place | Date | Hour | Summary of Events and Information STRENGTH:- OFFS - 40, ORS - 956 | Remarks and references to Appendices |
|---|---|---|---|---|
| ST OMER. | 1/7/18 | 8.00 a.m. | Battn detrain at ST OMER; and march to billets at ST MARTIN AU LAERT. Remainder of day spent in resting and cleaning up. | |
| BOIS DE BEAUVOORDE | 2/7/18 | 2.30 a.m. | Operation Order 85 issued re Move to ABEELE Area | |
| | | 8.30 a.m. | Dismounted personnel of Battn move to WATOU by motor bus; and march from there to BOIS DE BEAUVOORDE (K33 & 34); bivouac there. Transport move by road to near EBBLINGHEM. | |
| | 3/7/18 | | Transport rejoin dismounted personnel; lines near STEENVOORDE. Operation Order R1 issued. POPERINGHE Reserve Line reconnoitred. Advance parties sent to Front Line. | |
| | 4/7/18 | 3 p.m. | Battn move to relieve the 4/21st French Infantry Regiment in the front line in the LOCRE Sector. Halt for tea near R2 a (27) | |
| | | 9 p.m. | March resumed; French Guides picked up at LOYE Cross roads. L35 d 1.3 (27). | |
| | 5/7/18 | 1.30 a.m. | Relief completed without incident. Bn HQ. M17 c 15.35. (28). Casualties 1 OR - K/A, 3 OR - W/A | |
| | 6/7/18 7/7/18 | | Casualties in line 1 OR - K/A 3 OR - W/A. | |
| | 8/7/18 | | 1 OR - K/A O.O. R2 issued | |
| BOESCHEPE | 9/7/18 | 1 a.m. | Battn relieved in front line by 18 Lan Fus. Move back into reserve area near BOESCHEPE. | |

A7092 Wt. W128 9/M1293 750,000. 1/17. D. D & L. Ltd. Forms/C2118/14.

Instructions regarding War Diaries and Intelligence Summaries are contained in F. S. Regs., Part II. and the Staff Manual respectively. Title pages will be prepared in manuscript. (Sheet 2.)

# WAR DIARY
*or*
# INTELLIGENCE SUMMARY.
*(Erase heading not required.)*

Army Form C. 2118.

| Place | Date | Hour | Summary of Events and Information | Remarks and references to Appendices |
|---|---|---|---|---|
| BOESCHEPE | 10/7/18 | | Day spent in cleaning up, Rifle Inspection etc. | |
| | 11/7/18 | 9 pm | Z Coy move off to relieve reserve Coy of 19 D.L.I. (Support Battn). O. Order R.3 issued. | |
| | 12/7/18 | 9 pm | Battn (less Z Coy) move up to relieve 19 D.L.I. in support. Relief completed without incident by 12 mid. W and Y Coys forward. Z and X Coys support | |
| | 13/7/18 | | 2 O.R. - W/A | |
| | 16/7/18 | | 3 O.R. - W/A Battn relieve 19 D.L.I. in front line. Relief completed without incident by 11 30 pm. W and Z Coys front line; Y and X Coys in support | |
| | 17/7/18 | | 3 O.R. - K/A Very heavy bombardment from 2 am to 3.30 a.m. Shells of all calibres | |
| | 18/7/18 | | 2 O.R. - K/A 4 O.R. - W/A. | |
| | 19/7/18 | | LT T W M GREENWELL, Northd. Fus., attached - K/A. during heavy bombardment. 2 O.R. - K/A 2 O.R. - W/A 2/LT W H BREARLEY - wounded/A. 2/LT J GALBRAITH + party of 23 O.R. attached to R.E. for tunnelling. 2 LT W D STOTT and 6 O.R. of W Coy bomb an enemy post inflicting casualties. | |
| | 20/7/18 | | 1 O.R. - K/A. 5 O.R. - W/A. Battn relieved by 18 Bn Lancs Fus. Relief completed by 11 30 pm without incident. Battn move back into reserve billets near BOESCHEPE | |
| | 21/7/18 | | Day spent resting and cleaning up arms, equipment etc. | |

A7092 Wt. W128 9/M1293 750,000. 1/17. D. D & I. Ltd. Forms/C2118/14.

Instructions regarding War Diaries and Intelligence Summaries are contained in F. S. Regs., Part II. and the Staff Manual respectively. Title pages will be prepared in manuscript. (Sheet 3)

# WAR DIARY
*or*
# INTELLIGENCE SUMMARY.
*(Erase heading not required.)*

Army Form C. 2118.

| Place | Date | Hour | Summary of Events and Information | Remarks and references to Appendices |
|---|---|---|---|---|
| ROGSCHEPE | 22/7/18 23/7/18 | | Spent in cleaning up, Lewis Gun classes, Bathing etc. | |
| | 24/7/18 | | O O Q 6 issued. Battn. move into support, leaving at 9 p.m, and relieve 19 DLI. Y and Z Coys forward in intermediate line. W and Z in support. Two platoons of W Coy occupy the Redoubt line, freeing two platoons of the 19 DLI for a raid. Relief completed without incident. | |
| | 25/7/18 | | Work carried out wiring and improving line. | |
| | 26/7/18 | | do. | |
| | 27/7/18 | | 3 OR – K/A. 2 OR W/A. O O Q 7 issued. | |
| | 28/7/18 | 12.5 a.m. | 19 DLI carry out a raid capturing 2 prisoners and killing a no. of the enemy. Very little enemy retaliation. | |
| | | | Battn relieve 19 DLI in the line. X + Y Coys in front line, W and Z Coys in support in Redoubt Line. Two platoons of 18 Lan Fus under W Coys command and two platoons of W Coy under 2 Lts W.D STOTT and J WORTHINGTON remain in support Bn to practise for a raid on MINDEN DAY. Relief completed without incident by midnight. | |
| | 29/7/18. | | Wiring and strengthening of line carried on. 1 OR – K/A. Patrolling actively carried out. 2/Lt E E Benson W/A. | |
| | 30/7/18 | | O.O. re raid on MINDEN DAY issued. | |

A7092 Wt. W125 9/M1293 750,000. 1/17. D. D & L. Ltd. Forms/C2118/14.

Army Form C. 2118.

# WAR DIARY
*or*
# INTELLIGENCE SUMMARY.
*(Erase heading not required.)*

Instructions regarding War Diaries and Intelligence Summaries are contained in F. S. Regs., Part II. and the Staff Manual respectively. Title pages will be prepared in manuscript.

Sheet 4.

| Place | Date | Hour | Summary of Events and Information | Remarks and references to Appendices |
|---|---|---|---|---|
| | 31/7/18 | | 2 O R - W/A. | |
| | | | Casualties for month:- Offrs: K/A Lt. Twentymen (?) ; W/A —; M/A 2/Lt. W.H. Brearley (?), 2/Lt. C.C. Benson (?); D/W — | |
| | | | O.Rks: K/A 14; W/A 23 | |
| | | | Strength:- Offrs 39, O.Rks 918. | |
| | 3/8/18 | | G. Rackerth (?) Major for Lieut Colonel Commdg 14th (S) Batt. Lancashire Fusiliers. | |

A7092 Wt. W128 9/M1293 750,000. 1/17. D. D & I. Ltd. Forms/C2118/14.

35



(Confidential)

Vol 31

# War Diary

of

17th Service (1st S.E.L.) Battalion, Lancashire Fusiliers

1-8-18. to 31-8-18.

Volume 31.

31.V.
4 sheets

Army Form C. 2118.

Instructions regarding War Diaries and Intelligence Summaries are contained in F. S. Regs., Part II. and the Staff Manual respectively. Title pages will be prepared in manuscript.

# WAR DIARY
*or*
# INTELLIGENCE SUMMARY.
*(Erase heading not required.)*

REF MAPS Sheets 27 and 28 1/40,000.

STRENGTH OFFS 37 ORS [illegible]

| Place | Date | Hour | Summary of Events and Information | Remarks and references to Appendices |
|---|---|---|---|---|
| LOCRE | 1/8/18 | | Silent raid carried out by 2nd Lieuts J. Worthington and D.W. Scott, with 2 Pls ~~two~~ ~~[illegible]~~ of W Company. 2nd Lieut Scott reached his objective and assaulted enemy post. One man was [illegible], remainder fled. On a strong enemy counterattack being launched, our party was forced to withdraw. 2nd Lieut Worthington while preparing to assault his objective, was discovered and forced to withdraw. | |
| | | | Operation Order R.8. for relief by 27th Canadian Battn issued. | |
| | 2/8/18 | | Battn relieved by 27th Canadian Battn in front line, and moved into reserve billets at BOESCHEPE. | |
| | 3/8/18 | | "Minden Day" celebrated. | |
| | 4/8/18 | | Battn move into support, taking over from 18th Lan. Fus. Casualties 2 OR K/a 2 OR W/a Working, carrying and wiring parties. | |
| | 5/8/18 | | Casualties 1 OR K/a 1 OR SIW. As day before, working, carrying and wiring parties. | |
| | 6. | | Working, carrying and wiring parties. | |
| | 7. | | Casualties 1 OR K/a, 4 OR W/a | |
| | | | OPERATION ORDER R.11. for relief by 7th Royal Irish Regt issued. | |
| | | | Working parties. | |
| | 8. | | Battn relieved in support by 7th Royal Irish Regt (30th Div) and move to rest billets between BOESCHEPE and GODEWAERSVELDE. | |
| | 9. | 4.30pm | Battn march to billets near CASSEL, via GODEWAERSVELDE and STEENVOORDE. | |
| | 10. | | Spent in cleaning up. | |
| | 11. | | Divine Services. Lieut Col F. J. F. Cook D.S.O addressed the Officers and men of the Battn prior to leaving to assume command of a Battn in England. | |

A7092 Wt. W128.9/M1293. 750,000. 1/17. D. D & L. Ltd. Forms/C2118/14.

Instructions regarding War Diaries and Intelligence Summaries are contained in F. S. Regs., Part II. and the Staff Manual respectively. Title pages will be prepared in manuscript.

# WAR DIARY
*or*
# INTELLIGENCE SUMMARY.
*(Erase heading not required.)*

Army Form C. 2118.

STRENGTH 46 OFFS
915 ORS

| Place | Date | Hour | Summary of Events and Information | Remarks and references to Appendices |
|---|---|---|---|---|
| | 11/8/18 | | Major G. Mackereth M.C. (second in command) assumes command of the Battn. | [illegible] |
| | 12/8/18 | | Training from this date carried out by Platoons, according to the general lines laid down by Inspector General of Training. Operation Order R12 issued. | [illegible] |
| | 13/8/18 to 17/8/18 | | Training as outlined in B.O's. By platoons. Conference of Officers of Batt to discuss training. | [illegible] |
| | | | Capt S. A. Bull, R.A.M.C. M.O. in charge, awarded the Military Cross. | |
| | | | Operation Order R13 issued for move to LOTTINGHEN. | [illegible] |
| | 18/8/18 | 2pm. | Battn leaves CASSEL for Musketry Training at LOTTINGHEN. LIEUT H.C. Leavenworth joins Battn. | [illegible] |
| | 19/8/18 to 22/8/18 | | Musketry Training as per Battn Orders. | [illegible] |
| | | | Platoon Competitions. Musketry Competition winners. No 2 Platoon. Lewis Gun Competition winners. No 16 Platoon. | [illegible] |
| | 23/8/18. | | Operation Order R.R4. issued for return to CASSEL. | [illegible] |
| | 24/8/18 | | Battn leaves LOTTINGHEN for CASSEL. | [illegible] |
| | 25/8/18. | | Training as per B.O's resumed. By platoons. | [illegible] |
| | 26/8/18 to 29/8/18 | | Training continued | [illegible] |
| | | | Operation Order No R15 issued re move to 27/Q.2.C.6.4 (South of STEENVOORDE) | [illegible] |
| | 30/8/18 | | Training and preparations for move. | |
| | | 3.30pm | Move cancelled. | |
| | 31/8/18. | | Training | |

A7092 Wt. W128.9/M1293 750,000. 1/17. D. D & L. Ltd. Forms/C2118/14.

Instructions regarding War Diaries and Intelligence Summaries are contained in F. S. Regs., Part II. and the Staff Manual respectively. Title pages will be prepared in manuscript.

# WAR DIARY
*or*
# INTELLIGENCE SUMMARY.
*(Erase heading not required.)*

Army Form C. 2118.

| Place | Date | Hour | Summary of Events and Information | Remarks and references to Appendices |
|---|---|---|---|---|
| | | | Casualties for month – Officers K/ | |
| | | | K/A W/A M/A D/W | |
| | | | ORks 4 6 | |
| | | | S/W 1 | |
| | | | Strength Offrs 46. | |
| | | | ORks 915. | |
| | | | [illegible signature] | |
| | | | Lieut Colonel | |
| | | | Commanding | |
| | | | 17th (S) Bn Lancashire Fusiliers | |

A7092 Wt. W128 9/M1293 750,000. 1/17. D. D & I. Ltd. Forms/C2118/14.

35



(Confidential)

104/35

VR 32

# WAR DIARY

OF

The 17th Service (1st S.E.L.) Battalion,
The Lancashire Fusiliers

From 1.9.18 To 30.9.18.

Volume No 32.

32.V.
12 sheets

Instructions regarding War Diaries and Intelligence Summaries are contained in F. S. Regs., Part II. and the Staff Manual respectively. Title pages will be prepared in manuscript.

# WAR DIARY
*or*
# INTELLIGENCE SUMMARY.

SEPTEMBER, 1918. *(Erase heading not required.)*

Army Form C. 2118.

Ref. Maps. Sheets 27 & 28. [illegible]

| Place | Date | Hour | Summary of Events and Information | Remarks and references to Appendices |
|---|---|---|---|---|
| | | | Strength 1918 { Offrs: 45. O.Rks. 918. | |
| CASSEL | 1. | | Church Parades held. Batt. prepares to move to HERZEELE. | |
| | 2. | | Batt. moved by road to HERZEELE via the CASSEL – HERZEELE main road | |
| HERZEELE | 3 & 4 | | Days spent in Platoon Training. | |
| | 5. | | Batt. moved to ERIE CAMP H.11.a. east of POPERINGHE marching to CROIX ROUGE, entraining there on the light railway and proceeding by rail as far as RED FARM on [illegible] POPERINGHE – VLAMERTINGHE Road. Billets were taken over at ERIE CAMP from the 120th Regt. 30th (AMERICAN) Division | |
| ERIE CAMP | 6 | | Day spent in training [illegible] Baths | |
| | 7 | | Training [illegible] Operation Order for relief of 15th [illegible] received | |
| FRONT LINE | 8. | | Batt. relieved 15th [illegible] in front line [illegible] CANAL SECTOR south of YPRES. Batt. HQ [illegible] Coy. left [illegible] right front line [illegible] Coy. [illegible] | |
| | 9. | 5 am | Two strong patrols, each consisting of 1 officer [illegible] made [illegible] to secure identification but [illegible] Casualties [illegible] OR. Wounded [illegible] Missing [illegible] | |
| | 10 | | Patrols [illegible] attempted to obtain identification but [illegible] M.G. fire directed from [illegible] BANK [illegible] J. EDWARDS [illegible] Coy. [illegible] | |
| | 11 | | [illegible] LA CHAPELLE. Three patrols went out. [illegible] J. COOKE [illegible] Coy. reached BLAUWE POORT Farm I.27.b.6.4 and threw bombs into it. Casualties – 2 O.R. W.P. | |

A7092 Wt. W128 9/M1293 750,000. 1/17. D. D & L. Ltd. Forms/C2118/14.

Instructions regarding War Diaries and Intelligence Summaries are contained in F. S. Regs., Part II. and the Staff Manual respectively. Title pages will be prepared in manuscript.

# WAR DIARY
*or*
# INTELLIGENCE SUMMARY.
*(Erase heading not required.)*

Army Form C. 2118.

| Place | Date Sept. | Hour | Summary of Events and Information | Remarks and references to Appendices |
|---|---|---|---|---|
| FRONT LINE | 12. | | Operation Order for relief by 19 D.L.I. issued. | |
| | | 10.30 pm. | Relief reported complete without incident | |
| | | | A/Lt. Col. T. JONES, M.C., D.L.I. joined to command the Batt. A/Lt. Col. G. MACKERETH, M.C. resumes second in Command of Batt. | |
| BDE. RES. | 13 | | Batt. in relief moved back to Bde Reserve. Bn. HQ at ROAD CAMP. Z Coy at BELGIAN CHATEAU. X Coy at SQUARE KEEP. Y & W Coys at DINGO FARM (near H. 16. 17 + 23) | |
| | | | Working parties found for work on G.H.Q. line & front line under R.E. Lewis Gun & Musketry training under Coy arrangements. | |
| | 14. | | Working parties and training | |
| | 15. | | do do [illegible] for [illegible] | |
| | 16. | | Batt. relieved during afternoon by 17th H.L.I. and moved back to Reserve Bde. area. Bn. HQ at SKIE FARM. | |
| | 17. | | Day spent in cleaning up [illegible] etc. Scheme of Batt. in pursuit practised. | |
| | 18. | | Scheme of Batt. in pursuit & marching [illegible] practised. | |
| | 19 + 20 | | Scheme of "pursuit" practised. | |
| | 21. | | do do [illegible] Corps Comdr. | |
| | 22. | | Preparing for the line. | |
| | | 6 pm. | Batt. moved to line, relieving part of the 1st Royal [illegible] & part of the 18 H.L.I. making an alteration in the [illegible] of the [illegible] Sub Sector. Relief complete by 11. 30 am. 23/9/18. | |

A7092 Wt. W128 9/M1293 750,000. 1/17. D. D & L. Ltd. Forms/C2118/14.

Army Form C. 2118.

Instructions regarding War Diaries and Intelligence Summaries are contained in F. S. Regs., Part II. and the Staff Manual respectively. Title pages will be prepared in manuscript.

# WAR DIARY
*or*
# INTELLIGENCE SUMMARY.
*(Erase heading not required.)*

| Place | Date | Hour | Summary of Events and Information | Remarks and references to Appendices |
|---|---|---|---|---|
| | 22. | | Batt. H.Q. at SWAN CHATEAU, I.19.c. X Coy Right Front Line, Z Coy Left Front Line; Y Coy Support in G.H.Q. Line; W Coy in Reserve around SWAN CHATEAU. | |
| | 23. | | Assembly positions reconnoitred in view of proposed attack. Jumping off positions for the other two Battns of the Bde. taped out by Major MACKERETH M.C. Casualties – 2 OR. K/A. 1 OR. W/A. 1 OR W/A (at duty) | |
| | 24. | | Operation Order for relief of Batt. partly by [illegible] & partly by 10th [illegible] issued. Casualty. 1 OR K/A. | |
| | 25 | 12.30 am | Relief completed, & Batt. moved back to Bde Reserve around VANCOUVER FARM in H.8 & 14. Day spent in cleaning up, making up deficiencies [illegible]. Bde Operation Order for attack on VERBRANDENMOLEN – STIRLING CASTLE RIDGE received. | |
| | 26. | | Day spent in preparations for coming attack. | |
| | 27 | 2 pm | Further Orders [illegible] for Attack. (App attached). | |
| | | 9.30 pm | Batt. moved into line to take up Assembly position at I.21.c.6.2 for attack. Positions reached without incident except for heavy enemy gas shelling. Casualties – 1 OR K/A 2 OR W/A. | |
| | 28 | 5.30 am | Attack on VERBRANDENMOLEN – STIRLING CASTLE RIDGE commenced. The artillery barrage was excellent & the attacking Battns of the Bde – 18th Lan. Fus & 19 D.L.I. – easily reached their objective, the KLEIN ZILLEBEKE LINE. | |
| | | 7.30 am | Orders received to move from Assembly positions at 8 am & pursue the enemy beyond the KLEIN ZILLEBEKE LINE as far as ZANDVOORDE in P.3. | |

A7092 Wt. W128.9/M1293 750,000. 1/17. D. D & I. Ltd. Forms/C2118/14.

Instructions regarding War Diaries and Intelligence Summaries are contained in F. S. Regs., Part II. and the Staff Manual respectively. Title pages will be prepared in manuscript.

# WAR DIARY
*or*
# INTELLIGENCE SUMMARY.
(*Erase heading not required.*)

Army Form C. 2118.

| Place | Date Sept. | Hour Sept. | Summary of Events and Information | Remarks and references to Appendices |
|---|---|---|---|---|
| | 28. | 8.am. | Batt. moved off passing through a very heavy barrage about the railway in I 21 d + I 22 c by HILL 60 to KLEIN ZILLEBEKE. Only a few casualties were sustained in passing through the barrage. Z Coy led followed by X, Y, HQ + W. | |
| | | 9.40am | KLEIN ZILLEBEKE, I.36.c and the positions taken there by the 18 [illegible] were passed, and the Batt. moved on in "attack" formation, ("Z" Coy at the head of the diamond, "X" Coy on the right flank, Y Coy on the left flank, Bn HQ + W Coy in the rear) to take JEHOVAH TRENCH running through J. 31. a. + c. This was found to be occupied by enemy machine gunners but these retired at the advance of the Batt. [and] JEHOVAH TRENCH was ours by 11.30 am.<br>The Batt. then proceeded to push on frontally towards ZANDVOORDE, Y + Z Coys pushing out strong reconnaissance, but such heavy M.G. fire was directed on them from the valley of the "BASSEVILLEBEEK" in P.2 and from the ZANDVOORDE RIDGE in P.5. that Lt Col JONES decided that a frontal attack would be too costly and that a flanking attack would have more success.<br>Having made a personal reconnaissance + discovered that the left Bde was meeting with less resistance + was advancing quickly on its objective – ALASKA HOUSES at J.33.b. – he swung the Batt round + pushed forward through J.31 a + b. W Coy leading followed closely by Y + Z Coys to the road in J.32.c. Meantime X Coy engaged the enemy on the ridge.<br>Heavy M.G. fire was directed on the Batt. while in J.32.c. from the ZANDVOORDE RIDGE in P.2. c + d. but W + Y Coys closely followed by Z Co. | |

A7092 Wt. W128_9/M1293 750,000. 1/17. D. D & I. Ltd. Forms/C2118/14.

Army Form C. 2118.

Instructions regarding War Diaries and Intelligence Summaries are contained in F. S. Regs., Part II. and the Staff Manual respectively. Title pages will be prepared in manuscript.

# WAR DIARY
*or*
# INTELLIGENCE SUMMARY.
*(Erase heading not required.)*

| Place | Date | Hour | Summary of Events and Information | Remarks and references to Appendices |
|---|---|---|---|---|
| | Sep 28 | | pushed across the BASSEVILLEBEEK at P.2.a.7.8. and, attacking southwards, drove the enemy from the ridge. | |
| | | | Most of the enemy did not await the attack, but ran off under our fire. The crew of one A-A. gun however showed fight, but a shower of rifle bombs from a platoon of W Coy made them withdraw [illegible]. | |
| | | 4 pm | ZANDVOORDE RIDGE in our possession. | |
| | | | The position won was consolidated. W, Y + Z Coys in the front line and X Coy in Reserve. | |
| | | | The line taken up ran from P.2.c.8.1. to P.3.c.1.8. along the forward slopes of the spur [illegible] of the village of ZANDVOORDE. | |
| | | | During the attack & the subsequent consolidation the following were wounded, viz:- | |
| | | | Capt R.S. HEAPE, M.C. O.C. Z Coy | |
| | | | Lieut J.A.S. PEARSTON. O.C. Y Coy | |
| | | | Lieut A. BELL W. Coy | |
| | | | Casualties to other ranks were fairly heavy. | |
| | | | All ranks showed the greatest dash & endurance. The day had opened very wet & cold, & everyone was [illegible] to the skin. | |
| | | | Fortunately about noon the weather cleared & made the going [illegible]. | |
| | | 6-30 pm | The enemy, about 100 strong, was seen emerging from the [illegible] of TEN BRIELEN, [illegible] up for [illegible] at about P.9.d. but were heavily engaged by rifle + L.G. fire & dispersed. | |
| | | | During the day [illegible] 8 prisoners + 7 guns were captured. | |
| | | | Casualties: Other ranks - K/A. 13. W/A 78 M/A 5 W(at duty) 1 | |

A7092 Wt. W128.9/M1293 750,000. 1/17. D. D & L. Ltd. Forms/C2118/14.

Instructions regarding War Diaries and Intelligence Summaries are contained in F. S. Regs., Part II. and the Staff Manual respectively. Title pages will be prepared in manuscript.

# WAR DIARY
*or*
# INTELLIGENCE SUMMARY.
*(Erase heading not required.)*

Army Form C. 2118.

| Place | Date | Hour | Summary of Events and Information | Remarks and references to Appendices |
|---|---|---|---|---|
| | Sept 29 | | During the night 28th/29th, strong reconnoitring patrols were pushed out but no enemy were encountered. | |
| | | | When the morning of the 29th dawned the enemy became very active with his artillery & his M.Gs pushed forward into the eastern outskirts of ZANDVOORDE & made the position unpleasant. | |
| | | 2pm | The 105th Inf Bde (in conjunction with the 106th Inf Bde on the left) attacked through the Batt and carried the villages of ZANDVOORDE and TENBRIELEN. | |
| | | | The Batt was relieved on the ZANDVOORDE RIDGE by the 19 D.L.I. Relief completed by 10.30pm. | |
| | | | On relief the Batt moved back to JEHOVAH and KLEIN ZILLEBEKE TRENCHES with Batt HQ at CANADA TUNNELS in I.30.c. | |
| | | | CASUALTIES - Other ranks - W/a. 8 M/A. 2. | |
| | 30 | 2pm | Batt moved forward with rest of the Bde to attack towards the WERVICQ - MENIN Road. 18 Lan Fus & 19 D.L.I in front. Batt in support. Area of AMERICA CABARET P.12.d.7.8. Route via ZANDVOORDE - TENBRIELEN to Q 14 a & c | |
| | | | The 18 Lan Fus & 19 D.L.I encountered strong opposition from Q.8.c. & were unable to advance further than a line running from Q.13 central to Q.7.d.7.5. | |
| | | | The Batt remained in support in P.12.c. | |
| | | | Casualty 1 O.R. W/Duty. | |

Instructions regarding War Diaries and Intelligence Summaries are contained in F. S. Regs., Part II. and the Staff Manual respectively. Title pages will be prepared in manuscript.

# WAR DIARY
*or*
# INTELLIGENCE SUMMARY.
*(Erase heading not required.)*

Army Form C. 2118.

| Place | Date | Hour | Summary of Events and Information | Remarks and references to Appendices |
|---|---|---|---|---|
| | | | Casualties for month:- | |
| | | | Officers - Capt R S HEAPE, M.C W/A 28. 9. 18. | |
| | | | Lieut J. A. SHEARSTON W/A 28. 9. 18. | |
| | | | Lieut A. BELL. W/A 28. 9. 18. | |
| | | | 2/Lt J. EDWARDS W/A 10. 9. 18. | |
| | | | Other Ranks:- Killed in Action - 24. | |
| | | | Wounded in Action - 91. | |
| | | | Missing in Action - 9. | |
| | | | Wounded & Missing - 4. | |
| | | | Wounded (at Duty) - 1. | |
| | | | Strength of Batt. 30/9/18 - | |
| | | | Officers - 44. | |
| | | | Other Ranks - 744. | |
| | | | J. Jones. Lieut Colonel<br>Comdg 1/4 Lancs Fusiliers | |

A7092 Wt. W128 9/M1293 750,000. 1/17. D. D & L. Ltd. Forms/C2118/14.

Secret **OPERATION ORDER D.23.** Copy No. 3

**Ref. Maps.** Sheets 28 N.W.4. 28.N.E.3. 28.S.E.1. & 28.S.W.2. Scale - 1:10,000.

27: Sept. 1918.

**1. INTENTION:** On morning of 28th September the 104th Inf. Bde will attack the VERBRANDENMOLEN - STIRLING CASTLE RIDGE (within the Brigade boundaries). 18 Lan Fus on the right, 19 D.L.I. on the left.
17 Lan. Fus will be in support during the first phase of the attack and will eventually move through the 18 Lan Fus and 19 D.L.I. on to ZANDVOORDE.

**2. ASSEMBLY:** During the night 27/28 Sept., the Batt will assemble in the area between the old front line and NORCO'S HOUSE, distributed by Coys in artillery formation. As soon as Coys are in their assembly positions they will report their arrival to Batt HQ. by runner. Coy. areas are allotted as under:-

Z Coy - at about I.21.c.4.3. (east of railway)
X Coy - at about I.21.c.0.2.
Y Coy - at about I.20.d.9.7.
W Coy - at about I.20.d.4.6.
Bn HQ - Trench at I.21.c.6.2.

If their Coys are heavily shelled in these areas Coy Commanders may use their discretion as to altering their dispositions, within the boundaries laid down. Any move of a Coy. H.Q. will be at once reported to Bn HQ.
Coys. will pass BELGIAN BATTERY CORNER on their way to the Assembly positions at the following times:-
Z Coy. at 11pm. X Coy. at 11.15pm. Y Coy. at 11.30pm.
W Coy. at 11.45pm. Bn HQ at 12 midnight
Movement will be by platoons at 100x interval. Route recommended is via SHRAPNEL CORNER - LILLE Gate - Tram crossing in I.19.d

**3. ZERO:** At ZERO, 18 Lan Fus and 19 D.L.I. will attack. The Batt will stand fast until the objective, the KLEIN ZILLEBEKE LINE is taken, but Coys will hold themselves in readiness to move forward to ZANDVOORDE. The actual order for the advance will be given, but the probable time seems to be 0 plus 2 hrs 20 mins, which will enable the Batt. to have a halt on the way up behind the Western slopes of HILL 60 - CANADA TUNNELS RIDGE and pass the first objective, the KLEIN ZILLEBEKE LINE at 0 plus 4 hrs 20 minutes.
On the word "PURSUE", the Batt. will move off by platoons at about 100x interval in the following order, Z, X, Y, HQ, W. Route - road I.21.d.40.45 - cross roads at BLUE FORT I.28.a.3.5. and on to KLEIN ZILLEBEKE, as per attached sketch. Just before reaching KLEIN ZILLEBEKE the Batt will break up into advanced guard formation, Z Coy in front. - X Coy. right flank - Y Coy left flank. - W Coy (+ Bn HQ) in rear - and advance to ZANDVOORDE the objective. Route - as per attached sketch. As their route is shorter, X Coy must regulate their advance by the advance of the main body.
As the Batt. passes the PAUSE LINE the troops of the 18 Lan. Fus. & 19 D.L.I. occupying that position will move forward on the flanks,
18 Lan Fus on the right flank of the Battalion
19 Dur. L.I. on the left flank of the Battalion

**4. OBJECTIVE:** On reaching ZANDVOORDE the following positions will be taken up south and east of the village - P.2.c.65.85
"X" Coy. from road junction at P.2.c.65.85. to approx. P.3.c.1.5.
Z Coy. from P.3.c.1.5., following 35 contour to P.3.d.40.85.
Y Coy. from P.3.d.35.85 to about TIN HOUSES J.33.d.20.35.
W Coy will be in reserve on both sides of road at P.3.a.35.70. facing S.E.
Bn HQ will be at approx P.3.a.0.9. near road junction
The flanking troops of the 18 Lan Fus will take up a position along the line PIONEER HOUSE - POTSDAM - CIRQUE POINT.
The flanking troops of 19 D.L.I. will form the connecting link between the Battalion's left and the 106 Inf. Bde. at ALASKA HOUSES

**5. MACHINE GUNS** C Coy 35th Bn M.G.C. will be assembled near Batt HQ. I.21.c.6.2. not later than 0 plus 2 hrs. ready to move on receipt of orders.
1 Section will move with X Coy on the right flank
2 guns will move with Y Coy on the left flank
2 guns will move with Z Coy in front
1 Section will move in reserve with Bn HQ.

6. ARTILLERY. A special detachment of artillery will follow up the Battalion's advance, and assist in covering the advance or breaking up a counter attack as may be required.

7. AEROPLANES. A contact patrol Aeroplane (marked by one BLACK flap projecting from each lower plane and by one streamer flying from the tail) will fly along the front of the attack at about one hour after ZERO and thereafter at every clock hour.

Coys will show their positions by lighting flares, flashing tin discs in groups of three, or by displaying strips when the aeroplane demands recognition signal by sounding the letter 'A' in Morse on the Klaxon Horn or by firing a single WHITE light.

A counter-attack Aeroplane will patrol the front from 0 + 40 minutes onwards and will signal the development of an enemy counter attack by firing a RED PARACHUTE FLARE and flying in the direction of the enemy who are massing for the attack.

Batt. H.Q. will be indicated by ground signal sheets and strips and will communicate by means of the POPHAM PANEL

8. AMMUNITION. Aeroplanes have been instructed to look out for the 'V' signal calling for ammunition, at cross roads P.3.a.6.8 about 12 noon on 28th Sept.

9. PRISONERS. All prisoners of war will be disarmed and passed back to WOODCOTE HOUSE.

10. BATTN. HQ (1). At the commencement of the attack Bn. HQ will be in trench at I.24.c.6.2.
(2) During the Battn's advance BHQ will move in front of W. Coy.
(3) When objective is captured BHQ will be at approx. P.3.a.65.90.

11. ZERO HOUR will be intimated later. P 3. a 65 90

12. SYNCHRONISATION of Watches. Coys will each send one officer to Bn HQ at 4.30 pm Sept 27 and one hour after ZERO on Sept. 28th to synchronise watches.

13 SIGNALLING. Signalling Officer will arrange to make best use of all the apparatus at his disposal so as to maintain communication.

14. RATIONS and WATER. The Transport Officer will be prepared to bring up rations & water to Bn. HQ, ZANDVOORDE using the KLEIN ZILLEBEKE – ZANDVOORDE Rd on night Sept. 28/29.

On night 27/28 Sept. tea will be made at present billets and taken up to Assembly positions in Hot Food Containers on pack mules (2 containers per Coy.) The tea will be issued out and the containers returned before ZERO hour.

Coys. will arrange to take in with them 2 tins of water per platoon for use before the advance. Men must be instructed that their waterbottles must NOT be touched until they reach ZANDVOORDE

L.G. limbers will move with their Coys as far as EMBER FARM, H.17.c.30.45. Lewis Guns etc will thereafter be carried on the man.

15. MEDICAL ARRANGEMENTS. At commencement of operation there will be RAPs in GHQ 1. Line and at SWAN CHATEAU.

R.M.O. will move forward as attack progresses.

16. REPORTS. Reports on progress will be sent as frequently as possible to Batt. HQ.

17. GENERAL. Every effort must be made to overcome speedily any resistance met. The essence of success is speed. When ZANDVOORDE has been gained, the success must be exploited, and strong patrols pushed out from each Coy.

Physical contact will be established between Coys and on the flanks.

18. ACKNOWLEDGE.

Issued at 2.0pm.

R. Irvine
Captain
Adjt. 10V1.

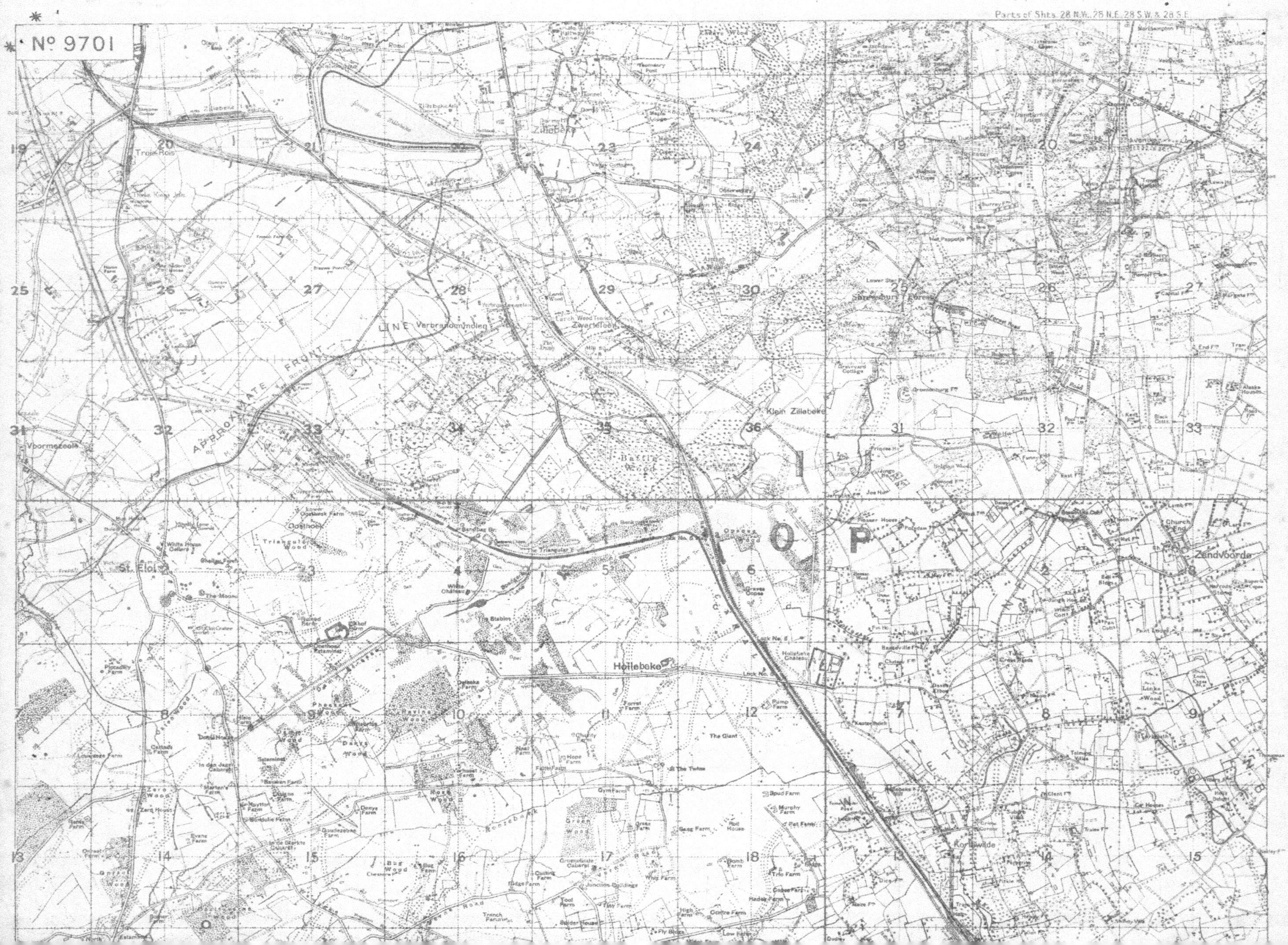

Nº 9701
Parts of Shts. 28 N.W., 28 N.E., 28 S.W. & 28 S.E.
Zillebeke
Trois Rois
Vbormezeele
St. Eloi
Oosthoek
Verbrandenmolen
Zwarteleen
Klein Zillebeke
Battle Wood
Hollebeke
Zandvoorde
Kortewilde
APPROXIMATE FRONT LINE
The Triangular Fm
White Château
The Stables
Triangular Wood
The Giant
The Twins
Gym Farm
Green Wood
Rose Wood
Bug Wood
Spud Farm
Murphy Farm
Roll House
Bomb Farm
Trio Farm
Centre Farm
Low Farm
High Farm
Whiz Farm
Junction Buildings
Tool Farm
Trench Farm
Dug Farm
Denys Wood
Denys Farm
Caterpillar
Hill 60
Larch Wood Tunnels
Shrewsbury Forest
Groenenburg Fm
North Fm
Lower Star Post
Graveyard Cottage
Pioneer House
Church End
Lock No. 6
Lock No. 8
Hollebeke Château
Pump Farm
Jay Wood
Zero Wood
Ravine Wood
The Mound
Cottage Farm
Goudezeune Farm

**To**..........................................................................................

**From**..........................................................................................(Rank and Name)

..........................................................................................(Company)

..........................................................................................(Regiment)

Date..................................................191

Time..................a.m. or ..............p.m.

Place..........................................................................................

I am now at..........................................................................................(give map reference and mark on map with a cross)

I have scouts at..........................................................................................

I want { S.A.A.
Bombs.
Water.

The nearest Germans are now at..........................................................................................

I am in touch with..........................................at..........................................................
on right and with..........................................................................................on left.

Enemy is retiring along..........................................................................................road.

Enemy is advancing along..........................................................................................road.

Other Information :—

*(Signature)*

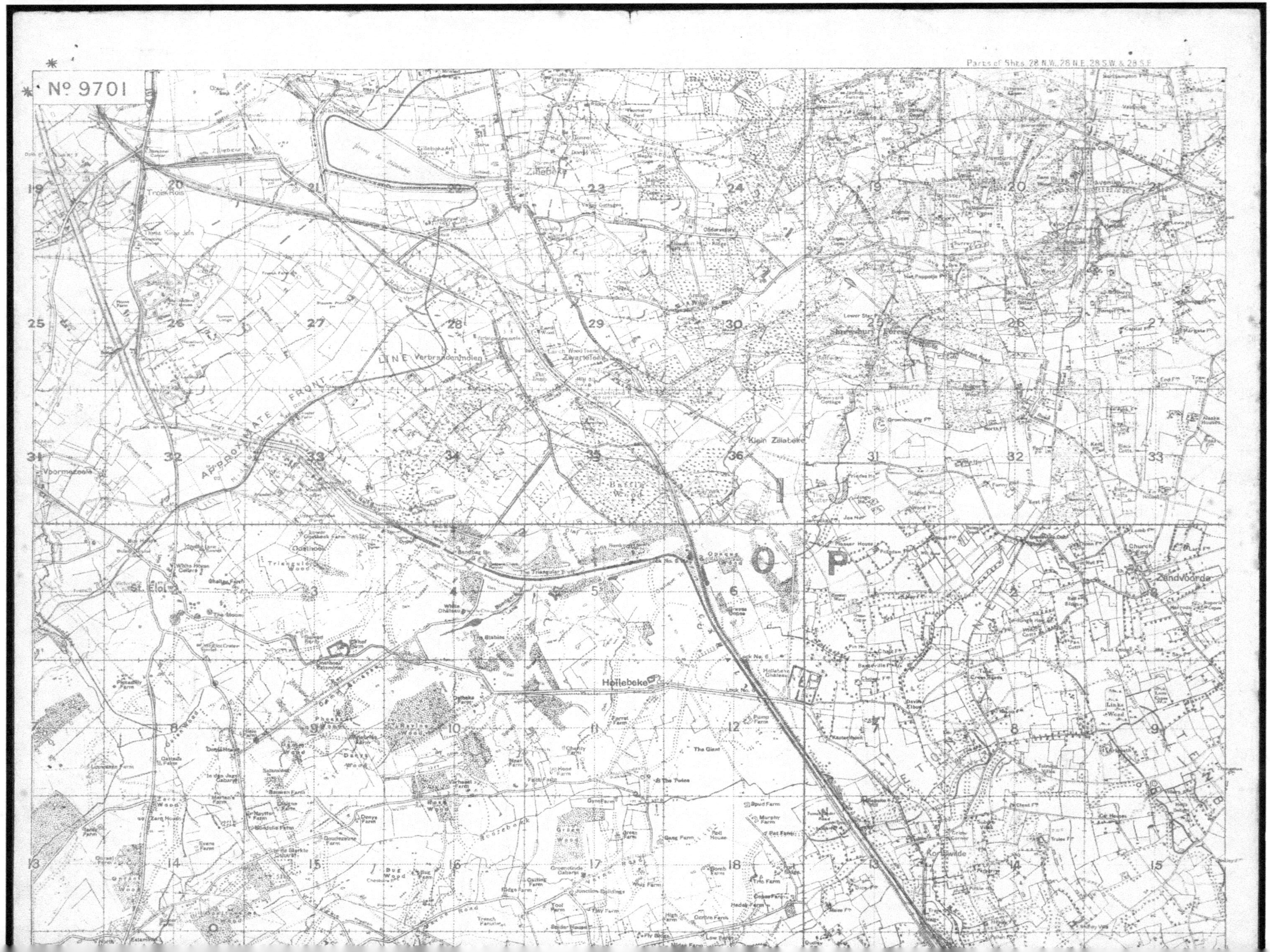
Nº 9701
Parts of Shts. 28 N.W., 28 N.E., 28 S.W. & 28 S.E.
Zillebeke
Verbrandenmolen
Zwarteleen
Klein Zillebeke
Battle Wood
Shrewsbury Forest
Hollebeke
Zandvoorde
Kortewilde
St. Eloi
Voormezeele
Oosthoek
White Château
The Bluff
Church End
LINE
APPROXIMATE FRONT
O P
The Caterpillar
The Mound
The Twins
The Grenadier

**To**..............................................................................................

**From**..............................................................................................(Rank and Name)

..............................................................................................(Company)

..............................................................................................(Regiment)

Date.........................................................1918.

Time... ...........a.m. or ..............p.m.

Place..........................................................................

I am now at...........................................................................(give map reference and mark on map with a cross)

I have scouts at..................................................................................................

I want { S.A.A.
Bombs.
Water.

The nearest Germans are now at..........................................................................

I am in touch with...................................at...................................................
on right and with.............................................................................................on left.

Enemy is retiring along.......................................................................... ..road.

Enemy is advancing along.................................................... ......................road.

Other Information:—

(*Signature*)

To O.C. ______________ Message No.

I am at ______________

I am not in touch with ______________ on left

I am not in touch with ______________ on right

MESSAGE MAP

Scale 1/40,000 Part Sheet 28

Ammunition required at ______________

Enemy Movement seen at ______________

Send up ______________

Signature ______ Commanding ______ Date ______ Time ______

Traffic Bridge ⩸ Foot Bridge

To O.C. ______________ Message No. ______

I am at ______________

I am-not-in touch with ______________ on left

I am-not-in touch with ______________ on right

MESSAGE MAP

Scale 1/40,000

Part - Sheet 28

Ammunition required at ______________

Enemy Movement seen at ______________

Send up ______________

Signature ______ Commanding ______ Date ______ Time ______

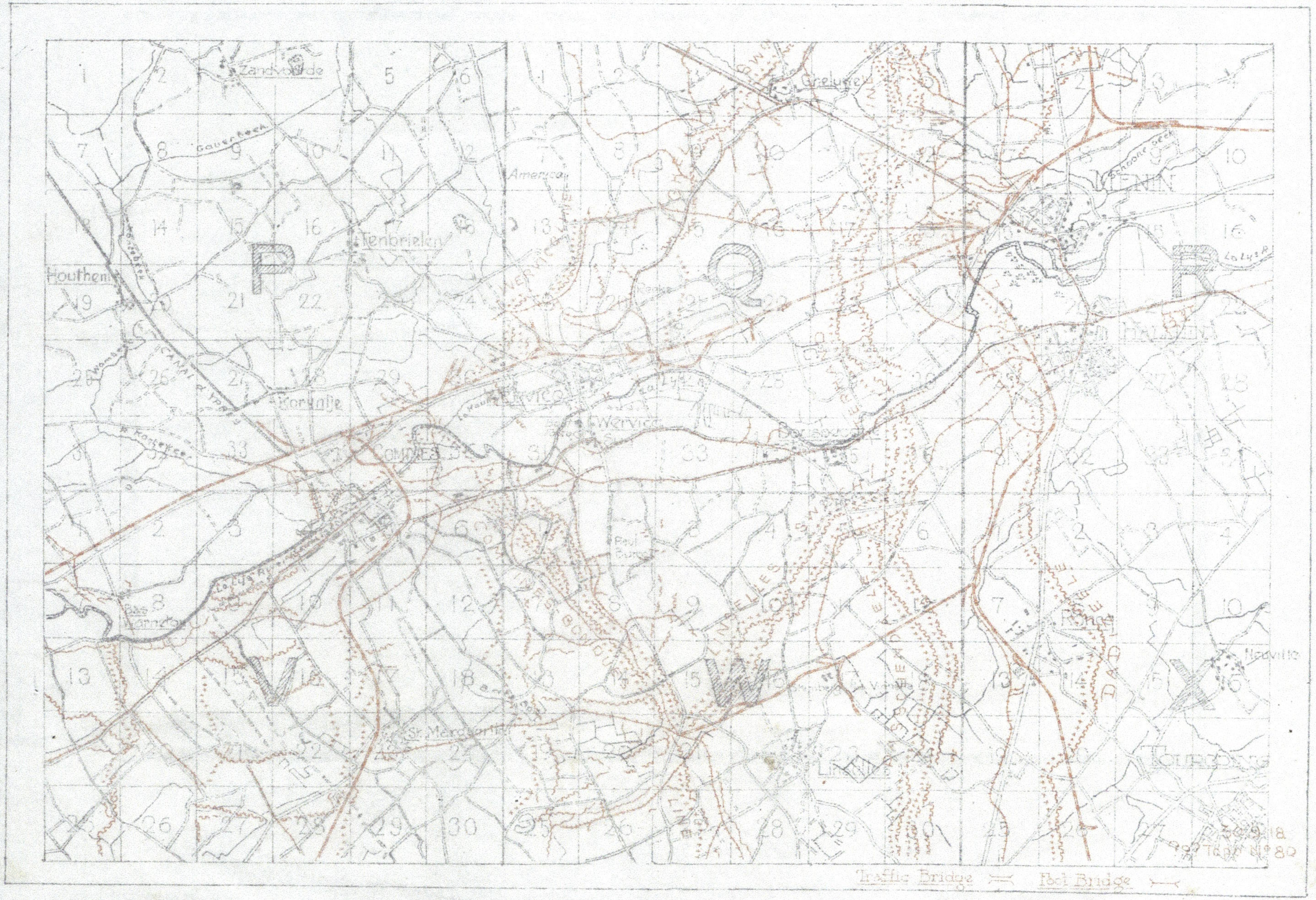

APPENDIX 2.

Copy No.

[illegible]

E.g.

10.2.17.

1. The Advance [illegible] [illegible] this morning [illegible]

2. [illegible]

3. [illegible]

[illegible]

4. [illegible] Bombers have [illegible]

[illegible]

5. [illegible]

6. [illegible]

[illegible]

7. [illegible]

[illegible] Copy No. 1
[illegible] 2
[illegible] 3
[illegible] 4
[illegible] 5

[illegible] Cmdg. [illegible]

Issued at 9.30 AM.

(Confidential)

# WAR DIARY

OF

The 17th Service (1st S.E.L.) Battalion
The Lancashire Fusiliers

From 1.10.18 To 31.10.18

Volume No 33.

Instructions regarding War Diaries and Intelligence Summaries are contained in F. S. Regs., Part II. and the Staff Manual respectively. Title pages will be prepared in manuscript.

# WAR DIARY
*or*
# INTELLIGENCE SUMMARY.
*(Erase heading not required.)*

Army Form C. 2118.

OCTOBER 1918. REF. MAPS. Sheets 27, 28, 29 1/40,000

| Place | Date | Hour | Strength 1.10.18 Offrs - 44 OR - 744. Summary of Events and Information | Remarks and references to Appendices |
|---|---|---|---|---|
| W of WERVICQ - AMERICA CABT. | 1. | | Battalion in support at P12c./28. During the evening relieved 19 DLI in line east of AMERICA CABT. Battn HQ. - P12 d 8.8. Relief completed by 2330 h. Blackness of night delayed relief. | |
| do. | 2. | 0700h. | At 0700 h X Coy attacked ridge in Q20 a. (REEKE) but made no progress owing to extremely heavy M.G. fire. Casualties. 2/Lt W. BROOKES, X Coy. W/A OR. - 3 K/A 17 W/A. W Coy endeavoured on the left to outflank the ridge but without success. During the evening the Battn. was relieved by SCOTTISH RIFLES, 34th Div. Relief completed 2345 h. Battn moved back to shelters in J35 near KRUISEECKE X RDS | |
| ZILLEBEKE LAKE | 3 | 1130h | Battn marched back to shelters S of ZILLEBEKE LAKE I22C. | |
| do | 4. | | Bathing at VLAMERTINGHE. Cleaning up of arms and equipment. | |
| do | 5. | | Cleaning up and resting. | |
| do. | 6. | | 1030h. - Church Parade. 1330 h. Battn moved to front line through BERCELAERE - TERHAND, relieving 18 HLI Halt was made for teas at J23 b. | |

A7092 Wt. W128/9/M1293 750,000. 1/17. D. D & L. Ltd. Forms/C2118/14.

Army Form C. 2118.

Instructions regarding War Diaries and Intelligence Summaries are contained in F. S. Regs., Part II. and the Staff Manual respectively. Title pages will be prepared in manuscript.

# WAR DIARY
*or*
# INTELLIGENCE SUMMARY.
(*Erase heading not required.*)

| Place | Date (OCTOBER) | Hour | Summary of Events and Information | Remarks and references to Appendices |
|---|---|---|---|---|
| | 6. | | Battn HQ. - K 22 C 3·6. W and Y Coys front line. X and Z Coys support. | |
| Front Line | 7 | | Relief completed 0100 h. Assembly positions for attack reconnoitred. Battn. HQ moved to K23 a 2·9. Casualties - 3 OR W/A | |
| do. | 8. | | Line further reconnoitred with a view to attack. { 2Lt. J. GALBREATH W/A. 3 OR - W/A } Relieved during the evening by 18th H.L.I. Relief completed 2300 h. Battn on relief moved back to shelters in J 20 near GHELUVELT. | |
| J 20. | 9. | | Day spent in cleaning up, resting, etc. | |
| do | 10. | | Do. Preliminary instructions for attack received and issued | |
| do. | 11. | | Further Instructions for attack received and issued. | |
| | | 1530h | Battn. moved into the line, relieving 18 HLI. Battn HQ - K 23 C 6·6. Y and W Coys front line. Z and X Coys support. Relief completed by 2200 h. | |

A7092 Wt. W125 9/M1293 750,000. 1/17. D. D & L. Ltd. Forms/C2118/14.

Instructions regarding War Diaries and Intelligence Summaries are contained in F. S. Regs., Part II. and the Staff Manual respectively. Title pages will be prepared in manuscript.

# WAR DIARY
*or*
# INTELLIGENCE SUMMARY.
*(Erase heading not required.)*

Army Form C. 2118.

| Place | Date (OCTOBER.) | Hour | Summary of Events and Information | Remarks and references to Appendices |
|---|---|---|---|---|
| FRONT LINE. | 12 | | Assembly positions again reconnoitred. During night patrol of W Coy went out under 2LT. H. COOK towards GOLDFLAKE FARM. An enemy post was encountered and attacked. 2LT COOK shot two of the enemy. Our casualties were 1 OR - K/A. Reconnoitring patrol went out from Y Coy front under 2LT. G.G. PEET. | |
| do | 13 | | Enemy put down heavy counter preparation from 0430 h to 0500 h. At 2300 h. Battn moved into Assembly positions for attack. 1 OR W/A. | |
| | 14 | 0430 h | Enemy put down heavy counter preparation until 0500 h. Casualties slight. | |
| do | 14 | 0535 h. | Battn attacked, under cover of barrage. Y Coy on right, W on left, Z right support, X left support. Battn HQ moved in front of rear waves. 105 Inf Bde attacked on ~~left~~ right, 36th Ulster Div on left. Starting line - K24 a + b. Considerable short shooting from our guns was experienced. Enemy opposition was the more easily overcome ~~because~~ of the dense mist that prevailed. Numerous machine gun nests and infantry posts were encountered and put out of action. 2LT F. ASPDEN, 2LT. A.C. STEPHENSON, 2LT. H. DRUMMOND, and CAPT. C.S. ATKINSON M.C. distinguished themselves ~~by~~ in overcoming hostile resistance. | |

A7092 Wt. W125 9/M1293 750,000. 1/17. D. D & L. Ltd. Forms/C2118/14.

Instructions regarding War Diaries and Intelligence Summaries are contained in F. S. Regs., Part II. and the Staff Manual respectively. Title pages will be prepared in manuscript.

# WAR DIARY
*or*
# INTELLIGENCE SUMMARY.
*(Erase heading not required.)*

Army Form C. 2118.

| Place | Date | Hour | Summary of Events and Information | Remarks and references to Appendices |
| --- | --- | --- | --- | --- |
| FRONT LINE. | 14. | | The line of the ROULERS - MENIN railway - 1st pause - was reached to time. Final objective (L27 b 2 8) was captured at 0705 hours. and position was consolidated. 18 LAN. FUS and 19 DLI attacked through the Battn at 0710 h.<br>Captures - 100 prisoners, 6 Field Guns, 2 Trench Mortars, and 16 M.Gs.<br>Casualties. 2LT. F. ASPDEN., 2LT. H.T. LEIGH } K/A; LT. COL. J. JONES M.C. - Died of Wounds<br>2LT. S.R. WILLIAMS, 2LT J COOKE, 2LT J.P. PENDER } W/A<br>O.R. 18 - K/A. 102 - W/A. 7 - M/A | |
| ELBA CORNER L27 b.2.8. | 15. | | Day spent resting and cleaning up. MAJOR G. MACKERETH, M.C assumes command of Battn. | |
| do | 16 | | do. | |
| do | 17 | | do and platoon training. | |
| do | 18. | 1600h. | Battn moved forward through MOORSEELE to G 26 c + d. 29. Officers reconnoitred crossings over LYS. At 2300h. Battn again moved forward, crossed the LYS by a footbridge [illegible] of MARCKE and took up assembly position for attack on the Eastern outskirts of MARCKE. | |

A5834 Wt. W4973/M687 750,000 8/16 D. D. & L. Ltd. Forms/C.2118/13.

Instructions regarding War Diaries and Intelligence Summaries are contained in F. S. Regs., Part II. and the Staff Manual respectively. Title pages will be prepared in manuscript.

# WAR DIARY
*or*
# INTELLIGENCE SUMMARY.
*(Erase heading not required.)*

Army Form C. 2118.

| Place | Date OCTOBER. | Hour | Summary of Events and Information | Remarks and references to Appendices |
|---|---|---|---|---|
| MARCKE. | 19. | 0300 h. | Battn in assembly positions. | |
| | | 0530 h. | Battn attacked under cover of creeping barrage. Barrage opened short causing casualties. Direction of attack - S.E. Final Objective MARIONETTE CABT; 29/N 14 c, and N 20 a reached by 7 a.m. No enemy encountered during attack. Success was at once exploited and the line advanced by X and Z Coys a further 1000x by 1015 h. Here considerable opposition was encountered from hostile M.Gs and further exploitation made impossible. Battn HQ established in N 13 b. Casualties - 4 OR - W/A. | |
| MARIONNETTE-BERG + | 20. | 0700 h. | Attack resumed in a S.E. direction, (without barrage) W and Y Coys in front, Z and X Coys behind. Attack carried out in diamond formation with scouts 500x in front. Slight opposition encountered from Field Guns and M.Gs. These were forced to withdraw and objective was gained, ground about N 35 d, by 0900 h. Patrols pushed out 500x in front. Battn HQ - N 35 a 7.6. Captures - 1 M.G. Casualties - 3 OR W/A. | |
| | | 1915 h. | The attack on the left was held up and at 1915 h the 106th Inf Bde passed through the Battn to roll up the right flank of the opposition. ? left | |

A5834 Wt. W4973/M687 750,000 8/16 D. D. & L. Ltd. Forms/C.2118/13.

Instructions regarding War Diaries and Intelligence Summaries are contained in F. S. Regs., Part II. and the Staff Manual respectively. Title pages will be prepared in manuscript.

# WAR DIARY
*or*
# INTELLIGENCE SUMMARY.
*(Erase heading not required.)*

Army Form C. 2118.

| Place | Date OCTOBER. | Hour | Summary of Events and Information | Remarks and references to Appendices |
|---|---|---|---|---|
| N35a. COURTRAI. | 21. | 0900h. | At about 0800h the 41st British Division passed through to resume the attack, and at 0900h the Battn moved back to billets S of COURTRAI. | |
| COURTRAI. | 22. | | Day spent resting, cleaning up. etc. { 2LT. J. GALBREATH rejoins from Hospital. Draft of 90 O.R. arrives. | |
| do | 23 | | do. Platoon training. Bathing. Draft of 60 O.R. arrives | |
| do | 24 | | do. do. do. Church Parade. | |
| do | 25. | | CAPT. P.J. McKEVITT, LT. A.E. VEITCH, 2LT. J. JENKINS evacuated to Hospital sick. CAPT C.S. ATKINSON M.C. leaves to act as instructor at Cadet School in U.K. REV. H.M. CRABBE, chaplain, evacuated to Hospital. sick. | |
| | | 1530h. | Battn move to the line via SWEVELGHEM and KROTE. Halt at KROTE for tea. Relieve 10th Queens, 41st Division in the line at AVELGHEM on the western bank of L'ESCAUT. Relief completed by 2300h. W and Y Coys in front line, X (two platoons forward with W) and Z in support. Battn HQ at BOSCH. P21 d. | |
| AVELGHEM. | 26. | 0400h. | Battn HQ move to P20 c 8.9. | |
| | | 0500h. | Z Coy attack in a N.E. direction in conjunction with 18 L.F. on left. Strong opposition encountered. Line advanced about 200x but was withdrawn to original position about 1200h owing to heavy Artillery, T.M. + M.G. fire. Captures - 3 prisoners Casualties - 1 OR K/A 17 O.R. W/A. 12 OR M/A. | |

A5834 Wt. W4973/M687 750,000 8/16 D. D. & L. Ltd. Forms/C.2118/13.

Instructions regarding War Diaries and Intelligence Summaries are contained in F. S. Regs., Part II. and the Staff Manual respectively. Title pages will be prepared in manuscript.

# WAR DIARY
*or*
# INTELLIGENCE SUMMARY.
*(Erase heading not required.)*

Army Form C. 2118.

| Place | Date OCTOBER. | Hour | Summary of Events and Information | Remarks and references to Appendices |
|---|---|---|---|---|
| AVELGHEM. | 27. | 0430h. | Hostile counter-preparation. Heavy Artillery fire directed on our position throughout the day. Casualties - 2 O.R. K/A. 16 O.R. W/A.<br>Relieved in evening by 19 DLI. Relief complete by 2300h.<br>On relief Battn moved to billets near KROTE - O.5. | |
| KROTE | 28. | | Day spent resting, refitting etc. | |
| do | 29 | | Do. Orders received for attack on morning of 31st. | |
| do | 30. | | Orders issued for attack. At 1700h. Y Coy move up and take over Battn sector from 19 DLI. Remainder of Battn move off to Assembly positions at 2359 h. Assembly positions reached without accident. | |
| AVELGHEM. | 31. | 0525h. | Battn attacked N.E. along L'ESCAUT, 19 DLI on right, 18 LF. on left, Z Coy on right W Coy on left, X Coy left support, X Coy left support. - under cover of barrage. A large amount of smoke was put down by our guns on Eastern bank of L'ESCAUT to hinder enemy observation from MONT DE L'ENCLUS Starting point - line of road in 29/P29 a. | |

A5834 Wt. W4973/M687 750,000 8/16 D. D. & L. Ltd. Forms/C.2118/13.

Instructions regarding War Diaries and Intelligence Summaries are contained in F. S. Regs., Part II. and the Staff Manual respectively. Title pages will be prepared in manuscript.

# WAR DIARY
*or*
# INTELLIGENCE SUMMARY.
*(Erase heading not required.)*

Army Form C. 2118.

| Place | Date | Hour | Summary of Events and Information | Remarks and references to Appendices |
|---|---|---|---|---|
| | OCTOBER | | | |
| AVELGHEM. | 31. | | Considerable MG and Artillery fire encountered. MG posts mopped up and put out of action by successful flanking fire from Lewis Guns and line of first objective - WAERMAERE - TIEGHEM Road reached to time:- 0646h. Patrols pushed out with sweep of barrage and formed line in front. | |
| | | 0849h | Attacks resumed - Y Coy on right, X Coy on left, behind barrage. M.G. opposition again encountered and again successfully overcome. Enemy used tracer ammunition which gave the position of his guns away. Final objective - KERKHOVE - VARENT, Q 15 + 9. taken by 0955h. | |
| | | | Battn redistributed as follows X Coy - VARENT, Y Coy VOSSENHOEK, Z and W Coys behind VOSSENHOEK, - in depth. | |
| | | 1430h. | Patrols of X Coy reached EEUWHOEK near MEERSCHE and established themselves there. | |
| | | | Captures. - 150 prisoners, 30 M.Gs., 1 T.M., and 2 Motor Ambulances. The casualties to the enemy were extremely heavy. Numerous civilians were liberated. | |
| | | | Casualties: 2LT. H.R.E. IRVING. K/A; 2LT. H. DRUMMOND K/A; CAPT. R.C.R. ROBINSON W/A.; LT. C.G. PEET W/A.; 2LT C.S. DICKINSON W/A.; 2LT H. COOK W/A.; 2LT [illegible] HALSTEAD W/A. O.R. 8 - K/A. 63 - W/A. 13 - M/A. | |

A5834 Wt. W4973/M687 750,000 8/16 D. D. & L. Ltd. Forms/C.2118/13.

Instructions regarding War Diaries and Intelligence Summaries are contained in F. S. Regs., Part II. and the Staff Manual respectively. Title pages will be prepared in manuscript.

# WAR DIARY
*or*
# INTELLIGENCE SUMMARY.
*(Erase heading not required.)*

Army Form C. 2118.

| Place | Date | Hour | Summary of Events and Information | Remarks and references to Appendices |
|---|---|---|---|---|
| | | | Casualties for month :- | |
| | | | Officers :- Lieut Col. J. Jones. M.C. Died of Wounds. 14.10.18. | |
| | | | 2/Lt. F. Aspden. K/A. 14.10.18. | |
| | | | 2/Lt. H.T. Leigh K/A 14.10.18 | |
| | | | 2/Lt. H. Drummond K/A 31.10.18. | |
| | | | 2/Lt H.R.E. Irving K/A 31.10.18. | |
| | | | 2/Lt. J. Galbreath. W/A. 7.10.18. (since rejoined) | |
| | | | 2/Lt. S.R. Williams. W/A 14.10.18 | |
| | | | 2/Lt. J. Cooke. W/A 14.10.18. | |
| | | | 2/Lt. J.P. Pender. W/A 14.10.18. | |
| | | | A/Capt. R.C.R. Robinson. M.C. W/A. 31.10.18. | |
| | | | 2/Lt. C.G. Peet. W/A 31.10.18. | |
| | | | 2/Lt. C.S. Dickinson. W/A 31.10.18. | |
| | | | 2/Lt. H. Cook W/A 31.10.18. | |
| | | | 2/Lt. J. Halstead W/A 31.10.18. | |
| | | | Other Ranks. Killed in Action — 29 | |
| | | | Wounded in Action — 217 | |
| | | | Missing in Action — 32. | |
| | | | Wounded & Missing — nil. | |
| | | | Wounded (at Duty) — nil. | |
| | | | Strength of Battalion 31/10/18. | |
| | | | Officers — 30. | |
| | | | Other Ranks. — 670. | |
| | | | G. Rackuth. Lieut Colonel. Comdg 17th Lancs. Fusliers. | |

A5834 Wt. W4973/M687 750,000 8/16 D. D. & L. Ltd. Forms/C.2118/13.

Instructions regarding War Diaries and Intelligence Summaries are contained in F. S. Regs., Part II. and the Staff Manual respectively. Title pages will be prepared in manuscript.

# WAR DIARY
*or*
# INTELLIGENCE SUMMARY.
*(Erase heading not required.)*

Army Form C. 2118.

| Place | Date | Hour | Summary of Events and Information | Remarks and references to Appendices |
|---|---|---|---|---|
| | | | Honours Gained by the Battalion during the Period 1st – 31st October, 1918. | |
| | | | Award. | |
| | | | LT / A/LT.COL J. JONES, M.C. 19 DLI. (attached) (died of wounds – 14:10:18) — D.S.O. | |
| | | | T/2LT. F. ASPDEN, K/A 14:10:18 — M.C. | |
| | | | T/2LT. (A/CAPT) R.C.R. ROBINSON, W/A. 31:10:18. — M.C. | |
| | | | 24740 Sig. B REES MM. – D.C.M. 14430 Sgt. Sig J. LORD M.M – Bar to Mil. Medal. | |
| | | | The following have been awarded the MILITARY MEDAL. | |
| | | | 15323 Pte. J. NICHOLLS. — 35889 Cpl A FIELDING. | |
| | | | 14144 Cpl (L/Sgt) R HARTILL — 14032 Pte. C.P. HOWITT. | |
| | | | 46974 Pte (A/Sgt) E. SEDDON. — 3302 Pte J.H. MEAKIN. | |
| | | | 56695 Pte. P. RIVETT. — 5736 Pte E HOLLAND | |
| | | | 15402 Pte P ALMOND. — 35992 Pte W. CARRADUS | |
| | | | 14162 L/c J. RIGBY. — 14686 L/c C. HOLMES. | |

A5834 Wt. W4973/M687 750,000 8/16 D. D. & L. Ltd. Forms/C.2118/13.

SM 513

Secret

"ZOVI"

10th October 1918

## Preliminary Instructions for Attack.

Ref Maps: Sh 28. 1/40000: DADIZEELE 1/10000

1. The following preliminary instructions are issued to enable Coy. Commanders to make their preparations for the Attack.

2. On night J-3/J-2 the Batt will move into the line, as previously held. – except that Batt. H.Q. may move to pill box near LINKSFIELD FARM.

3. At Zero on J. night the Batt will attack, with W. Coy on Left Front, Y. Coy on Right Front, X Coy Left Support and Z Coy Right Support.

4. The Batt will assemble east of the road and railway running through K.24 a and K.23.d. at an hour on J. night to be intimated later.

5. The 105th Inf. Bde. will attack on the [illegible] right
The Bde. and Divisional boundaries, and the rough lines of the objective have been marked on maps already issued to Coys.
The creeping barrage will be 100x in two minutes. The barrage will begin at H-2 minutes
There will be a pause of 15 minutes after every 1500x
~~At the first pause W and Y Coys will consolidate and X and Z Coys will "leap frog" and continue the advance.~~
At the second pause ~~X and Z~~ ALL Coys will consolidate and the 18th Lan. Fus. (?) and 19th Div. L.I. will "leap frog" and continue the advance towards the LYS.

6. The Batt. must push towards its objective irrespective of the troops on right and left.

7. It must be explained to all ranks that the barrage will be diagonal to the line of the advance and care must be taken not to lose direction and move S.E. Compass bearings will be taken and landmarks noticed. The Battalion's left is well defined by the TERHAND– MOORSEELE Road.
The right of the 105th Inf. Bde. will be marked by Thermite Shells.

8. The 106th Inf. Bde will be in Reserve.

9. The barrage will start, approx. on the line L.19.c 55.85 to K.30.c.75.80. Heavy artillery will shoot on selected points behind.

10. Further details will be issued later.

R. [illegible]
Captain
Adjt. "ZOVI."

10.10.18.

Adjt

12th [illegible]

Overnight 13/14 2 [illegible]

14th – 4 [illegible] 13th —

4 pack mules.
each 2 boxes
1 [illegible] 1 bandolier

Coy dumps. 1 [illegible]
[illegible] under Coy orders
Dumps formed [illegible]

Rum 13/14

Tea in containers
13/14.

9850 630

## 17th (S) Battn. LANCASHIRE FUSILIERS

**Secret.** **OPERATION ORDER R27.** Copy No. [illegible]

**Ref. Map 29 S.E. 20000.** **30.10.18.**

1. **INTENTION:** The Battn. will resume the attack on Thursday 31st Oct. at an hour to be notified later.
   1st Objective: Along road running S.E. from P.18.d.5.6. to Q.19.c.5.8.
   2nd Objective: Along road running S.E. from Q.9.c.0.3. to road junction Q.15.a.2.4.

2. **ATTACK:** The attack will be carried out within the boundaries indicated by Coy. Commanders yesterday 29th Oct.
   First Objective will be taken by "Z" Coy on the right & W Coy on the left.
   Second Objective " " " " "Y" " " " " "X" " " "

3. **FORMING UP:** (a) W & Z Coys will form up on line immediately E. of road from LANGESTRAAT to P.23.b.8.0. with a fringe of scouts 150 yds in advance.
   (b) X & Y Coys will form up on line immediately W. of road mentioned in (a).
   **Formation:** Diamond formation by Coys. Sections in blobs with scouts, 2 from each section in front.

4. **MOVEMENT:** On opening of barrage, ie at O. Batt. will move forward, to follow 100 yds behind barrage – X & Y Coys 250 yds in rear of W & Z Coys. W & Z Coys will carry forward bridges for crossing SCHEEBEEK (probably 3 each) and will carry them forward. [illegible] per Coy. front, which will be left over the SCHEEBEEK, & the [illegible] for the crossing of that stream. After crossing the SCHEEBEEK, X & Y Coys will halt and follow 500 yds in rear of W & Z Coys.

5. **DIRECTION:** As a considerable number of smoke shells will be used, the importance of utilizing compasses for maintaining direction must be observed to the utmost. The centre of the Batt advance is on a Magnetic bearing of 72°.

6. **ARTILLERY:** Barrage will advance at rate of 100 yds in 3 minutes resting 3 minutes on Zero line.
   The following pauses must be accurately observed.
   O + 36. pause of 6 minutes
   O + 81. " " 2 hrs. & 3 minutes
   O + 204. Artillery will reopen fire and the advance to second objective will be resumed.
   O + 231. pause of 6 minutes
   O + 273 Final objective should be reached.

7. On reaching First Objective, X & Y Coys will move forward in readiness to resume the advance to Second Objective at O + 204 minutes.
   Z Coy will move back & take up a position in vicinity of HULSTRAAT.
   W Coy will occupy first objective.
   On reaching Second Objective, "X" Coy will consolidate the position & Y Coy will move back & take up a position in area S. of VOSSENHOEK.
   Every effort must be made to conceal the whereabouts of the troops after the final objective has been secured.

8. **Bn. HQ:** established initially at P.28.a.8.9. & will move along the N. boundary.
9. **PRISONERS:** will be sent back at once to Batt. HQ.
10. **AID POST** will be established at P.22.d.2.3.
11. **REPORTS** on progress must be sent back at each pause for communication back to Bde. This is of the greatest importance.
12. **AEROPLANES.** A contact patrol plane will fly along front at O+60, O+90 and O+120. Forward troops will show their positions by lighting flares 1 man in 3.
13. **ACKNOWLEDGE.**

Issued at 1815 hrs.
Distribution – Normal.

R. Jervis [illegible]
Captain
Adjutant 17th Lancs. Fusrs.

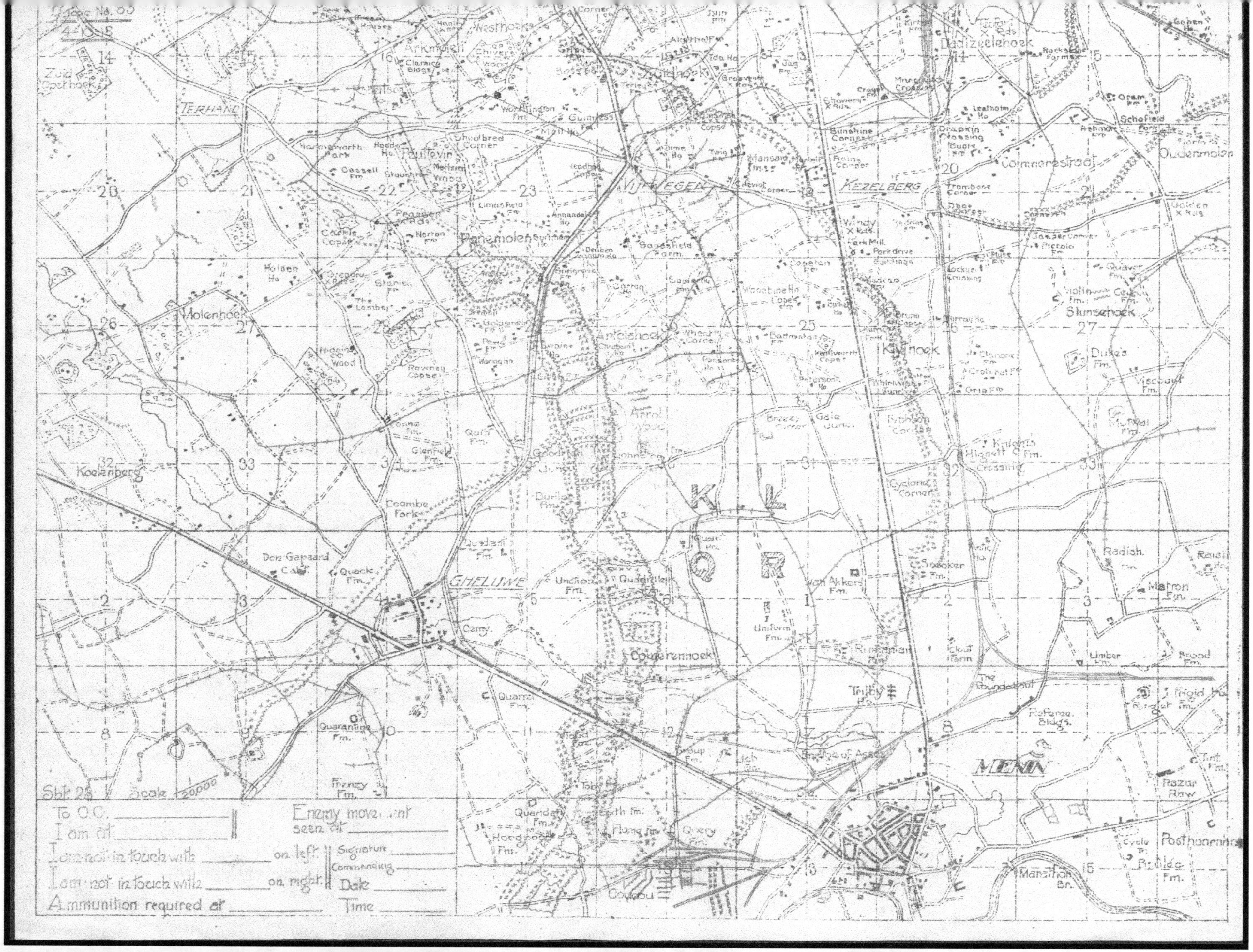

Zuid Ostrhoek
Terhand
Westhoek
Ankmolen
Zuidhoek
Dadizeelehoek
Oudenmolen
Kezelberg
Vijfwegen
Commerestraat
Molenhoek
Koelenberg
Anteishoek
Kruishoek
Slunsehoek
Ghelune
Coucerennoek
Menin
Coucou
Quarantine Fm.
Frenzy Fm.
Den Gapaard Cabt.
Coombe Fork
Uniform Fm.
Trilby Ho.
Bridge of Asses
Marathon Br.
Razar Row
Posthoornhk
The Roundabout
Referee Bldgs.
Sbt. 28
Scale 1/20000
To O.C.
I am at
I am not in touch with on left.
I am not in touch with on right.
Ammunition required at
Enemy movement seen at
Signature Commanding
Date
Time

Nº 9308
Busseboom
Reninghelst
Ouderdom
Dickebusch
Zevecoten
Westoutre
Hallebast
La Clytte
St Hubertushoek
G
H
M
N
Scale 1:20,000

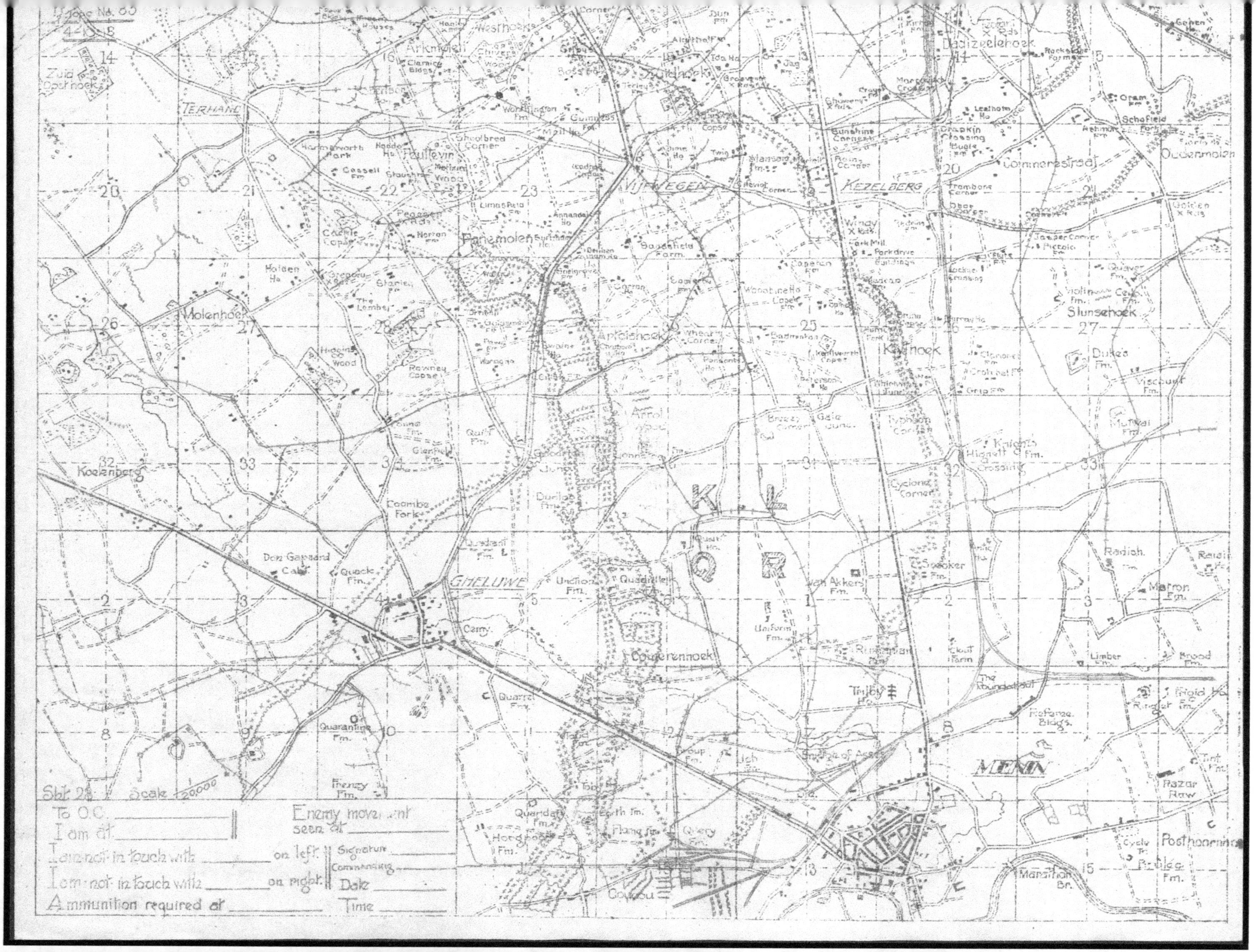

Westhoek
Arkmolen
Zuidhoek
Dadizeelehoek
Oudermolen
Commenestraat
Kezelberg
Vijfwegen
Terhand
Paddevin
Molenhoek
Anfolshoek
Kruiphoek
Slunsehoek
Koelenberg
Gheluwe
Coupernhoek
Menin
Postboerderie
Scale 1/20000
To O.C. ____
I am at ____
I am not in touch with ____ on left.
I am not in touch with ____ on right.
Ammunition required at ____
Enemy movement seen at ____
Signature Commanding ____
Date ____
Time ____

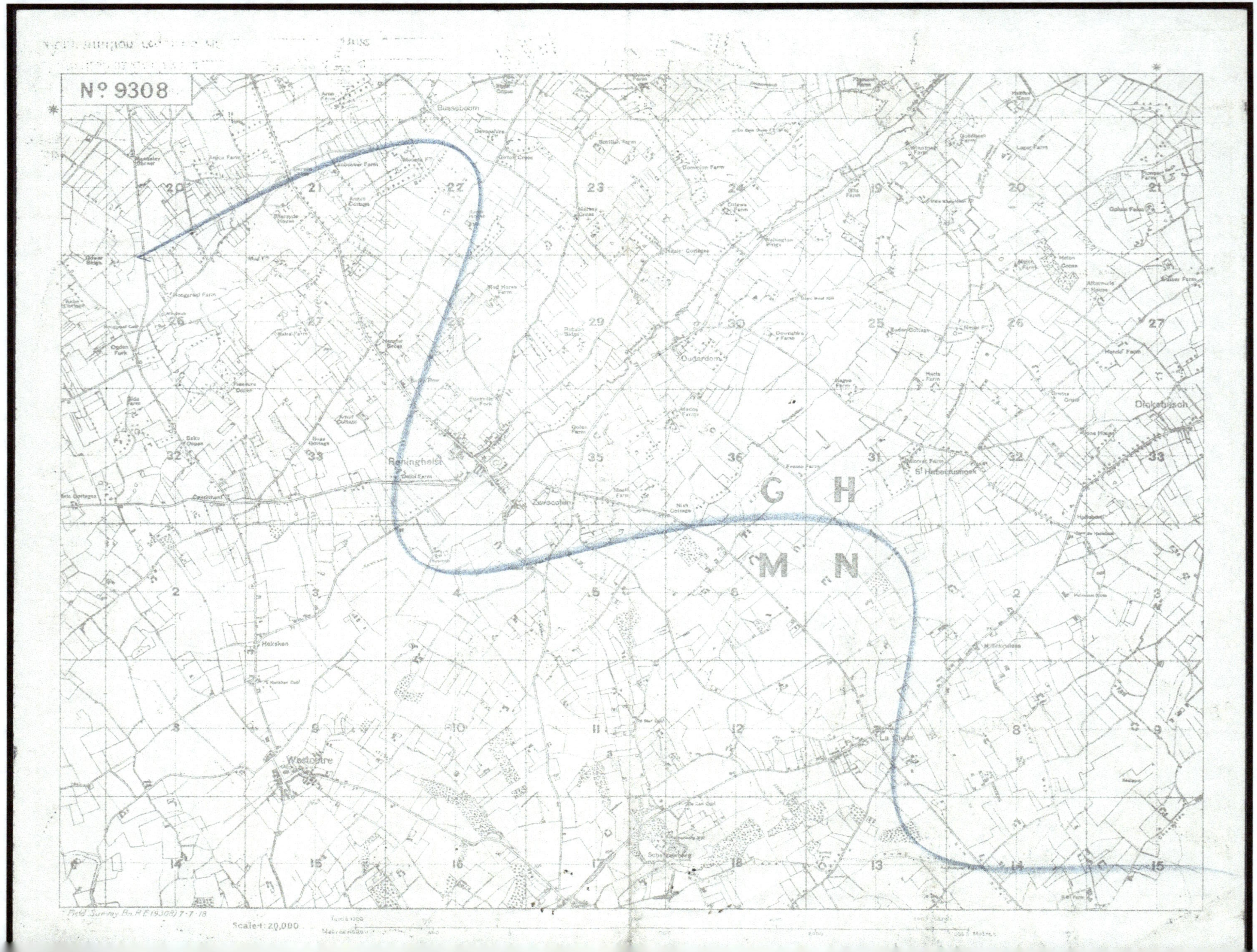

Nº 9308
Busseboom
Reninghelst
Ouderdom
Zevecoten
Westoutre
Dickebusch
St Hubertushoek
La Clytte
Hekskon
G
H
M
N
Field Survey Bn. R.E. (9308) 7-7-18
Scale 1:20,000

Nº 9252
TRENCHES CORRECTED FROM INFORMATION RECEIVED UP TO 6.7.18
Babington Camp
Bermuda Camp
Devon Camp
Barossa Camp
Devon wood
Shoe Wood
Kimberley Camp
Wedge Wood
Scherpenberg
Victoria Camp
Fermoy Farm
Fermoy Camp
Pompier Camp
Au Pompier Est
Clydesdale Camp
Jasper Camp
Kim Camp
Garden Farm
Garden Farm A Camp
Nut Farm
Garden Farm B Camp
Dettingham Camp
Fairy House Camp
Butterfly Farm Camp
Brulooze
Sebastopol Camp
Leeds Camp
Boiler Camp
FRONT
Cyclists Camp
Redan Camp
APPROXIMATE
Hospice
Kemmel Shelters
Gordon
Brulooze
Mont Kemmel
Artillery Road
Kemmel Windmills
Beaver Hall Camp
Cupola Dugouts
Norfolk Lines
Swindon
Taro Camp
12
8
18
13
14
24
19
20
30
25
26
36
31
32
M
N

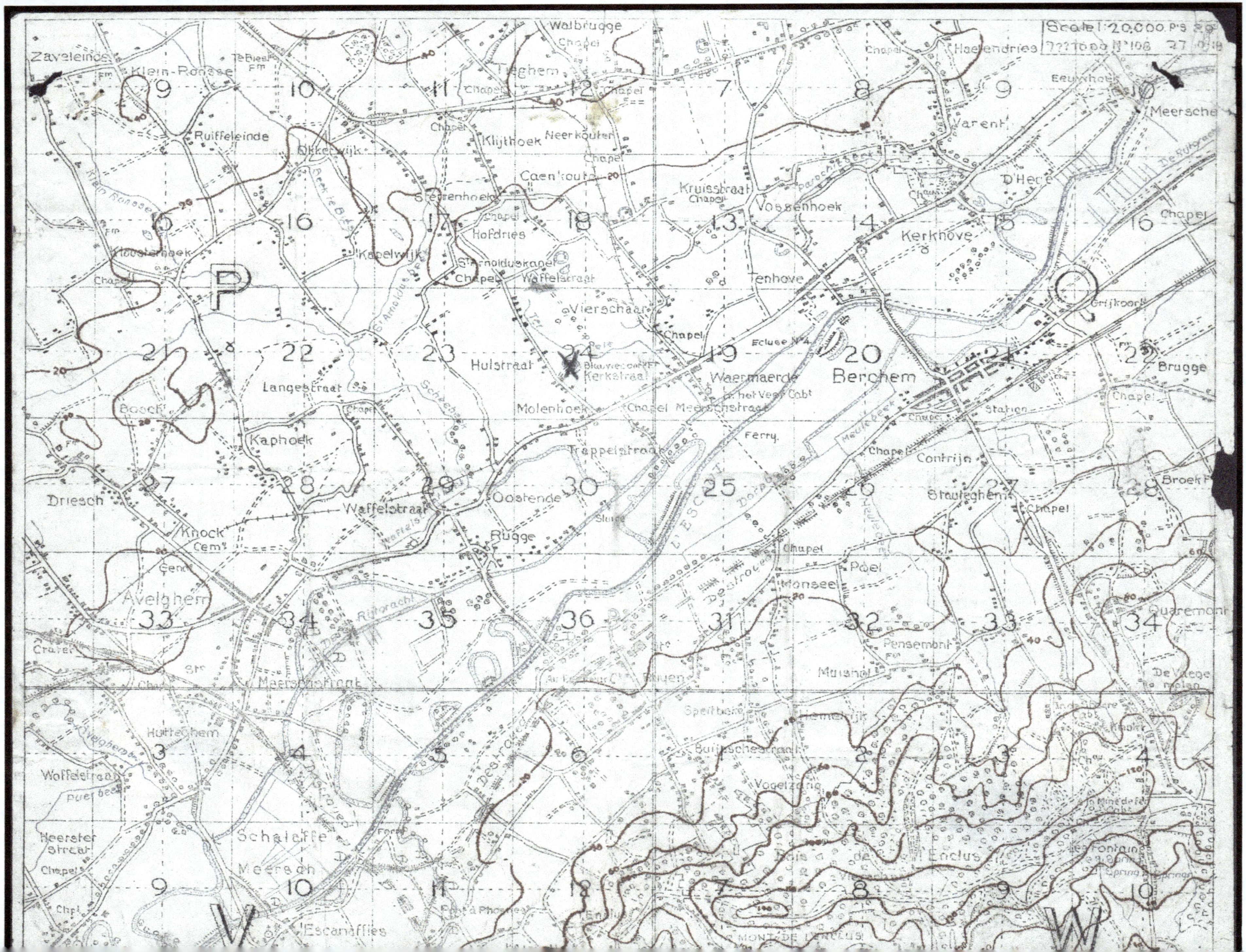

Scale 1:20,000
Zaveleinde
Klein-Ronsse
Walbrugge
Tieghem
Haelendries
Meersche
Ruiffeleinde
Okkerwijk
Klijthoek
Neer Kouter
Caenkouter
Varent
D'Hecre
Kruisstraat
Vossenhoek
Kerkhove
Hofdries
Kapelwijk
Waffelstraat
Vierschaar
Tenhove
Grijkoort
Hulstraat
Kerkstraat
Waermaerde
Berchem
Brugge
Langestraat
Molenhoek
Meerschstraat
Ferry
Station
Kaphoek
Trappelstraat
Contrijn
Broek
Driesch
Waffelstraat
Oostende
Rugge
Stauleghem
Knock
Poel
Monseel
Avelghem
Quaremont
Pensemont
Muisnol
Meerschstraat
Hutteghem
Woffelstraat
Heerster Straat
Schalaffe
Meersch
Escanaffles
Vogelzang
Bois de Enclus
MONT DE L'ENCLUS
L'Escaut
Eclusе No. 4
Chapel
P
V
W

No. 9252
TRENCHES CORRECTED FROM INFORMATION RECEIVED UP TO 6.7.18
Babington Camp
Ferns Camp
12
8
Riviere
Bermuda Camp
Devon Camp
Barossa Camp
Devon wood
Shoe wood
Kimberley Camp
Pandora
Wedge Wood
Scherpenberg
Victoria Camp
Clydesdale Camp
Jasper Camp
Pompier Camp
Fermoy Farm
Fermoy Camp
18
13
14
Au Pompier Est.
Nut Rd
Kim Camp
Garden Farm
Garden Farm A Camp
Nut Farm
Dettingham Camp
Garden Farm B Camp
Fairy House Camp
Butterfly Farm Camp
Brulooze
Sebastopol Camp
De Brulooze Cab.
Leeds Camp
Bailey Camp
FRONT
Cyclists Camp
24
19
20
Redan Camp
APPROXIMATE
Kemmel Shelters
Gordon
Hospice
Brulooze
Mont Kemmel
Tower
Road
Artillery
30
25
26
Kemmel Windmill
Cuppa Dugouts
Norfolk Lines
Construction
Beaver Hall Camp
Swindon
M
N
Tyro Camp
36
31
32

Scale 1:20,000
Zaveleinde
Klein-Ronsse
Walbrugge
Tieghem
Haelendries
Meersche
Ruiffeleinde
Klijthoek
Neer Kouter
Caenkouter
Kruisstraat
Vossenhoek
Kerkhove
D'Hede
Varent
Hofdries
Kapelwijk
Koutenhoek
Waffelstraat
Vierschaar
Tenhove
Grijkoort
Hulstraat
Kerkstraat
Waermaerde
Berchem
Brugge
Station
Langestraat
Molenhoek
Chapel Meersschstraat
Ferry
Kaphoek
Trappelstraat
Contrijn
Stautegem
Broek
Driesch
Oostende
Rugge
L'Escaut
Knock
Avelghem
Poel
Monseel
Quaremont
Pensemont
Maerschstraat
Muishol
De Vlegge molen
Speilberg
Hutteghem
Waffelstraat
Heerster Straat
Vogelzang
Schaleffe
Meersch
Escanaffles
Bois de l'Enclus
Mont de l'Enclus
P
V
W
Chapel

35

Army Form C. 2118.

Instructions regarding War Diaries and Intelligence Summaries are contained in F. S. Regs., Part II. and the Staff Manual respectively. Title pages will be prepared in manuscript. (Confidential)

# WAR DIARY
*or*
# ~~INTELLIGENCE SUMMARY.~~

*(Erase heading not required.)*

V8 34

| Place | Date | Hour | Summary of Events and Information | Remarks and references to Appendices |
|---|---|---|---|---|
| | | | The 17th Service (1st S.E.L.) Battalion | |
| | | | The Lancashire Fusiliers | |
| | | | From 1-11-18 To 30-11-18. | |
| | | | Volume No. 34 | |

34. V.
10 sheets

A5834 Wt. W4973/M687 750,000 8/16 D. D. & L. Ltd. Forms/C.2118/13.

Army Form C. 2118.

Instructions regarding War Diaries and Intelligence Summaries are contained in F. S. Regs., Part II. and the Staff Manual respectively. Title pages will be prepared in manuscript.

# WAR DIARY
*or*
# INTELLIGENCE SUMMARY.
*(Erase heading not required.)*

NOVEMBER, 1918. REF. MAPS. Sheets 29 + 30. 1/40,000

| Place | Date | Hour | Strength 1-11-18 Offs – 30. O.R. – 670. Summary of Events and Information | Remarks and references to Appendices |
|---|---|---|---|---|
| TENHOVE | 1. | | Line captured consolidated. During the evening relieved by 41st Division. Relief completed by 2200 hrs. On relief Battn. moved back to billets at Lock No. 6. (O.2.b.) | |
| | | | 2ND LIEUT. TURNER joined for duty. | |
| O.2.b. | 2. | 1300 | Battn. moved to HOOGE area S.E of COURTRAI. | |
| HOOGE. | 3. | | Cleaning up & resting. Baths. | |
| do. | 4. | | do & Platoon Training. | |
| do. | 5. | | Stand by to move to HARLEBEKE area 1400 hrs. – Move cancelled. | |
| do. | 6. | | Platoon Training. LIEUT. J. GOODIER joined for duty. | |
| do. | 7. | 1200 | Battn. moved to ESSCHER area I 31 + 32. | |
| ESSCHER | 8. | | Platoon Training. | |
| do. | 9. | 0930 | Battn. moved to OKKERWIJK P.10.d. | |
| | | 1700 | Battn. crossed L'ESCAUT & billeted in BERCHEM. Q 20 + 21. | |

A5834 Wt. W4973/M687 750,000 8/16 D. D. & L. Ltd. Forms/C.2118/13.

Instructions regarding War Diaries and Intelligence Summaries are contained in F. S. Regs., Part II. and the Staff Manual respectively. Title pages will be prepared in manuscript.

# WAR DIARY
*or*
# INTELLIGENCE SUMMARY.

(*Erase heading not required.*)

Army Form C. 2118.

| Place | Date (NOVEMBER.) | Hour | Summary of Events and Information | Remarks and references to Appendices |
|---|---|---|---|---|
| BERCHEM | 10 | 0720 | Battn. moved forward, 18th L.F. acting as Advanced Guard. | |
| | | 1300 | Having reached AUDENHOVE M.34.d. the Battn. billeted there. All Entrances to the village were picqueted. The Outpost line, held by 18th L.F. was established about 4000x E. of AUDENHOVE. | |
| AUDENHOVE | 11 | 0400 | At 0400 hrs. orders were received from 104 Bde. to move through Outpost line (then held by 18th LAN.FUS.) at 0900 hrs, as advance guard to 104 Bde, taking as the first objective a general line O.22.c.0.0. to U.3 central & then, if situation allowed, to push on & seize the crossing of the DENDRE at GRAMMONT. | |
| | | | 2 Platoons of XIX Corps Cyclists, 1 Battery of M.M.G.C. & 1 Battery (R.F.A. 159) of field guns are placed at tactical disposal of Battn. Commander. | |
| | | 0715 | At 0715 hrs. the Battn. moved from AUDENHOVE, with X Coy as advance guard. | |
| | | | The composite advanced guard assembled in rear of the outpost line & No. 1 Platoon Cyclists, with one M.M.G. attached, were ordered to occupy & hold high ground E. of PARICKE, No 2 Platoon Cyclists, with one M.M.G. attached, being ordered | |

A5834 Wt. W4973/M687 750,000 8/16 D. D. & L. Ltd. Forms/C.2118/13.

Instructions regarding War Diaries and Intelligence Summaries are contained in F. S. Regs., Part II. and the Staff Manual respectively. Title pages will be prepared in manuscript.

# WAR DIARY
*or*
# INTELLIGENCE SUMMARY.
*(Erase heading not required.)*

Army Form C. 2118.

| Place | Date (NOVEMBER) | Hour | Summary of Events and Information | Remarks and references to Appendices |
|---|---|---|---|---|
| AUDENHOVE | 11 | 0715 | to occupy & hold high ground in O.32.b. & report on position of enemy. | |
| | | 0900 | The Battn advanced through the outpost line at 0900 hrs. with X Coy. as advanced guard, operating in two columns. | |
| | | 1015 | At 1015 hrs. Cyclist Platoons reported no sign of enemy. Orders were at once issued for the two Cyclist Platoons to push on to GRAMMONT & secure the bridges as rapidly as possible. | |
| | | 1030 | Battn. reached the general line of first objective. X Coy. pushed down to GRAMMONT in support of the Cyclist Platoons, the remaining guns of the M.M.G.C. being held in readiness to support this forward move. Meanwhile C Battery R.F.A. 159 was ordered to come into action covering the GRAMMONT Bridgehead. | |
| | | 1105 | Message was received that an armistice had been signed & hostilities ceased at 1100 hrs; the line as held at 1100 hrs. to be established as an outpost line. At this time the cyclists & M.M.G's had established themselves on the E. side of GRAMMONT & had secured the DENDRE crossings. X Coy were well on their way to the same place. | |

A5834 Wt. W4973/M687 750,000 8/16 D. D. & L. Ltd. Forms/C.2118/13.

Instructions regarding War Diaries and Intelligence Summaries are contained in F. S. Regs., Part II. and the Staff Manual respectively. Title pages will be prepared in manuscript.

# WAR DIARY
*or*
# INTELLIGENCE SUMMARY.
*(Erase heading not required.)*

Army Form C. 2118.

| Place | NOVEMBER Date | Hour | Summary of Events and Information | Remarks and references to Appendices |
|---|---|---|---|---|
| AUDENHOVE | 11 | 1120 | The Divisional Commander passed in a Staff Car returning from GRAMMONT, having previously passed through the infantry scouts of X Coy. on his way towards GRAMMONT. | |
| | | | The Divisional Commander issued verbal orders that only the bridges themselves were to be held & no British troops were to cross the DENDRE. As soon as possible the Cyclists & M.M.G's were recalled from the E. edge of the town & took up a position covering the bridges over the DENDRE & W. of that river. | |
| | | 1130 | X took over the bridges & established a position. | |
| | | | At this time, 1130 hrs, some French Cavalry pushed through our outpost line & took up the position vacated by the two cyclist platoons. | |
| | | | No enemy were seen & no hostile action was encountered. | |
| | | | Later in the day 11 enemy surrendered, having hidden in cellars. | |
| | | | In the evening about 200 returned British prisoners were received & cared for. | |

A5834 Wt. W4973/M687 750,000 8/16 D. D. & L. Ltd. Forms/C.2118/13.

Army Form C. 2118.

Instructions regarding War Diaries and Intelligence Summaries are contained in F. S. Regs., Part II. and the Staff Manual respectively. Title pages will be prepared in manuscript.

# WAR DIARY
*or*
# INTELLIGENCE SUMMARY.
*(Erase heading not required.)*

| Place | Date NOVEMBER | Hour | Summary of Events and Information | Remarks and references to Appendices |
|---|---|---|---|---|
| Vicinity of GRAMMONT | 12 | | Resting + cleaning up. | |
| do. | 13 | 1200 | Battn. moved to SCHOORISSE M. 11. c., arriving at 1530 hrs. | |
| SCHOORISSE | 14 | | Resting + cleaning up.<br>Returned British prisoners of war sent to Divisional Reception Camp | |
| do. | 15 | | Section Rifle Competition won by H.Q. Section of W Coy. | |
| do. | 16 | | Section Walking Race won by No. 5 Section of Z Coy. | |
| do. | 17 | | Recreational Training + Divine Services. | |
| do | 18 | 1130 | Battn. moved from SCHOORISSE to BERCHEM, arriving at 1500 hrs. | |
| BERCHEM | 19 | 1000 | Battn. moved from BERCHEM to HARLEBEKE H. 12. a., arriving at 1430 hrs. where they billeted | |
| HARLEBEKE | 20 | | Resting + cleaning up. | |
| do. | 21 | | Battn. Medical Inspection.<br>Cleaning up — Eight officers reported for duty. | |

A5834 Wt. W4973/M687 750,000 8/16 D. D. & L. Ltd. Forms/C.2118/13.

Instructions regarding War Diaries and Intelligence Summaries are contained in F. S. Regs., Part II. and the Staff Manual respectively. Title pages will be prepared in manuscript.

# WAR DIARY
*or*
# INTELLIGENCE SUMMARY.

*(Erase heading not required.)*

Army Form C. 2118.

| Place | Date NOVEMBER | Hour | Summary of Events and Information | Remarks and references to Appendices |
|---|---|---|---|---|
| HARLEBEKE | 22 | | Arm Drill, Recreational Training & Baths. | |
| do | 23 | | Arm Drill & Recreational Training. | |
| do | 24 | | Divine Services. | |
| do | 25 | | Arm Drill, Squad Drill, Ceremonial Drill & Recreational Training. | |
| do | 26 | | Fitting of Marching Order, Physical Training, Arm Drill & Foot Inspection. | |
| do | 27 | | Battn. Route March. | |
| do | 28 | | Arm & Ceremonial Drill. | |
| do | 29 | 0850 | Battn: marched to MENIN, billeting on arrival at 1400 hours. | |
| MENIN | 30 | 0900 | Battn. moved to VLAMERTINGHE, arriving at 1600 hours. | |

A5834 Wt. W4973/M687 750,000 8/16 D. D. & L. Ltd. Forms/C.2118/13.

Instructions regarding War Diaries and Intelligence Summaries are contained in F. S. Regs., Part II. and the Staff Manual respectively. Title pages will be prepared in manuscript.

# WAR DIARY
*or*
# INTELLIGENCE SUMMARY.
*(Erase heading not required.)*

Army Form C. 2118.

| Place | Date | Hour | Summary of Events and Information | Remarks and references to Appendices |
|---|---|---|---|---|
| | | | Honours gained by the Battalion during the period 1st — 30th November, 1918. | |
| | | | award. | |
| | | | CAPT. C.S. ATKINSON. M.C. — Bar to M.C. | |
| | | | LIEUT. C. HUNTLY. North'd Fus. (attached) — M.C. | |
| | | | T/LIEUT. P.J. McKEVITT. — M.C. | |
| | | | 2ND LIEUT. A.C. STEPHENSON. E. Yorks. R. (attached) — M.C. | |
| | | | 57435 Pte. A. WALMSLEY — D.C.M. | |
| | | | 14689 Sgt. H. ROOKE. M.M. — Bar to M.M. | |
| | | | 14956 Sgt. F. TETLOW M.M. — Bar to M.M. | |
| | | | 14718 Pte. L.G. BRIERS. M.M. — Bar to M.M. | |

A5834 Wt. W4973/M687 750,000 8/16 D. D. & L. Ltd. Forms/C.2118/13.

Instructions regarding War Diaries and Intelligence Summaries are contained in F. S. Regs., Part II. and the Staff Manual respectively. Title pages will be prepared in manuscript.

# WAR DIARY
*or*
# INTELLIGENCE SUMMARY.
(*Erase heading not required.*)

Army Form C. 2118.

| Place | Date | Hour | Summary of Events and Information | Remarks and references to Appendices |
|---|---|---|---|---|
| | | | Honours gained by the Battalion (continued) | |
| | | | The following have been awarded the MILITARY MEDAL. | |

| | | | | | | |
|---|---|---|---|---|---|---|
| 19724 | C.S.M. | C.W. CHAMBERLAIN. | | 35711 | Pte. | J.M. GREGSON. |
| 32129 | Sgt. | R.H. GARNETT. | | 62953 | Pte. | J.E. MINCHER. |
| 14910 | Sgt. | C. PARSONS. | | 46428 | Pte. | C.P. GRAY. |
| 32109 | Sgt. | F.J. ROWLANDS. | | 46438 | Pte. | H. KNOWLES. |
| 15541 | Cpl. | T. PEMBERTON. | | 46403 | Pte. | G. WILKIE. |
| 40976 | Lce Cpl. | J. FRANCIS. | | 34322 | Pte | R.T. KERSHAW. |
| 41938 | Lce Cpl. | S. KENDALL. | | 14102 | Pte. | A. MOLE. |
| 12320 | Pte. | W. THOMAS. | | 35027 | Pte. | J. PENDELL. |
| 9522 | Pte. | E. SPEAR. | | 34531 | Pte. | I. WINSTANLEY. |
| 22289 | Pte. | C.B. HODGKISS. | | 305764 | Pte. | W. WILLIAMS. |
| 46792 | Pte. | C. LANE. | | 26640 | Pte | W. CONNOR. |
| 21962 | Pte. | P. BROUGHTON. | | 12688 | Dmr. | R. HOWARTH. |
| 20442 | Pte. | J. HOLDEN. | | | | |

A5834 Wt. W4973/M687 750,000 8/16 D. D. & L. Ltd. Forms/C.2118/13.

Instructions regarding War Diaries and Intelligence Summaries are contained in F. S. Regs., Part II. and the Staff Manual respectively. Title pages will be prepared in manuscript.

# WAR DIARY
*or*
# INTELLIGENCE SUMMARY.
*(Erase heading not required.)*

Army Form C. 2118.

| Place | Date | Hour | Summary of Events and Information | Remarks and references to Appendices |
|---|---|---|---|---|
| | | | Casualties for month:- | |
| | | | Officers - NIL | |
| | | | Other Ranks - NIL | |
| | | | Strength of Battalion:- 30th November, 1918. | |
| | | | Officers:- 39 | |
| | | | Other Ranks - 684. | |
| | | | G. Rackwith [signature] Lieut. Colonel, Commanding 17th (S) Bn. Lancs. Fusiliers. | |

A5834 Wt. W4973/M687 750,000 8/16 D. D. & L. Ltd. Forms/C.2118/13.

(Confidential.)

Instructions regarding War Diaries and Intelligence Summaries are contained in F. S. Regs., Part II. and the Staff Manual respectively. Title pages will be prepared in manuscript.

# WAR DIARY
*or*
~~INTELLIGENCE~~ SUMMARY.

*(Erase heading not required.)*

35

Army Form C. 2118.

Vol 35

| Place | Date | Hour | Summary of Events and Information | Remarks and references to Appendices |
|---|---|---|---|---|
| | | | The 17th Service (1st S.E.L.) Battalion | |
| | | | The Lancashire Fusiliers | |
| | | | From 1-12-1918 to 31-12-1918. | |
| | | | VOLUME No 35. | |

17th (S) BATTN.
LANCASHIRE
FUSILIERS.
No. 0346
Date 2 1 1919

35 V.
6 sheet

D. D. & L., London, E.C.
(A7883) Wt. W803/M1672 350,000 4/17 Sch. 52a Forms/C/2118/14

Army Form C. 2118.

Instructions regarding War Diaries and Intelligence Summaries are contained in F. S. Regs., Part II. and the Staff Manual respectively. Title pages will be prepared in manuscript.

# WAR DIARY
*or*
# ~~INTELLIGENCE SUMMARY.~~
*(Erase heading not required.)*

DECEMBER, 1918

REF. MAP – HAZEBROUCK 1/100,000.

| Place | Date | Hour | Summary of Events and Information | Remarks and references to Appendices |
|---|---|---|---|---|
| VLAMERTINGHE | 1 | 08-40 | Battalion moved to St. SYLVESTRE CAPPEL billetting on arrival at 1600 hours. | |
| ST. SYLVESTRE CAPPEL | 2 | 08-20 | Battalion moved to MERCKEGHEM arriving at 1500 hours. | |
| MERCKEGHEM | 3 | | Resting and cleaning up. | |
| " | 4 | | Ceremonial drill, physical and recreational training. | |
| " | 5 | | Company drill, physical and recreational training, Battalion Bathed. | |
| " | 6 | | Ceremonial drill, physical and recreational training and Education. | |
| " | 7 | | do. do. | |
| " | 8 | | Divine Services. | |
| " | 9 | | Ceremonial drill, physical, recreational and educational training. | |
| " | 10 | | do. do. | |
| " | 11 | | do. do. | |
| " | 12 | | do. do. G.O.C. 104th Inf Bde. lectured | |
| | | | officers and other ranks on "Whether it is worth while staying on in the Army" | |
| " | 13 | 11.30 | Medal presentation by Major. General MARINDIN in the Square, BOLLEZEELE. | |
| " | 14 | | Ceremonial drill, Cross. Country run. Educational Training. | |
| " | 15 | | Divine Services. | |

D. D. & L., London, E.C.
(A7893) Wt. W803/M1672 350,000 4/17 Sch. 52a Forms/C/2118/14

2.

Instructions regarding War Diaries and Intelligence Summaries are contained in F. S. Regs., Part II. and the Staff Manual respectively. Title pages will be prepared in manuscript.

# WAR DIARY
*or*
~~INTELLIGENCE SUMMARY.~~
*(Erase heading not required.)*

Army Form C. 2118.

| Place | Decr. Date | Hour | Summary of Events and Information | Remarks and references to Appendices |
|---|---|---|---|---|
| MERCKEGHEM | 16. | - | Musketry, Ceremonial drill, Physical and Recreational Training. Education. | |
| " | 17. | - | do. do. | |
| " | 18. | - | do. do. and Baths. | |
| " | 19. | - | do. do. | |
| " | 20. | - | do. do. a/Capt. R. Irvine, M.C. Adjutant, left Battalion on being demobilized and a/Capt. C. Huntly, M.C. took over the duties of Adjutant, Lieut. A.E. Veitch taking over duties of Education Officer. | |
| " | 21. | - | Training, education, and bathing continued. | |
| " | 22 | - | Divine Services. | |
| " | 23. | - | Training, education and bathing continued. | |
| " | 24. | - | do. | |
| " | 25. | - | Xmas Day - Holiday - Church parades. G.O.C. 104th Inf. Bde. visited the men at dinners. | |
| " | 26 | - | No parades. | |
| " | 27 | - | Training and Education continued. G.O.C. 104th Inf. Bde. delived a lecture to the Education classes on the "Soudan, &c" | |

D. D. & L., London, E.C.
(A7883) Wt. W803/M1672 350,000 4/17 Sch. 52a Forms/C/2118/14

3.

Instructions regarding War Diaries and Intelligence Summaries are contained in F. S. Regs., Part II. and the Staff Manual respectively. Title pages will be prepared in manuscript.

# WAR DIARY

*or*

~~INTELLIGENCE SUMMARY.~~

*(Erase heading not required.)*

Army Form C. 2118.

| Place | Decr. Date | Hour | Summary of Events and Information | Remarks and references to Appendices |
|---|---|---|---|---|
| MERCKEGHEM. | 28. | – | Training and Education continued. | |
| " | 29. | – | Divine Services. | |
| " | 30 | – | Salvage, Training and Education resumed. Baths. | |
| " | 31. | – | do | |

D. D. & L., London, E.C.
(A7883) Wt. W803/M1672 350,000 4/17 Sch. 52a Forms/C/2118/14

Army Form C. 2118.

Instructions regarding War Diaries and Intelligence Summaries are contained in F. S. Regs., Part II. and the Staff Manual respectively. Title pages will be prepared in manuscript.

# WAR DIARY
*or*
~~INTELLIGENCE SUMMARY.~~
*(Erase heading not required.)*

| Place | Date | Hour | Summary of Events and Information | Remarks and references to Appendices |
|---|---|---|---|---|
| | | | Casualties for month — | |
| | | | Officers — NIL. | |
| | | | Other Ranks — NIL. | |
| | | | Strength of Battalion — 31st December, 1918 | |
| | | | Officers — 39. | |
| | | | Other Ranks — 689. | |
| | | | [illegible] | |
| | | | Lieut Colonel, | |
| | | | 2nd January, 1918. Commanding, 17th (S.) Bn. Lan. Fusiliers. | |

D. D. & L., London, E.C.
(A7883) Wt. W593/M1672 350,000 4/17 Sch. 52a Forms/C/2118/14

Army Form C. 2118.

# WAR DIARY
*or*
~~INTELLIGENCE SUMMARY.~~
*(Erase heading not required.)*

Instructions regarding War Diaries and Intelligence Summaries are contained in F. S. Regs., Part II, and the Staff Manual respectively. Title pages will be prepared in manuscript.

| Place | Date | Hour | Summary of Events and Information | Remarks and references to Appendices |
|---|---|---|---|---|
| | | | Honours gained by the Battalion during the period | |
| | | | 1st – 31st December, 1918. | |
| | | | AWARD. | |
| | | | 2nd LT. W. D. Stott — Military Cross. | |
| | | | 2nd LT. H. R. E. IRVING Killed/A — do. | |
| | | | Capt. H. G. LEAVER, M.C. — Croix de Guerre (Corps). | |
| | | | Capt. R. IRVINE, M.C. — do. (Division). | |
| | | | No. 33615, Pte. A. WARD. — Distinguished Conduct Medal. | |
| | | | " 18099, Cpl. J. WARD. — Croix de Guerre (Brigade). | |

D. D. & L., London, E.C.
(A7883) Wt. W803/M1672 350,000 4/17 Sch. 52a Forms/C/2118/14

35

Confidential.

Instructions regarding War Diaries and Intelligence Summaries are contained in F. S. Regs., Part II. and the Staff Manual respectively. Title pages will be prepared in manuscript.

# WAR DIARY
*or*
# ~~INTELLIGENCE~~ SUMMARY.

(*Erase heading not required.*)

Army Form C. 2118.

Vol 36

| Place | Date | Hour | Summary of Events and Information | Remarks and references to Appendices |
|---|---|---|---|---|
| | | | The 17th Service (1st S.E.L.) Battalion<br>The Lancashire Fusiliers.<br><br>From 1-1-1919 to 31-1-1919.<br><br>VOLUME 36. | |

36. V. 6 mnt

A5834 Wt. W4973/M687 750,000 8/16 D. D. & L. Ltd. Forms/C.2118/13.

Confidential.

Army Form C. 2118.

# WAR DIARY

or

~~INTELLIGENCE SUMMARY.~~

(*Erase heading not required.*)

Instructions regarding War Diaries and Intelligence Summaries are contained in F. S. Regs., Part II. and the Staff Manual respectively. Title pages will be prepared in manuscript.

JANUARY - 1919.

REF. MAPS - HAZEBROUCK 1:100,000. CALAIS 1:40,000

| Place | Date | Hour | Summary of Events and Information | Remarks and references to Appendices |
|---|---|---|---|---|
| MERCKEGHEM | 1 | – | New Year's Day – Holiday | |
| " | 2 | – | Training, Salvage and Education resumed. | |
| " | 3 | – | do. G.O.C. 104th Inf. Bde lectured Education classes on "the South African Campaign". | |
| " | 4 | – | Training, Salvage and Education. | |
| " | 5 | – | Divine Services | |
| " | 6 | – | Training, Salvage and Education. | |
| " | 7 | – | do. Lecture on "India" by G.O.C. 104th Inf Bde. | |
| " | 8 | – | Training, Salvage and Education | |
| " | 9 | – | do | |
| " | 10 | – | do. | |
| " | 11 | – | do | |
| " | 12 | – | Divine Services. | |
| " | 13 | – | Training, Salvage, ~~and~~ Education and Baths. | |
| " | 14 | – | do do. | |

D. D. & L., London, E.C. (A7883) Wt. W80/M1672 350,000 4/17 Sch. 52a Forms/C/2118/14

Confidential

Instructions regarding War Diaries and Intelligence Summaries are contained in F. S. Regs., Part II, and the Staff Manual respectively. Title pages will be prepared in manuscript.

# WAR DIARY

~~or~~

~~INTELLIGENCE SUMMARY.~~

(Erase heading not required.)

Army Form C. 2118.

| Place | Date | Hour | Summary of Events and Information | Remarks and references to Appendices |
|---|---|---|---|---|
| | January, 1919 | | | |
| MERCKEGHEM | 15 | – | Training, Salvage and Education. Battalion Cross Country Race in afternoon. | |
| " | 16 | – | Training, Salvage and Education. | |
| " | 17 | – | do. | |
| " | 18 | – | do. | |
| " | 19 | – | Divine Services. | |
| " | 20 | – | Training, Salvage, Education and Baths. | |
| " | 21 | – | do do | |
| " | 22 | – | Training, Salvage and Education. "Gibraltar" was the subject of a lecture by the G.O.C. Brigade. | |
| " | 23 | – | Training, Salvage and Education. Major A.J. SCULLY, M.C. Manchester Regiment, arrived and took over command of the Battalion from a/Lt. Col. G. Mackereth, M.C. | |
| " | 24 | – | Training, Salvage and Education. Amalgamation of Companies making a two-Company Battalion. | |
| " | 25 | – | do. | |
| " | 26 | – | Divine Services. | |

D. D. & L., London, E.C.
(A7883) Wt. W803/M1672 350,000 4/17 Sch. 52a Forms C/2118/14

Confidential.

Instructions regarding War Diaries and Intelligence Summaries are contained in F. S. Regs., Part II. and the Staff Manual respectively. Title pages will be prepared in manuscript.

# WAR DIARY
*or*
~~INTELLIGENCE SUMMARY.~~
*(Erase heading not required.)*

Army Form C. 2118.

| Place | Date | Hour | Summary of Events and Information | Remarks and references to Appendices |
|---|---|---|---|---|
| | January, 1919. | | | |
| [illegible]ERCKEGHEM | 27 | – | Training, Salvage and Education. | |
| " | 28 | – | do. | |
| " | 29 | – | Battalion paraded at 0700 hours leaving a few details behind and route marched to WATTEN where it entrained for CALAIS. This hurried move was in connection with a very serious mutiny amongst returning leave men. Men of Battalion billetted in No 5 Leave Camp for night. | |
| [illegible]ALAIS | 30 | 11 | The Battalion, in conjunction with the remainder of the brigade, marched to the camp occupied by the mutineers, entered the camp and took up its allotted position. The outbreak was peacefully settled by 1300 hours today. Battalion remained in No 5 Camp. | |
| " | 31 | — | Cleaning up. | |

3/2/1919

A. [illegible] Lieut Colonel,
Commanding 17th (S) Bn
Lancashire Fusiliers

A5834 Wt. W4973/M687 750,000 8/16 D. D. & L. Ltd. Forms/C.2118/13.

Instructions regarding War Diaries and Intelligence Summaries are contained in F. S. Regs., Part II. and the Staff Manual respectively. Title pages will be prepared in manuscript.

# WAR DIARY
*or*
# INTELLIGENCE SUMMARY.
*(Erase heading not required.)*

Army Form C. 2118.

| Place | Date | Hour | Summary of Events and Information | Remarks and references to Appendices |
|---|---|---|---|---|
| | | | Honours gained by the Battalion during the period 1st – 31st January, 1919 | |
| | | | Award | |
| | | | Lt Col. G. MACKERETH — Croix de Guerre Belge | |
| | | | 2nd Lt J. WORTHINGTON — do | |

A5834 Wt. W4973/M687 750,000 8/16 D. D. & L. Ltd. Forms/C.2118/13.

Instructions regarding War Diaries and Intelligence Summaries are contained in F. S. Regs., Part II. and the Staff Manual respectively. Title pages will be prepared in manuscript.

# WAR DIARY
*or*
# INTELLIGENCE SUMMARY.

*(Erase heading not required.)*

Army Form C. 2118.

| Place | Date | Hour | Summary of Events and Information | Remarks and references to Appendices |
|---|---|---|---|---|
| | | | Casualties for month —<br>Officers — NIL.<br>Other ranks — NIL.<br><br>Strength of Battalion — 31st January, 1919<br>Officers — 32<br>Other Ranks — 480.<br><br>3rd February, 1919.<br><br>A. [signature] Lieut Colonel<br>Commanding, 17th (S) Bn. Lan. Fusiliers. | |

A5834 Wt. W4973/M687 750,000 8/16 D. D. & L. Ltd. Forms/C.2118/13.

Confidential

Instructions regarding War Diaries and Intelligence Summaries are contained in F. S. Regs., Part II. and the Staff Manual respectively. Title pages will be prepared in manuscript.

FEBRUARY 1919

# WAR DIARY
*or*
# INTELLIGENCE SUMMARY.
*(Erase heading not required.)*

17 L F

Army Form C. 2118.

Ref. Maps HAZEBROUCK 1:100.000 CALAIS 1:40000

18 34

| Place | Date | Hour | Summary of Events and Information | Remarks and references to Appendices |
|---|---|---|---|---|
| CALAIS | 1 | — | The Battalion at No. 5 Camp – men employed in running the camp for leave men | |
| | 2 | — | The Battalion moved at 0915 hours to No 5 Labour Group Camp at BOULOGNE | |
| BOULOGNE | 3 | — | Training and cleaning up. – 38 men to 47th P.O.W. Coy. | |
| | 4 | — | —— do —— | |
| | 5 | — | —— do —— | |
| | 6. | — | Congratulatory message from Major General expressing appreciation of the soldierly manner in which all ranks carried out their duties during the last few days. The Good discipline particularly noted. | |
| | 7 | — | Training under company arrangements. | |
| | 8 | — | —— do —— | |
| | 9 | — | Divine Services. | |
| | 10 | — | The Battalion employed in escort duties for P.O.W. work | |
| CALAIS | ~~#~~ | — | At 1300 hours the Battalion moved to No. 6. Camp CALAIS | |
| | 11 | — | Lt. Col A. J. SCULLY. M.C. and Capt. C. HUNTLY. M.C. took over the duties of CAMP COMMANDANT and CAMP ADJUTANT respectively. | |
| | 12 | — | Capt. J. H. B. CRAWFORD took charge of the portion of the Battalion at No. 6. Leave Camp. The men employed in the running of the camp. | |

37. V. 2 sheets

A5834 Wt. W4973/M687 750,000 8/16 D. D. & L. Ltd. Forms/C.2118/13.

Confidential

Instructions regarding War Diaries and Intelligence Summaries are contained in F. S. Regs., Part II. and the Staff Manual respectively. Title pages will be prepared in manuscript.

FEBRUARY 1919

# WAR DIARY
*or*
# INTELLIGENCE SUMMARY.

*(Erase heading not required.)*

Army Form C. 2118.

Ref Maps: HAZEBROUCK 1:100000; CALAIS 1:40000

| Place | Date | Hour | Summary of Events and Information | Remarks and references to Appendices |
|---|---|---|---|---|
| CALAIS | 13 | — | The Battalion employed in duties involved in running of No 6 Leave Camp | |
| | 14 | — | — do — | |
| | 15 | — | — do — | |
| | 16 | — | Divine Services | |
| | 17 | — | The Battalion running No 6 Leave Camp. | |
| | 18 | — | — do — | |
| | 19–27 | — | The Battalion employed as Police, Cookhouse orderlies escorts etc in the running of No 6. LEAVE CAMP. | |
| BEAUMARAIS | 28 | | The Battalion moved at 1400 hours to No 5 CAMP BEAUMARAIS | |

3/3/19.

[signature] Lieut Colonel
Commanding 17th (S) Bn Lancashire Fusiliers

A5834 Wt. W4973/M687 750,000 8/16 D. D. & L. Ltd. Forms/C.2118/13.

Instructions regarding War Diaries and Intelligence Summaries are contained in F. S. Regs., Part II. and the Staff Manual respectively. Title pages will be prepared in manuscript.

# WAR DIARY
*or*
# INTELLIGENCE SUMMARY.
*(Erase heading not required.)*

Army Form C. 2118.

| Place | Date | Hour | Summary of Events and Information | Remarks and references to Appendices |
|---|---|---|---|---|
| | | | Honours gained by the Battalion during the period 1st — 28th February 1919 | |
| | | | 48962 Pte. CRITCHLEY. J. — AWARD Military Medal | |
| | | | 22415 Pte ROBINSON. J. — do — | |
| | | | (both attached to 104. Bde. H.Q.) | |

A5834 Wt. W4973/M687 750,000 8/16 D. D. & L. Ltd. Forms/C.2118/13.

Instructions regarding War Diaries and Intelligence Summaries are contained in F. S. Regs., Part II. and the Staff Manual respectively. Title pages will be prepared in manuscript.

# WAR DIARY
*or*
# INTELLIGENCE SUMMARY.
*(Erase heading not required.)*

Army Form C. 2118.

| Place | Date | Hour | Summary of Events and Information | Remarks and references to Appendices |
|---|---|---|---|---|
| | | | Casualties for the month— | |
| | | | Officers — NIL | |
| | | | O.Rs — NIL | |
| | | | Strength of Battalion — 28th February 1919 | |
| | | | Officers — 29 | |
| | | | O.Rs. — 288. | |
| | | | 3rd March. 1919. | |
| | | | [illegible] Lieut-Colonel. | |
| | | | Commanding. 1st (S) Bn Lancashire Fusiliers | |

A5834 Wt. W4973/M687 750,000 8/16 D. D. & L. Ltd. Forms/C.2118/13.

CONFIDENTIAL

Instructions regarding ~~War Diaries and Intelligence~~ Summaries are contained in F. S. Regs., Part II. and the Staff Manual respectively. Title pages will be prepared in manuscript.

**WAR DIARY**
*or*
**~~INTELLIGENCE SUMMARY~~.**
*(Erase heading not required.)*

Army Form C. 2118.

Vol 38

| Place | Date | Hour | Summary of Events and Information | Remarks and references to Appendices |
|---|---|---|---|---|
| | | | The 11th Service (1st S.E.L) Battalion. | |
| | | | The Lancashire Fusiliers | |
| | | | From 1-3-19 to 31-3-19. | |
| | | | VOLUME 38 | 38. V 5 sheets |

A5834 Wt. W4973/M687 750,000 8/16 D. D. & L. Ltd. Forms/C.2118/13.

CONFIDENTIAL

Instructions regarding War Diaries and Intelligence Summaries are contained in F. S. Regs., Part II. and the Staff Manual respectively. Title pages will be prepared in manuscript.

# WAR DIARY
*or*
# INTELLIGENCE SUMMARY.
*(Erase heading not required.)*

Army Form

~~Feb~~ MARCH. 1919

REF. MAP. HAZEBROUCK 1:100000

| Place | Date | Hour | Summary of Events and Information | Remarks and references to Appendices |
|---|---|---|---|---|
| BEAUMARAIS | 1 | – | Battalion organized as HQ. and 1 Coy. | |
| | 2 | – | Divine Services. | |
| | 3 | – | Training and Working Parties. | |
| | 4 | – | Move from BEAUMARAIS to MERCEGHEM to the same camps as occupied previously. | |
| MERCEGHEM | 5 | – | Training and Working Parties. | |
| | 6 | – | do | |
| | 7 | – | The Colours were consecrated by the Rev H M Crabbe C.F and presented by Maj Gen. Marindin, G.O.C 35th Division to the Battalion on Battalion Parade under Lt Col A J Scully M.C. in BOLLEZEELE Square. Lieut R. Cressy carried colours. | |
| | 8 | – | Training & working parties as usual | |
| | 9 | – | Divine Services. | |
| | 10 | – | Training & working parties. | |
| | 11 | – | do: | |
| | 12 | – | do. | |
| | 13 | – | do | |
| | 14 | – | do. | |

A5834 Wt. W4973/M687 750,000 8/16 D. D. & L. Ltd. Forms/C.2118/13.

CONFIDENTIAL.

Instructions regarding War Diaries and Intelligence Summaries are contained in F. S. Regs., Part II. and the Staff Manual respectively. Title pages will be prepared in manuscript.

# WAR DIARY
~~or~~
# ~~INTELLIGENCE SUMMARY.~~
(Erase heading not required.)

Army Form C. 2118.

MARCH 1919. REF. MAP. HAZEBROUCK 1:100000

| Place | Date | Hour | Summary of Events and Information | Remarks and references to Appendices |
|---|---|---|---|---|
| MERCEGHEM | 15 | – | Training and working Parties. | |
| | 16 | – | Divine Services | |
| | 17 | – | Training & working Parties. | |
| | 18 | – | Battalion parade with colour in square BOLLEZEELE for presentation of medal ribbons by Brig. Gen. J.W. Sandilands, C.M.G. | |
| | 19 | – | Training & working parties | |
| | 20 | – | do | |
| | 21 | – | do | |
| | 22 | – | do | |
| | 23 | – | Divine Services. | |
| | 24 | – | Training & working parties. | |
| | 25 | – | do. | |
| | 26 | – | do | |
| | 27 | – | do | |
| | 28 | – | do | |
| | 29 | – | do | |
| | 30 | – | Divine Services. | |
| | 31 | – | Training & working parties. | |

31-3-19

A5834 Wt. W4973/M687 750,000 8/16 D. D. & L. Ltd. Forms/C.2118/13.

[signature] Lieut-Colonel
Commanding 17th (S) Bn. Lancashire Fusiliers

Instructions regarding War Diaries and Intelligence Summaries are contained in F. S. Regs., Part II. and the Staff Manual respectively. Title pages will be prepared in manuscript.

# WAR DIARY
*or*
# INTELLIGENCE SUMMARY.
*(Erase heading not required.)*

Army Form C. 2118.

| Place | Date | Hour | Summary of Events and Information | Remarks and references to Appendices |
|---|---|---|---|---|
| | | | Honours gained by the Battalion during the period 1st — 31st March 1919: — Nil | |

A5834 Wt. W4973/M687 750,000 8/16 D. D. & L. Ltd. Forms/C.2118/13.

Instructions regarding War Diaries and Intelligence Summaries are contained in F. S. Regs., Part II. and the Staff Manual respectively. Title pages will be prepared in manuscript.

# WAR DIARY
*or*
# INTELLIGENCE SUMMARY.
*(Erase heading not required.)*

Army Form C. 2118.

| Place | Date | Hour | Summary of Events and Information | Remarks and references to Appendices |
|---|---|---|---|---|
| | | | Casualties for the month :— | |
| | | | Officers — Nil | |
| | | | O.R's — Nil | |
| | | | Strength of Battalion — March 31. 1919. | |
| | | | Officers — 16. | |
| | | | O.R's — 260. | |
| | | | 31st March 1919 | |
| | | | A. [illegible] Lieut Colonel | |
| | | | Commanding 17th (S) Bn Lancashire Fusiliers | |

A5834 Wt. W4973/M687 750,000 8/16 D. D. & L. Ltd. Forms/C.2118/13.

www.ingramcontent.com/pod-product-compliance
Lightning Source LLC
Chambersburg PA
CBHW080913230426
43667CB00015B/2671